KETO PASSPORT

Energy-boosting, fat-burning, low-carb
cuisine from across the globe

by Layla McGowan
and Lindsay Taylor, Ph.D.

Library of Congress Control Number: 2018960032

Hardcover ISBN: 978-1-7326745-0-9
Ebook ISBN: 978-1-7326745-1-6

Publisher: Bradventures LLC
Please contact the publisher at theusefuldish@gmail.com with any questions, concerns, and feedback.
Please contact Midpoint Trade Books at orders@midpointtrade.com to obtain quantity discounts.

Art Director and Book Design: Caroline De Vita
Photography: Layla McGowan
Indexer: Tim Tate

DISCLAIMER: The ideas, concepts, and opinions expressed in this book are intended to be used for educational purposes only. This book is sold with the understanding that the authors and publisher are not rendering medical advice of any kind, nor is this book intended to replace medical advice, nor to diagnose, prescribe, or treat any disease, condition, illness, or injury. It is imperative that before beginning any diet, exercise, recipes, or lifestyle program, including any aspect of the methodologies mentioned in *Keto Passport*, you receive full medical clearance from a licensed physician. If you are currently taking medication for health conditions, are pregnant or a growing youth, or have a current or past condition such as cardiovascular disease, cancer, diabetes, or other serious health condition, major dietary changes should be considered with extreme caution and the guidance of a trusted medical professional. The authors and publisher claim no responsibility to any person or entity for any liability, loss, or damage caused or alleged to be caused directly or indirectly as a result of the use, application, or interpretation of the material in this book. If you object to this disclaimer, you may return the book to publisher for a full refund.

Printed in the U.S.A.

WELCOME & THANKS..............................v

INTRODUCTION.................................vi

KETO PASSPORT FAQS xii

REGION: AFRICA 1
Bamya Alich'a (Ethiopian-style Okra).........3
Berbere Spice Blend........................5
Bobotie 6
Chicken "Groundnut" Stew 8
Doro Wat 11
Jollof Rice with Chicken 12
Malata 15
Nigerian Meat Stew........................17
Niter Kibbeh 20
Ras el Hanout Spice Blend 23
Shrimp Piri Piri 24
Suya......................................27
Tibs Wat 29

REGION: EAST ASIA.......................31
Bok Choy with Mushroom 33
Keto-Friendly Sriracha....................35
Bulgogi 39
Chasu Pork Belly..........................41
Do Chua (Vietnamese Pickled Vegetables)...43
Kimchi 45
Omurice 47
Larb Lettuce Cups 51
Okonomiyaki Sauce 53
Japanese-style Mayonnaise 53
Pork Satay 54
Shoyu Tamago 57
Variation: Quail Shoyu Tamago.............57
Sokkori Gomtang (Oxtail Soup) 59
Spicy Mayo 63
Tak Bokkeum Tang 64
Thit Heo Nuong Xa (Vietnamese-style
    Pork Chops) 67
Tom Yum Goong 69
Yogurt Probiotic Shots....................71
Zoodle Ramen 72

REGION: SOUTH ASIA 75
Bhindi Pyaz (Okra with Onions) 77
Chicken Biryani 78
Chicken Korma 81

Madras Curry Spice Blend..................83
Curried Fish..............................84
Ghee 87
Indian-spiced Roasted Brussels Sprouts....89
Indian-Style Cauliflower Rice.............91
Lassi (3 Ways) 93
    Mint Lassi 93
    Saffron Avocado Lassi.................94
    Salted Margarita Lassi................95
Palak Paneer 97
Paneer 99
Pol Sambol (Coconut Sambal)..............101
Tandoori Chicken 103

REGION: MIDDLE EAST 105
Baked Cod with Tahini Sauce..............107
Beef Khoresh 109
Cauliflower Tabbouleh 111
Chicken Kebabs 113
Yogurt 115
Cucumber Yogurt Sauce 119
Fried Halloumi with Za'atar..............121
Israeli Salad 123
Jeweled Cauliflower Rice.................124
Kebab-e Barg.............................127
Tahini...................................129
Tahini Turmeric Dressing.................131
Toum 133
Za'atar Spice Blend......................135

REGION: MEDITERRANEAN 137
Caldo Verde 139
Caprese Salad (Insalata Caprese).........141
Chicken Cacciatore, Umbrian Style........143
Coquilles St. Jacques (Scallops in
    Mushroom Cream Sauce)................144
Dolmas 146
Greek Salad 149
Lamb Souvlaki 151
Lemon Garlic Sardines....................153
Moussaka 154
Porcini Mushroom Beef Stew 156
Spinach Ricotta Dumplings 159
Tapas Assortment 161
    Champinones al Ajillo (Garlic Mushrooms)...161
    Aioli 162

Asparagus and Serrano Ham...................... 163
Faux Patatas Bravas................................ 164
Gildas... 165
Tonnato Sauce 167
Vitello Tonnato (Beef Tongue with
   Tonnato Sauce) 168

REGION: EASTERN EUROPE 171
Bacon Borscht 173
Beet Kvass 175
Bigos 176
Blini 179
Blini with Smoked Salmon and
   Herbed Crème Fraîche 181
Chlodnik 183
Kajmak...185
Kapusta (Cabbage and Mushrooms) 187
Mushroom Julienne 189
Palačinke 191
Easy Palačinke Filling Ideas....................192
   Spinach and cheese............................. 192
   Strawberry cheesecake 192
Polish Dill Pickles 193
Russian Mushroom Soup 197
Salata od Hobotnice (Octopus Salad) 199
Tarator 201
Zrazy 202

REGION: WESTERN EUROPE........ 205
Asparagus and Celery Root Vichyssoise. 207
Coq au Vin 209
Sauerkraut..211
Gribenes 215
Moules Marinière 216
Pork with Camembert 218
Rabbit Stew..221
Rotkohlsalat mit Spek (Red Cabbage
   with Bacon)...................................... 223
Sauce Gribiche 225
Schmaltz 227
Schweinehaxe 229
Shrimp Provençal 231

Steak and Kidney Pie 233
Ratatouille 235

REGION: NORTH AMERICA.............239
Avocado Crema 241
Beef Cheek Barbacoa.............................243
Chicken Crackling Poutine......................245
Blue Cheese Dip.................................... 249
Boliche...251
Curtido Rojo 253
Buffalo Wings 256
Cretons 259
Caldo de Res 260
Deviled Eggs (3 Ways) 263
   Your Mama's Deviled Eggs 263
   *Not Your Mama's Deviled Eggs: Bacon
      and Butter Eggs*............................. 264
   *Not Your Mama's Deviled Eggs:
      Wasabi Eggs* 265
Dilly Beans... 266
Eggs Benedict.......................................270
Basic Mug Muffins 271
Smoked Salmon and Gribiche Benedict...273
Jerk Chicken...274
Snapper Veracruz 277

REGION: SOUTH AMERICA 279
Aji Dd Gallina 281
Brazilian Chopped Salad 283
Causa Limeña....................................... 285
Empanadas 287
Chimichurri 291
Charquican (Jerky Stew)......................... 292
Fermented Chimichurri 294
Crema de Aguacate (Avocado Soup)....... 297
Churrasco Chicken Hearts...................... 298
Moqueca (Brazilian Seafood Stew) 300
Pollo Asado Columbiano........................ 303
Shrimp Ceviche 305
Sopa de Aceitunas (Black Oliva Soup) 307

INDEX 308

WELCOME & THANKS

Welcome to the wide world of keto! We are so happy to bring you this collection of flavorful and exciting low-carb recipes from around the world. As long-time keto enthusiasts ourselves, we often hear keto folks lament that they struggle to add variety to their ketogenic diets; they figure out a few low-carb recipes that work for them early on—egg muffins, lettuce-wrapped hamburgers, and fatty coffee usually—and then they get stuck in a keto rut. Low-carb and ketogenic food doesn't have to be boring or repetitive! When you explore different ethnic cuisines, you find that there are a huge number of traditional recipes and regional favorites that fit a ketogenic way of eating or that are easily adaptable with a few strategic ingredient swaps.

We have curated over 130 recipes from around the world, some of which were pretty much keto-friendly already and some of which required some culinary gymnastics to get them in shape. Before we dive in to the recipes, we provide an overview of what it means to eat a ketogenic diet. Because the popularity of the ketogenic diet has grown so rapidly in the past few years (it is now the most Googled health term!), there are a lot of people calling themselves "experts" and promoting their own versions of keto, some frankly better than others. Our goal is to guide people to eat delicious, nutrient-dense food that promotes overall health and wellness. We believe a ketogenic diet should include plenty of vegetables, fresh herbs, and sustainably and humanely raised animal and seafood products. We also believe keto food should taste fantastic and never ever be dull. Accordingly, the recipes included in this book comprise a wide variety of ingredients, techniques, and flavor profiles that are sure to please keto and non-keto eaters alike.

No matter what style of eating you follow, you should truly enjoy your food. It is really unfortunate that the ketogenic diet is called a "diet" because that word implies struggling and suffering, and restricting and depriving yourself of food. We promise you, neither of us suffers or feels deprived because of how we eat. No, we don't eat bread, pasta, processed snack foods, or any of the many other modern foods that are making people sick, tired, and overweight. Nor do we want to. We genuinely love the foods we do eat. Eating real food prepared with love that nourishes you from the inside out is the greatest act of self-care you can do.

Thank you for making us part of your keto journey. Keto on!
~Layla and Lindsay

INTRODUCTION

WHAT IS "KETO?"

So what is "keto" anyway? Presumably if you purchased this book you are at least somewhat interested in following a ketogenic diet. First things first, let's agree from the outset to call it a ketogenic *way of eating*. The word "diet" is so emotionally fraught for many of us, and it also implies that the only, or the best, reason to "go keto" is to lose weight. Although keto can be a great way to drop excess body fat, the potential benefits are much greater than that, so it's a shame to pigeonhole keto as a weight-loss strategy. From here on out, no more "diet" talk. If you're hoping to drop a few pounds, terrific! Keto can support that goal! We expect that you'll soon find there are a great many other reasons to embrace a low-carb lifestyle as well.

Back to business. You are interested in a ketogenic way of eating, or keto. If you have done any research on the topic, you are possibly a little bewildered—or maybe totally overwhelmed—by the amount of information out there about what it means to be keto, what foods you should and should not be eating, how much to eat, and whether or not to supplement. It is really quite simple, though. In order to be keto, you need to significantly restrict your carbohydrate intake. That's it! Everything else is just details.

Keto falls under the broad category of low-carb, high-fat (LCHF) ways of eating, along with variants of Paleo, primal, Atkins, and others with which you might be familiar. Compared to the others, keto is generally lower carb and higher fat, but it's really the low-carb part that's important. A lot of people make the mistake of eating copious amounts of fat because they think they are "supposed to" when starting keto, thinking that's where the magic happens. When you dramatically reduce your carb intake, you also reduce the number of calories you are consuming. Fat intake must increase accordingly to provide calories to meet your daily energy needs. (At the same time, many people who come to keto from a typical low-fat dietary approach enjoy the newfound freedom of eating delicious high-fat foods that were previously off the table, no pun intended. There is a reason that keto is disparagingly called the "bacon and butter diet"—keto newbies often "rediscover" their love for those with gusto!) However, keto is really more about what you *don't* eat: grains, sugar, and a lot of high-carb fruits and tubers, which drive up your blood glucose and your insulin.

Let's back up a little and do a very brief Biochemistry 101 refresher here. The two main sources of energy on which your body generally relies are glucose (sugar) and fat. We get these from the food we eat, and we also store them in our tissues for later use. Glucose is stored as *glycogen* in the liver and muscles, and fat is stored as fatty acids mostly in adipose tissue (i.e., body fat). Most of our cells can burn either glucose or fatty acids, but there are a few types that cannot use the latter. Most importantly, the brain is highly dependent on glucose for energy... unless ketones are available.

> *Glucose is the predominant fuel source for your hard-working brain and body... unless ketones are available.*

You see, glycogen can only be stored in limited quantities, so the brain needs a plan B to fuel itself when glucose availability is low. This is where ketones come in. Ketones are an additional fuel source that your liver manufactures from fatty acids when glycogen stores in your liver are depleted. This can occur during periods of starvation—the ability to produce and use ketones evolved to keep us alive during periods of food scarcity—or when we fast or purposefully eat very few carbohydrates over a sustained period of time. You are said to be *in ketosis* if you have blood ketones measured at 0.5 mmol/L or higher, according to leading experts Drs. Stephen Phinney and Jeff Volek. If you get into ketosis by restricting carbohydrate intake, this is called being in *nutritional ketosis*.

As it turns out, there are advantages to running on ketones (and fat) rather than being *carb-dependent*, or relying so heavily on carbohydrates (glucose) for the bulk of our energy needs. For example, doctors have known for more than a century that eating a therapeutic ketogenic diet is highly effective for controlling epileptic seizures. Today researchers are examining whether keto (and low-carbohydrate diets in general) can be used to treat and even reverse many of the diseases that have become endemic in modern society, such as type 2 diabetes and obesity, autoimmune disorders, cancer, reproductive problems, Alzheimer's disease and dementia, and more. We don't want to get ahead of the science, but suffice it to say that the current research into the benefits of keto has us *very* excited. Some of the health benefits are undoubtedly due to the removal of harmful processed and highly inflammatory modern "carbage" (high-carbohydrate junk food) from one's diet, but there is also growing evidence that ketones in and of themselves have anti-inflammatory and other health-promoting properties.

Beyond the possible applications to treat specific diseases and dysfunctions, we both believe strongly in ancestral health principles, which means we think that the best way to achieve optimal health and longevity is to eat and live much as our ancestors did, within reason. We aren't building huts and giving up cell phones (we wrote this book on our laptops, after all). However, we aim to eat fresh, local, in-season foods as our ancestors did, to align our sleep with our circadian rhythms, move frequently, manage chronic stress, and get plenty of sunshine. It is clear that for most of human history, fat and ketones were the dominant energy sources for our bodies. Being carb-a-holics is a *modern* human condition, one that is undeniably harming our species' health and wellbeing immensely. By returning to our roots as fat- and ketone-burners, we can mitigate much of the damage done by modern diets like the Standard American Diet (i.e., the SAD).

SO HOW DO I BECOME A FAT- AND KETONE-BURNER?

This one is easy: eat fewer carbs. Stop providing your body with so much glucose. When your body doesn't have enough glucose available to meet its energy needs, it will switch to burning more fat, either from the food you eat or from body fat, or usually a combo. If you have spent decades eating a mostly high-carbohydrate diet, your body will essentially need to "relearn" how to burn fat efficiently. This is what we mean when we talk about *becoming fat- and keto-adapted*.

As a side note, many people get confused about the difference between being fat-adapted and keto-adapted. "Fat-adapted" simply means that you efficiently use fat for energy. You can be a good fat-burner without spending any significant time in ketosis if you eat a somewhat low-carb but not *very* low-carb diet. For example, a typical Paleo or primal eater who has removed grains and refined sugars from his or her diet but who still eats fruit, root vegetables, and maybe maple syrup and honey occasionally would likely be fat-adapted but not keto-adapted. However, to become keto-adapted, you *must also* become fat-adapted. Ketones are only made when fat is being metabolized, so individuals who become keto-adapted also become good at burning fat (i.e., fat-adapted) along the way.

It is pretty easy to "turn on" your fat- and ketone-burning capabilities by changing what you eat. However, once you get into the nitty-gritty of how to eat ketogenically, it can get confusing. Keto is the hottest dietary trend right now, in no small part because it *is* very effective for weight loss and for helping to manage many disease states. Consequently, there is a *lot* of (often conflicting) information being dispensed on the Internet right now. It can be overwhelming for the average person who is simply trying to figure out how to eat! The fact is there is no one single version of keto that is "right" or that will work for all people. The success of any particular way of eating for a given individual depends in how well it matches his or her unique needs and goals, biochemistry, and health status. That said, there are some basic guidelines that can get you started without getting bogged down in details.

MEET THE MACROS

A ketogenic diet is all about the macros—how much carbohydrate, protein, and fat you eat. Your macros are measured in grams. Each gram of carbohydrate and protein has 4 calories, while fat has 9 calories per gram. How much you eat of each depends on how many calories you aim to eat on a typical day, your exercise and fitness goals, metabolic health, and personal preferences. As an example, a moderately active person who wants to eat 1900 calories per day might aim for:

50 grams of carbohydrate	50 x 4 = 200 calories from carbohydrate
80 grams of protein	80 x 4 = 320 calories from protein
150 grams of fat	150 x 9 = 1350 calories from fat
	TOTAL = 1870 calories (close enough!)

As we said earlier, for a way of eating to qualify as ketogenic, the only condition that needs to be met is that it is very low carb. However, there is even disagreement among experts as to what constitutes "very low." We favor the recommendations laid out by Mark Sisson and Brad Kearns in *The Keto Reset Diet*: First, keep carb intake below 50 *total* grams per day (with a little wiggle room if the majority of your carbs come from above-ground green, leafy veggies and avocados). Aim for 0.7 to 1.0 grams of protein per pound of lean body mass. Eat as much fat as you need to meet your daily caloric goals. These recommendations are a great starting point for anyone interested in keto, and you can always tweak them as you go if necessary. Type 2 diabetics, for example, might need to reduce their daily carb intake further until they resolve their underlying insulin dysregulation. Bodybuilders might want more protein. We strongly encourage self-experimentation and finding the version of keto that works best for you.

One reason we strongly recommend these macros (i.e., this balance of carbs, protein, and fat) is that they allow for substantial intake of colorful vegetables. We find this to be a very sustainable and enjoyable way of eating. It is much less restrictive than other keto regimens that, for example, strictly limit carbs to 20 grams per day for everyone and *significantly* constrain the amount of vegetables one can eat; but for us it is just as effective. Because we are able to enjoy a daily array of fresh vegetables, we get our vitamins, minerals, and micronutrients from food instead of having to rely on supplements.

Of note, we do *not* believe that it is necessary to stuff our faces with arbitrary quantities of fat to be keto. Yes, we eat significantly more fat than we did when we were eating traditional

SAD diets, but we are not eating sticks of butter, or wrapping everything in bacon (only some things!), or slathering our food with cream cheese to "balance out" protein and carbohydrate. Our diets revolve around sustainably raised meat and poultry, wild seafood, lots of vegetables (opting for locally grown organic and/or pesticide-free whenever possible), pastured eggs, nuts and seeds, dark chocolate, and some full-fat dairy for Lindsay. (Sorry about that dairy intolerance, Layla!) We consume plenty of healthy fats from coconuts, olives, and avocados (the fruits and the derivative products), as well as the fat that naturally occurs in animal products and nuts. We cook with butter and ghee, lard and tallow, and the aforementioned oils (never polyunsaturated vegetable and seed oils like canola or soybean).

The recipes in this book reflect what we consider to be the healthiest version of keto. We encourage you to check out *The Keto Reset Diet* and our Keto Reset community on Facebook (we are both active moderators there) for more information about the science and rationale underlying these recommendations, as well as the Keto Reset method of transitioning to a ketogenic way of eating in a way that minimizes stress and maximizes your chances of success.

The recipes in this book reflect what we consider to be the healthiest version of keto—meat, poultry, seafood, lots of vegetables, eggs, nuts and seeds, full-fat dairy, and plenty of healthy fats.

FINAL WORDS

Preparing and eating food should be pleasurable experiences no matter what way of eating you pursue. It is absolutely possible to love your food *and* support your health and longevity goals. If you're struggling to find your way in keto, or if you've become bored with eating typical keto fare, *Keto Passport* is for you.

You might notice that the recipes in our book don't adhere strictly to typical macronutrient ratios (i.e., 70 to 75 percent of calories from fat, 20 to 25 percent from protein, 5 to 10 percent from carbs). Remember, it is not necessary that each individual dish—or even each entire meal, or *even* each entire day—be perfectly proportioned. Each of the recipes in this book centers on nutrient-dense foods that can support a ketogenic way of eating. We tried to keep the recipes to less than 15 grams of carbohydrate per serving, with most coming in well under that. Depending on how many carbs you aim to eat each day—and how many meals you divide those into—you might want to adjust serving sizes on some dishes. You may also exclude or swap out ingredients if you prefer. Likewise, if you wish to add more healthy fats, you always have that option. Think ghee for the Indian, Middle Eastern, and African dishes; sesame and coconut oils for East Asian; butter, sour cream, and avocado oil for East and West Europe, and North and South American; olive oil for Mediterranean.

We also included recipes for fermented foods throughout the book. Fermented foods are a staple of traditional cuisines because fermentation is one of the original methods of food preservation. In addition to being delicious, fermented foods contribute importantly to gut health because of the beneficial bacteria—probiotics—that facilitate the fermentation process. Doctors and researchers are increasingly appreciating the degree to which gut health is critical to overall health and wellbeing, both physical and mental. Fermented foods are so important that Dr. Cate Shanahan calls them one of the four pillars of "deep nutrition," also the title of her bestselling book. (Refer to the next section for more information about fermenting.)

Finally, we want to encourage you to use these recipes as jumping off points for your own kitchen adventures. If you want to follow the recipes exactly as written, that's great! If you want to use them as inspiration and see where your flights of fancy take you, fantastic! Let your creative juices flow and make kitchen magic.

KETO PASSPORT FAQS

SOURCING UNFAMILIAR INGREDIENTS

Most of the ingredients you will need to make the recipes in this book can be found in your everyday grocery store, and almost certainly in markets like Sprouts and Whole Foods. Look in the "ethnic foods," "Asian foods," or (the very imprecisely named) "Mexican foods" aisles for ingredients such as dried mushrooms and chilis, tamari, coconut cream, and the like. If you can't find something, ask! The ingredient you seek is probably hiding somewhere.

Harder-to-find ingredients such as dried powdered shrimp (Jollof Rice with Chicken, page 12), chicken hearts (Churrasco Chicken Hearts, page 298), or octopus (Salata od Hobotnice, page 199) might necessitate a trip to a local specialty market. Look in the phone book (haha, just kidding, Google it) to find Asian, Latin American, Indian, and nonspecific "international" grocers in your area. Not only will you probably find what you need, you can walk out with bags full of interesting, new-to-you produce, spices, and cuts of meat to try! Also check out the directory at eatwild.com to source locally produced meats, dairy, and eggs, as well as soup bones and cooking fat.

If you can't find ingredients locally, it is possible to order anything you need online. This is also a good option for ingredients that *can* be found in stores but often with objectionable ingredients you want to avoid, such as gochugaru (Kimchi, page 45); cleaner versions can be found online. Besides good ol' Amazon, we like to shop at HMart (hmart.com), U.S. Wellness Meats (grasslandbeef.com), and Vital Choice (vitalchoice.com).

HOT PEPPERS

Different varieties of chili peppers are staple ingredients in many regional cuisines. You might not be able to find exactly what you need in your local stores, but that's not a problem. Sometimes differences are in name only. For example, several recipes call for Thai chili or bird's eye chilis, which are simply two different names for the same plant. We tried to be true to what they would be called in the region from which we derived each recipe. For example, the chilis usually called bird or bird's eye chilis in Asia are piri piri chilis in Africa; everywhere else, they're Thai chilis.

Peppers differ in terms of both heat and flavor. Because of flavor differences, substituting one pepper for another in any of these dishes might subtly change the undertaste of the final dish, but not in a way that is likely to be unpalatable, so go ahead swap where necessary or desired.

Here is a list of peppers used in the recipes in this book, along with their heat ratings as measured by the standard Scoville scale. "SHU" means Scoville Heat Units; bigger numbers mean spicier peppers and more burn! If you're not a big fan of the burn, you may always select a milder pepper.

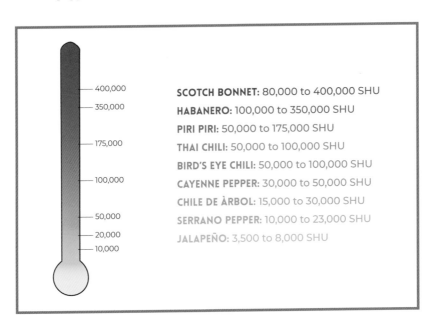

SCOTCH BONNET: 80,000 to 400,000 SHU

HABANERO: 100,000 to 350,000 SHU

PIRI PIRI: 50,000 to 175,000 SHU

THAI CHILI: 50,000 to 100,000 SHU

BIRD'S EYE CHILI: 50,000 to 100,000 SHU

CAYENNE PEPPER: 30,000 to 50,000 SHU

CHILE DE ÀRBOL: 15,000 to 30,000 SHU

SERRANO PEPPER: 10,000 to 23,000 SHU

JALAPEÑO: 3,500 to 8,000 SHU

THICKENING AGENTS

It can be tricky when eating primal/paleo, gluten-free, and keto to figure out how to thicken sauces, gravies, and soups without flour or cornstarch. We also generally avoid gums (xanthan gum, guar gum) because some people are sensitive to them and they yield inconsistent results in recipes. Nevertheless, you are not doomed to a life of watery gravy! Here are some options you can use:

Gelatin: Can be purchased in packets as unflavored gelatin or in canisters as beef or marine gelatin powder. A little goes a long way. Tends to impart a slightly gelatinous texture (no surprise).

Eggs: Whole eggs or egg yolks blended into liquids can thicken somewhat, but results will not be as dramatic as when using other thickening agents. Adds healthy fats and protein to dishes.

Mushrooms or cauliflower: When cooked until soft, can be blended into sauces, soups, and gravies (strain for smoother result). Flavors are fairly neutral, will not overpower dishes.

Arrowroot powder or tapioca starch: Whisk into cool water, nut milk, or coconut milk, then whisk into soup, stew, gravy, etc. As with gelatin, a little goes a long way, so the amount of carbs these impart per serving is usually small.

GRAIN-FREE FLOURS

We aren't big fans of making keto-fied baked goods, but every once in a while we will make a keto-friendly crust or pastry dough using almond and/or coconut flours (as in the Steak and Kidney Pie, page 233). Because their properties differ from wheat flours—coconut flour in particular absorbs much more liquid than wheat flour and behaves differently than almond flour—you cannot simply substitute one for another. We recommend following recipes that have already been tested rather than winging it when it comes to flour substitutions.

BAKING POWDER

A few recipes call for baking powder, to which some folks object because of the aluminum found in common brands. If you are concerned, seek out aluminum-free baking powder, or you can make your own replacement by combining 1 tablespoon arrowroot powder, 1 tablespoon cream of tartar, and ½ tablespoon baking soda in a small container. Use this mixture 1:1 for baking powder (e.g., 1 teaspoon baking powder = 1 teaspoon this mixture).

COOKING WITH ALCOHOL

Several of the recipes we wanted to include in this book called for wine. While we do not mind cooking with wine occasionally, this is an individual choice. *In general*, you may substitute a cup of chicken broth or beef broth plus 1 tablespoon of apple cider vinegar or lemon juice for a cup of wine in a recipe (scale appropriately). Understand that this will result in a somewhat altered final product, but in our tests they were still delicious (though perhaps slightly less "authentic").

PRESSURE COOKING

A handful of recipes call for using a countertop pressure cooker. The directions are written to be consistent with the brand we both use, Instant Pot, but they should be easily adaptable to other similar pressure cookers.

FERMENTING

Fermenting is an ancient method of preserving food that has been "rediscovered" as of late with the recent focus on the gut microbiome and its role in health and wellness. When food is fermented, anaerobic bacteria (oh-so-trendy "probiotics") consume the naturally occurring sugars in the foods you are fermenting and release lactic acid, creating an acidic environment in which harmful bacteria do not grow. Fermenting is exceptionally easy and costs only a tiny fraction of the price of refrigerated "live" fermented foods at your favorite market. Plus, it yields absolutely delicious and nutritious products.

However, care must be taken to ensure that it is done correctly so that harmful bacteria are not allowed to propagate. While a thorough lesson in the art of fermenting is outside the scope of this book, we do include a few beginner-friendly fermented recipes in this book for our fellow *fermentistas*. If you are totally new to fermenting, we recommend reading up about safe fermentation before diving in. Some of our favorite resources are:

- culturesforhealth.com/learn/recipe/natural-fermentation/sauerkraut/
- culturesforhealth.com/learn/natural-fermentation/how-to-ferment-vegetables/
- *Wild Fermentation* by Sandor Ellix Katz
- *Fermented Vegetables* by Kristen K. Shockey and Christopher Shockey

The most important things to keep in mind when fermenting are that you must (1) work in a clean environment and ensure that the equipment you are using has been properly sterilized, and (2) create an anaerobic environment for your fermenting foods, which means keeping them submerged in brine and not exposed to air. We favor a simple system that employs mason jars and glass fermentation weights to keep fermentables submerged, but you can purchase airlock systems or water seal crocks if you prefer. If all this is gibberish to you, check out the resources above. We strongly encourage you to delve into fermenting, as fermented foods *are* exceptional for gut health, not to mention for adding intense and addictive flavors to your meals.

Check out these fermented recipes: Kimchi, page 45; Sriracha, page 35; Yogurt Probiotic Shots, page 71; Yogurt, page 115; Polish Dill Pickles, page 193; Sauerkraut, 211; Curtido Rojo, page 253; Dilly Beans, page 266; and Fermented Chimichurri, page 294.

AFRICA

BAMYA ALICH'A (ETHIOPIAN-STYLE OKRA)

Okra gets a bad rap because of its admittedly sometimes gooey texture, but it's all about the preparation. We love this dish made with small, fresh okra that can be cooked whole.

INGREDIENTS

1½ pounds young okra, trimmed and, if large, sliced diagonally

2 tablespoons Niter Kibbeh (page 20) or ghee

1 small onion, thinly sliced

½ teaspoon Berbere Spice Blend (page 5 or store-bought) or ground cardamom

2 fresh piri piri chilis, seeded and diced

2 cloves garlic, minced

½-inch knob of fresh ginger, peeled and sliced into matchsticks

3 Roma tomatoes, diced

½ teaspoon salt

1. Bring a medium saucepan of filtered water to a boil and add the okra. Boil for 5 minutes, then drain the okra. Set aside.

2. Heat the niter kibbeh in a large skillet over high heat. Fry the onions until they just begin to soften, about 3 minutes. Add the berbere spice blend, chilis, garlic, and ginger to the pan and fry 2 minutes longer.

3. Stir in the cooked okra and cook for 3 minutes. Add the tomatoes and salt and stir to combine. Continue to cook for 3 to 5 minutes, stirring frequently, until the tomatoes are soft and the okra is tender.

4. Transfer to a serving dish. Serve hot or at room temperature.

NOTE: *Piri piri chilis are also known as Thai chilis and bird's eye chilis. You can substitute the slightly milder serrano pepper or the slightly hotter Scotch bonnet or habanero in its place. (Refer to discussion on page xii.)*

MACRONUTRIENTS PER SERVING
CALORIES: 87 · FAT: 5 G, 41 KCAL · CARBOHYDRATES: 11 G (7 G NET), 44 KCAL · PROTEIN: 3 G, 11 KCAL

BERBERE SPICE BLEND

MAKES ½ CUP

Berbere spice blend is a common ingredient in traditional Ethiopian cooking. It can be used on everything from meat to vegetables to fresh fruit for an unexpected kick.

INGREDIENTS

4 or 5 dried hatch chilis (aka New Mexico chilis), stems and seeds removed

½ tablespoon cardamom pods or 1 teaspoon whole cardamom seeds

½ tablespoon fenugreek seeds (see Note)

4 tablespoons paprika

1 tablespoon fine sea salt

1 teaspoon ground ginger

1 teaspoon onion powder

½ teaspoon ground garlic

½ teaspoon ground allspice

½ teaspoon ground cinnamon

½ teaspoon ground nutmeg

Pinch ground cloves

1. Using a spice grinder or small food processor, grind the hatch chilis until they create a medium-to-fine powder. Transfer to a small bowl.

2. Grind the cardamom and fenugreek together in the same spice grinder. Add to the bowl with the chilis. Add the paprika, salt, ginger, onion powder, garlic, allspice, cinnamon, nutmeg, and cloves, and mix well.

3. Store in an airtight container.

NOTE: *Fenugreek is actually a legume, and while there is no need to avoid it order to be keto-compliant, individuals who are allergic to peanuts might also react to fenugreek. If you are concerned, substitute ground mustard seed (though it will change the flavor somewhat).*

MACRONUTRIENTS PER SERVING
CALORIES: 5 KCAL · FAT: <1 G, 1 KCAL · CARBOHYDRATE: 1 G (1 G NET), 5 KCAL · PROTEIN: <1 G, 1 KCAL

BOBOTIE

MAKES 8 SERVINGS

Bobotie is a beautifully fragrant curried meat pie from South Africa. Don't be concerned about the small amount of fruit in the dish, the total carbohydrate per serving remains low.

INGREDIENTS

2 tablespoons ghee or butter

1 medium onion, finely diced

2 cloves garlic, smashed and minced

1 tablespoon Madras Curry Spice Blend (page 83)

1 teaspoon ground turmeric

½ teaspoon ground coriander

1½ pounds ground beef, lamb, or a mixture of both

2 tablespoons coconut oil or additional ghee or butter

4 unsweetened dried apricots, minced

¼ cup slivered almonds, lightly toasted

½ Granny Smith apple, peeled and grated

3 large eggs

Grated zest of ½ lemon

Juice of ½ lemon

1 cup heavy whipping cream, or substitute full-fat coconut milk

1 cup roughly-crumbled plain pork rinds

4 bay leaves, plus more for garnish

½ teaspoon salt

Pinch ground nutmeg

1. Preheat the oven to 350°F.

2. Melt the ghee in a large saucepan over medium-high heat. Add the onions and cook, stirring frequently, until translucent and soft, about 5 to 7 minutes. Add the garlic and cook for an additional minute. Stir in the Madras Curry Spice Blend, turmeric, and coriander, making sure to evenly coat the onion mixture. Cook for 5 minutes, stirring frequently, allowing the onions to become richly fragrant as the spices bloom.

3. Add the ground meat to the pan and cook until browned, about 7 to 10 minutes. As the meat cooks, stir well to incorporate the onions and spices, and breaking up any large pieces of meat. Remove the pan from the heat.

4. Liberally coat a large casserole or baking dish with butter or oil and set aside. In a large bowl, mix together the apricots, almonds, apple, 1 egg, lemon zest, lemon juice, ¼ cup of the cream, and pork rinds. Add the ground meat and onion mixture and stir well, then pour into the greased casserole. Space the bay leaves evenly inside the casserole dish and tuck about halfway into the meat, spooning extra meat on top to cover if necessary. Using the flat end of a spatula, pack the meat down until it is well compressed. Cover the casserole with a lid or foil and bake for 45 minutes.

5. Remove the casserole from the oven and increase the heat to 400°F. While the oven comes to temperature, whisk together the remaining 2 eggs, ¾ cup of cream, salt, and nutmeg. When the oven is ready, pour the egg mixture over top of the casserole, covering the entire surface. If desired, garnish the bobotie by topping the egg with additional bay leaves. Bake uncovered for 15 minutes or until the egg custard has set and turned golden brown. Allow to cool for 10 minutes.

6. To serve, cut the bobotie into squares and use a spatula to remove individual servings to plates. Be sure to instruct diners to discard the bay leaves.

MACRONUTRIENTS PER SERVING
CALORIES: 461 KCAL · FAT: 38 G, 346 KCAL · CARBOHYDRATE: 8 G (6 G NET), 32 KCAL · PROTEIN: 22 G, 88 KCAL

CHICKEN "GROUNDNUT" STEW

MAKES 6 SERVINGS

This adaptation of groundnut (peanut) stew has been made keto-friendly through strategic substitutions. Although it's generally a spicy dish, feel free to alter the amount of heat to suit your tastes.

INGREDIENTS

3 tablespoons coconut oil

12 ounces boneless, skinless chicken thighs, cut into 1½-inch chunks

Generous pinch fine sea salt, plus more to taste

1 medium white onion, thinly sliced

1 2-inch knob of ginger, peeled and sliced

2 dried bay leaves

1 cup halved radishes

1 or 2 scotch bonnet chilis, halved, ribs and seeds removed (optional)

4 Roma tomatoes, seeded and quartered

6 cups chicken bone broth or stock

2 tablespoons unsweetened almond butter

2 tablespoons unsweetened coconut butter

Freshly ground black pepper

8 ounces fresh leafy greens such as spinach, kale, collard, or mustard greens, chopped

2 tablespoons roughly chopped dry-roasted almonds, to garnish

1. Heat the oil over medium-high heat in a Dutch oven or deep casserole. While the oil warms, pat the chicken dry and season generously with salt. In the Dutch oven, brown the chicken for about 2 minutes per side until golden, working in batches so as not to crowd the pan. Remove the browned chicken to a plate and set aside.

2. Add the onion to the same pot and cook until just soft, about 4 or 5 minutes. Add the ginger and bay leaves to the pot and cook an additional 1 to 2 minutes until the aromatics become fragrant. Stir in the radish, chilis, and tomatoes.

3. Pour the bone broth over everything and stir to combine. Allow the liquid to come to a boil, then reduce the heat and cook uncovered on a low boil for about 10 to 15 minutes, until the radish is very soft.

4. Remove and discard the bay leaves. Purée the soup until smooth using an immersion blender, or carefully transfer the soup in batches to a blender or food processor, taking care not to burn yourself with hot splatter and steam. If using a blender or food processor, return the soup to the Dutch oven. Stir the chicken into the soup along with any juices that collected on the plate. Simmer for 10 minutes, until the meat is cooked through.

5. Slowly whisk in the almond and coconut butters. Taste the broth and adjust the seasoning with salt and pepper as needed. Stir in the greens and cook just until wilted. Spinach will wilt almost immediately, while heartier greens such as kale may require 3 or 4 minutes to become soft. Ladle into serving bowls and garnish with chopped almonds. >>

MACRONUTRIENTS PER SERVING
CALORIES: 294 KCAL · FAT: 20 G, 180 KCAL · CARBOHYDRATE: 10 G (6 G NET), 41 KCAL · PROTEIN: 21 G, 83 KCAL

DORO WAT

This traditional Ethiopian stew absolutely explodes with flavor. Traditionally it is eaten with *injera*, a spongy bread used to scoop up bites of food. Unfortunately, we have yet to find a good keto-friendly substitute for injera... so we just use forks.

INGREDIENTS

¼ cup Niter Kibbeh (recommended, page 20), unsalted butter, or ghee

2 medium onions, thinly sliced

1 tablespoon Berbere Spice Blend (page 5 or store-bought) or chili powder

¼ teaspoon ground cardamom

3 whole cloves

2 cloves garlic, smashed and minced

1½-inch piece of fresh ginger, peeled and minced

¼ teaspoon ground black pepper

1 teaspoon salt

1 tablespoon tomato paste

2 cups chicken bone broth or stock

¼ cup dry red wine, such as Cabernet Sauvignon (see Note)

4 pounds skin-on chicken drumsticks and thighs

2 whole hard-boiled eggs, peeled

2 tablespoons lime juice

1. On the stove, melt the niter kibbeh in a large Dutch oven over low heat. Add the onions and cook stirring occasionally until caramelized, about 10 to 15 minutes. Stir in the berbere spice blend, cardamom, cloves, garlic, ginger, pepper, salt, and tomato paste. Cook for 10 minutes longer.

2. Pour in the bone broth and wine, then add the chicken to the pot. Simmer for 30 minutes, occasionally stirring the sauce and turning the chicken pieces.

3. Add the eggs and lime juice and simmer for 10 minutes.

4. To serve, carefully remove the eggs and halve them or cut them into wedges. Serve the chicken with egg on the side and plenty of sauce spooned over top.

NOTE: *If you choose not to cook with red wine, you can substitute ¼ cup beef stock and ¾ teaspoon red wine vinegar or apple cider vinegar, but it will change the flavor somewhat.*

MACRONUTRIENTS PER SERVING
CALORIES: 680 KCAL · FAT: 46 G, 417 KCAL · CARBOHYDRATE: 6 G (5 G NET), 26 KCAL · PROTEIN: 59 G, 238 KCAL

AFRICA   11

JOLLOF RICE WITH CHICKEN

MAKES 4 SERVINGS

Jollof rice is a popular dish throughout many West African countries. This adaptation features cauliflower and most closely resembles joloff rice as it is prepared in Ghana.

INGREDIENTS

Approximately 3 pounds chicken leg quarters

3 cloves garlic, smashed and minced

1 tablespoon fresh ginger, peeled and minced

1 tablespoon salt

2 tablespoons olive oil or avocado oil

1 teaspoon chili powder

½ teaspoon ground coriander seed

½ teaspoon ground cumin

Pinch cinnamon

1 small onion, chopped

2 medium tomatoes, any variety, diced

2 tablespoons tomato paste

1½ to 2 cups chicken bone broth or stock

1 piri piri chili, seeded and minced (see Notes)

1 tablespoon dried powdered shrimp (see Notes)

2 cups riced cauliflower

2 scallions, white and green parts, thinly sliced

1. In a large bowl toss together the chicken, 1 clove of the garlic, 1 teaspoon of the ginger, and salt. Allow to rest at room temperature for 15 minutes.

2. In a deep skillet or Dutch oven, heat the olive oil over medium-high heat. Add the chicken, skin-side down and brown for 3 to 5 minutes per side. Remove the chicken to a bowl. To the skillet add the remaining garlic, ginger, chili powder, coriander, cumin, and cinnamon. Fry for 1 minute stirring constantly, until fragrant.

3. Add the onions, tomatoes, and tomato paste, and cook for 5 minutes, stirring frequently. Pour in 1 cup of the broth and reduce the heat to medium. Allow the tomatoes and onions to cook for 10 minutes longer, until the tomatoes become soft and begin to disintegrate.

4. Add the chicken to the tomato sauce along with any juices that collected in the bowl and stir well to coat. Stir in the chili and powdered shrimp. Bring to a boil, then reduce the heat and simmer for 5 minutes.

5. Add the riced cauliflower, scallions, and ½ cup bone broth to the pot and stir. Simmer for 10 to 15 minutes, until the chicken is cooked through. (Cooking time may vary due to the thickness of the chicken.) Add more broth to the pan as necessary to prevent the cauliflower rice from becoming too dry.

NOTES: *Piri piri chili is also known as bird chili, bird's eye chili, and Thai chili. You can substitute the slightly milder serrano pepper or the slightly hotter habanero or Scotch bonnet in its place. (Refer to the discussion on page xii.)*

If you are having difficulty finding dried powdered shrimp, check the Mexican section of your grocery store. In Spanish it is called camaron molido and is often sold in small bags for a very reasonable price.

MACRONUTRIENTS PER SERVING
CALORIES: 661 KCAL · FAT: 43 G, 387 KCAL · CARBOHYDRATE: 10 G (6 G NET), 40 KCAL · PROTEIN: 57 G, 228 KCAL

MALATA

Malata is clam dish from the southern African nation of Mozambique. As with any mollusks, it is important to select fresh clams that are still alive before cooking (see recipe Notes). Throw out any clams with chipped, damaged shells or those that do not close when tapped lightly on the counter, and of course if they have an off-putting odor.

INGREDIENTS

48 clams (littleneck variety preferred)

1½ tablespoons sea salt

Cold filtered water

2 tablespoons salted butter or ghee

2 tablespoons avocado oil

1 small yellow onion, diced

3 cloves garlic, chopped

1-inch piece fresh ginger, peeled and minced

¼ cup pine nuts

1 teaspoon red pepper flakes, or more to taste

4 ounces butternut squash, cut into 1-inch cubes

½ cup clam juice

1 cup chicken bone broth or stock (see Notes)

1 tablespoon apple cider vinegar

½ teaspoon fine sea salt

3 sprigs fresh thyme

4 cups fresh spinach leaves, roughly chopped

1. One or two hours before you intend to cook the clams, rinse the clams and use a brush to scrub off any dirt. Place a colander inside a large glass bowl and place the clams in the colander. Sprinkle the coarse sea salt over the clams and fill with filtered water to cover the clams. Place in the refrigerator.

2. Lift the clams out of the water, being careful to leave behind any sediment in the bottom of the soaking water. Rinse the clams with fresh water and place in a clean bowl.

3. Heat the butter and avocado oil in a large, deep pan over medium heat. Once the butter stops foaming, add the onion and sauté until just becoming soft, about 3 minutes. Stir in the garlic, ginger, pine nuts, and red pepper flakes (add more depending on how spicy you want the final dish to be) and cook for 1 minute more.

4. Stir in the butternut squash. Cover and cook for 10 minutes, stirring a few times. Remove the lid from the squash and stir in the clam juice, stock, vinegar, fine sea salt, and thyme. When the liquid begins to simmer, add the clams to the pan. Simmer for 8 to 12 minutes until the clams have opened. As they open, use tongs to transfer the clams to a clean bowl. Discard any clams that do not open. >>

5. Stir the spinach into the squash mixture and cook about 3 minutes until the spinach is wilted. Transfer the squash mixture to a wide, shallow serving dish, discarding the thyme stems if you wish. Nestle the clams among the squash. Serve immediately.

NOTES: *Live clams need to breathe, so transport them home from the store in an open plastic bag, then place them in a bowl covered with a damp kitchen towel in the fridge. Do not cover them with ice.*

This recipe generally calls for dry white wine. If you wish, you can use wine in place of the chicken stock and omit the apple cider vinegar.

Malata is a bit higher carb than our average recipe. Shellfish, especially mollusks, are surprisingly carb-heavy compared to other sources of protein, but they are worth it because they are absolutely packed with nutrients. If you wish to spare a few carbs in this dish, you may omit the butternut squash (3 grams of carbohydrate per serving).

MACRONUTRIENTS PER SERVING
CALORIES: 426 KCAL · FAT: 22 G, 196 KCAL · CARBOHYDRATE: 17 G (15 G NET), 69 KCAL · PROTEIN: 41 G, 162 KCAL

NIGERIAN MEAT STEW

MAKES 8 SERVINGS

This tomato-based stew is a staple food in Nigeria. This recipe calls for beef and chicken, but any combination of meat can be used. If you have access to a specialty butcher, try replacing the beef stew meat with lamb or even goat.

INGREDIENTS

1½ pounds oxtails

Filtered water

2 medium onions, one halved with skin on, one peeled and diced

1 tablespoon salt, plus more to taste

1 pound beef stew meat such as chuck or top round, cubed

3 tablespoons avocado oil

4 cloves garlic, smashed

1 or 2 habanero peppers, stems removed (optional)

1 pound boneless, skinless chicken thighs, cubed

1 teaspoon ground allspice

½ teaspoon Madras Curry Spice Blend (page 83)

1 teaspoon smoked paprika

14-ounce can San Marzano or Roma tomatoes

1 teaspoon dried thyme

2 teaspoons tomato paste

2 bay leaves

1. Place the oxtails in a deep pot and add water until the oxtails are fully covered by 1 inch. Add the halved onion and salt to the pot (save the diced onion for the next step). Bring the water to a boil over high heat, then lower the heat to a simmer. Simmer for 1½ hours uncovered. Add the beef to the pot and simmer for 1 hour longer, adding more water as necessary to keep the meat covered.

2. While the meat simmers, heat 2 tablespoons of oil over medium-high heat in a large Dutch oven. Add the onions and sauté until golden and translucent, about 5 minutes. Add the garlic and habanero pepper and sauté for 2 minutes longer. Use a slotted spoon to transfer the onion mixture to a blender and remove the pan from the heat (do not wipe out the oil, you will use it again in the step 4).

3. Add the allspice, Madras curry, paprika, tomatoes, thyme, and tomato paste to the blender and puree for about 1 minute, until smooth. Set this mixture aside while the meat cooks.

4. When the oxtails and stew beef are very tender, remove the pot from the heat and set aside. Heat the remaining tablespoon of oil over medium-high heat in the same Dutch oven in which you sautéed the onions. Sauté the chicken for about 5 minutes until browned on all sides. Season with salt. >>

5. Measure out 2½ cups of cooking liquid from the pot with the beef and pour it over the chicken, scraping the bottom of the Dutch oven to release any browned-on bits. Stir in the mixture from the blender. Use tongs to transfer the oxtails, beef, and bay leaves from the pot to the Dutch oven. (Discard the cooked halved onion and the remaining cooking liquid, or save the liquid to use in a different recipe.) Allow the mixture to simmer for 30 minutes.

6. Remove and discard the bay leaves. Ladle the stew into serving bowls. Oxtails may be served either whole on the bone or with the meat pulled off and bones discarded.

NOTE: *To make this recipe with a pressure cooker, instead of simmering the meat in the first step, place the oxtails and 2 cups of water in a pressure cooker. Cook for 40 minutes under high pressure, then release the pressure, open the lid, and add the stew meat. Seal the pressure cooker again and cook under high pressure for 20 minutes longer, then follow the remaining steps as written.*

MACRONUTRIENTS PER SERVING
CALORIES: 352 KCAL · FAT: 19 G, 167 KCAL · CARBOHYDRATE: 4 G (3 G NET), 17 KCAL · PROTEIN: 41 G, 162 KCAL

NITER KIBBEH

MAKES ABOUT 1½ CUPS

Niter kibbeh is an essential ingredient in Ethiopian cooking. This spiced, fragrant clarified butter imparts its delicious flavor to the Doro Wat (page 11), Tibs Wat (page 29), and Ethiopian-style Okra (page 3) in this book.

INGREDIENTS

1 pound butter (see Note)

½ onion, minced

1 clove garlic, smashed

1-inch knob of fresh ginger, peeled and sliced into thin strips

1 3-inch stick of cinnamon

2 bay leaves

1 teaspoon cardamom seeds or 10 whole pods

1 whole clove

½ teaspoon ground coriander

½ teaspoon cumin seeds

½ teaspoon fenugreek seeds (see Note on page 5)

¼ teaspoon ground turmeric

1. Melt the butter in a deep saucepan over medium heat, stirring occasionally. As soon as the butter has melted fully, reduce the heat to a simmer and cook for 10 to 15 minutes. As the butter cooks, the water will evaporate, causing it to bubble and foam. After the initial bubbling stops, you will begin to see light-colored whey solids floating to the top of the butter in the form of a thin foam. Skim the whey from the top with a spoon and reserve for another use, such as seasoning vegetables, if desired.

2. Soon after the whey solids stop rising to the top, the butter will become very fragrant and turn a bright translucent yellow color. Flakes of light-colored milk solids will collect at the bottom and sides of the pot. If you prefer light-colored, milder ghee, you may remove the ghee from the heat at this point and continue to step 3. If you prefer nuttier, richer ghee, allow the milk solids to brown slightly by cooking for an additional 2 to 3 minutes. Remove from heat.

3. Allow the ghee to cool slightly for a couple minutes, then strain through a fine mesh strainer lined with cheesecloth or a coffee filter to remove the milk solids. Place the strained ghee in a clean saucepan and return it to the stove.

4. Add the onion, garlic, ginger, and dry spices to the ghee. Simmer gently on low heat for 20 minutes to infuse the spices into the butter.

5. Strain the warm ghee through a fine mesh strainer lined with cheesecloth or a coffee filter into a clean glass jar. You may need to repeat this process in order to remove all of the spice residue. The finished niter kibbeh will be clear.

6. Discard the cooked onions and spices. Store the niter kibbeh in a sealed container in the refrigerator.

NOTE: *To save time, you can start with 8 ounces of ghee and skip the first three steps. Melt the ghee in a saucepan over low heat, then proceed with the fourth step.*

MACRONUTRIENTS PER 1 TEASPOON
CALORIES: 45 KCAL · FAT: 5 G, 45 KCAL · CARBOHYDRATE: 0 G, 0 KCAL · PROTEIN: 0 G, 0 KCAL

RAS EL HANOUT SPICE BLEND

MAKES ABOUT 3 TABLESPOONS

INGREDIENTS

2 teaspoons ground coriander

2 teaspoons ground cumin

1½ teaspoons ground turmeric

1 teaspoon ground cinnamon

½ teaspoon ground allspice

½ teaspoon ground ginger

½ teaspoon sweet paprika

¼ teaspoon ground cloves

¼ teaspoon ground nutmeg

¼ teaspoon ground black pepper

⅛ teaspoon cayenne pepper (optional)

Mix all the ingredients in a small bowl. Store in an airtight jar.

MACRONUTRIENTS PER SERVING (1 TEASPOON)
CALORIES: 3 KCAL · FAT: <1 G, 1 KCAL · CARBOHYDRATE: 1 G (1 G NET), 3 KCAL · PROTEIN: <1 G, 0 KCAL

AFRICA   23

SHRIMP PIRI PIRI

MAKES 4 SERVINGS AS AN APPETIZER OR 2 ENTRÉE PORTIONS

Good luck not getting addicted to these spicy shrimps! Piri piri sauce is fantastic on other proteins as well. For a complete meal, serve the warm piri piri shrimp atop a big salad.

INGREDIENTS

2 fresh piri piri chilis, red or green, seeds and ribs removed (see Note)

1 tablespoon fresh cilantro leaves, chopped

2 cloves garlic

2 tablespoons fresh lemon juice

1 tablespoon fresh parsley leaves, chopped

6 tablespoons avocado oil

12 ounces fresh or thawed large or jumbo shrimp, deveined (peeled or shell-on)

Lime wedges for serving

1. In a food processor, pulse piri piri chilis, cilantro, garlic, lemon juice, and parsley until just combined. Scrape down the sides of the bowl and add 4 tablespoons of the avocado oil. Process until the mixture forms a thick paste, stopping to scrape down the sides of the bowl as necessary.

2. Pour the mixture from the blender into a large glass bowl. Add the shrimp and toss to coat. Cover and refrigerate for 30 minutes.

3. Heat the remaining 2 tablespoons of avocado oil in a large skillet over medium-high heat. Remove the shrimp from the marinade and add to the pan. Cook 1 to 2 minutes per side, until just opaque. Work in batches if necessary. The shrimp will curl into a c-shape when they are done. (If they curl into tight o-shapes, they are overcooked.) Use tongs to transfer the shrimp to a serving plate.

4. Pour any remaining piri piri sauce into the skillet and heat until bubbling, stirring constantly. Remove from heat.

5. Serve the shrimp with the piri piri sauce drizzled over top and lime wedges on the side.

NOTE: *Piri piri chili is also known as bird chili, bird's eye chili, and Thai chili. You can substitute the milder serrano pepper or the slightly hotter habanero or Scotch bonnet in its place. (Refer to discussion on page xii.)*

MACRONUTRIENTS PER SERVING (AS AN APPETIZER, ¼ OF RECIPE)
CALORIES: 227 KCAL · FAT: 21 G, 186 KCAL · CARBOHYDRATE: 4 G (3 G NET), 16 KCAL · PROTEIN: 7 G, 28 KCAL

SUYA

MAKES 6 SERVINGS

Suya is often associated with Nigeria, but it is popular across West African cuisine. Traditional suya—meat skewers—are prepared with a spicy peanut-based rub. Since many primal/paleo folks avoid peanuts and other legumes, this recipe calls for almond meal instead. For the best flavor, select well-marbled cuts of meat. Also try this recipe with chicken.

INGREDIENTS

⅓ cup almond flour or meal

¼ teaspoon chili powder

1 teaspoon ground cinnamon

1½ teaspoons garlic salt

1½ teaspoons onion powder

1 teaspoon ground ginger

1 teaspoon paprika

1 teaspoon fine sea salt

1½ pounds well-marbled beef, such as ribeye or chuck roast

Equipment: 6 long skewers, metal or bamboo (see Note)

1. Prepare the spice rub by whisking together the almond flour, chili powder, cinnamon, garlic salt, onion powder, ginger, paprika, and salt.

2. Slice the beef into strips 1 inch wide by ¼ inch thick. Place the beef in a large bowl and toss it with spice rub, completely coating the meat on all sides. Gently massage the spice rub into the meat. Cover and refrigerate for 2 hours, or up to overnight.

3. Thread a generous amount of meat onto each skewer, folding it accordion-style.

4. TO BROIL: Preheat broiler to high and position a rack in the center of the oven, about 10 inches away from the heating element. (If using an under-oven broiler, set heat to low.) Broil the skewers for 15 minutes, turning them after 7 minutes.

   TO GRILL: Preheat a grill to high heat. Cook the skewers for 10 minutes, turning once. If the skewers are not cooked to the desired doneness, lower the heat and move the skewers so they are off direct heat. Cook with indirect heat until they reach the desired doneness.

5. Serve hot.

NOTE: *If you are using bamboo skewers, soak them in warm water for a minimum of 30 minutes prior to cooking in order to prevent them from burning.*

MACRONUTRIENTS PER SERVING
CALORIES: 331 KCAL · FAT: 25 G, 221 KCAL · CARBOHYDRATE: 3 G (2 G NET), 13 KCAL · PROTEIN: 24 G, 96 KCAL

TIBS WAT

MAKES 4 SERVINGS

Tibs wat is, for all intents and purposes, Ethiopian stir-fry, which means it's perfect for nights when you need a meal in a jiffy. The trick is to get your pan very hot before cooking the meat. This recipe is also delicious with cubed lamb.

INGREDIENTS

¼ cup Niter Kibbeh (page 20), unsalted butter, or ghee

½ medium red onion, thinly sliced

1 teaspoon salt

1½ pound skirt steak, cut into 1-inch cubes

1 tablespoon Berbere Spice Blend (page 5 or store-bought) or chili powder

¼ teaspoon ground black pepper

Pinch ground allspice

Pinch ground cinnamon

Pinch ground nutmeg

3 cloves garlic, minced

3 Roma tomatoes, finely chopped

2 jalapeños, seeded, ribs removed, thinly sliced

½ cup dry red wine, such as Cabernet Sauvignon (see Note)

1. Heat a skillet or wok over high heat. Melt the niter kibbeh. Add the onion and cook 2 minutes, stirring frequently.

2. Salt the meat well and add it to the skillet, cooking until browned, about 2 to 3 minutes per side. Add the berbere spice blend, pepper, allspice, cinnamon, and nutmeg. Cook for 1 minute, stirring well to coat the meat and onions.

3. Add the garlic, tomato, jalapeños, and wine. Lower the heat to a simmer and cook for 2 to 3 minutes, stirring occasionally, until the sauce thickens. Serve immediately.

NOTE: *If you choose not to cook with red wine, you can substitute ½ cup beef stock and ½ tablespoon red wine vinegar or apple cider vinegar, but it will change the flavor somewhat.*

MACRONUTRIENTS PER SERVING
CALORIES: 491 · FAT: 35 G, 313 KCAL · CARBOHYDRATE: 6 G (4 G NET), 22 KCAL · PROTEIN: 35 G, 140 KCAL

RUSSIA

MONGOLIA

CHINA

INDIA

STAN

KYRGYZSTAN

TAJIKISTAN

PAKISTAN

NEPAL

BHUTAN

BANGLADESH

MYANMAR
(BURMA)

LAOS

THAILAND

CAMBODIA

VIETNAM

SRI
LANKA

BRUNEI

MALAYSIA

INDONESIA

NORTH
KOREA

SOUTH
KOREA

JAPAN

TAIWAN

PHILIPPINES

PAPUA
NEW
GUINEA

TIMOR LESTE

SOLOMON
ISLANDS

NEW
CALEDONIA
(FRANCE)

AUSTRALIA

Pacific

Indian Ocean

EAST ASIA

BOK CHOY WITH MUSHROOM

MAKES 6 SERVINGS

Tender baby bok choy and richly umami shiitake mushrooms make the perfect pair for this braised vegetable dish. We recommend you allow the mushrooms to soak overnight if you have the time, as the longer soak causes them to become decadently plump and velvety.

INGREDIENTS

10 to 12 dried whole shiitake mushrooms

Filtered water

2 cups chicken bone broth or stock

2 tablespoons tamari

2 teaspoons coconut vinegar

1 teaspoon gelatin (optional, to thicken sauce)

1 teaspoon toasted sesame oil

2 tablespoons avocado oil

2 cloves garlic, smashed and minced

1½-inch knob fresh ginger, grated

1 pound small to medium baby bok choy, halved

1. Prepare the shiitake mushrooms for soaking by removing any visible sediment from the caps and rinsing with fresh water.

2. **TO SOAK OVERNIGHT (RECOMMENDED):** Place the mushroom caps in a medium-sized bowl and cover with several inches of room-temperature filtered water. Place in the refrigerator and soak for 8 hours or longer, until the mushrooms have become very plump.

   TO QUICK-SOAK: Bring a medium-sized saucepan of water to a boil and add the mushroom caps. Remove from heat and cover the pot with a lid. Allow the mushrooms to soak for 30 minutes, turning the caps occasionally, until the mushrooms have become tender.

3. Once the mushrooms have fully reconstituted, remove them from the water and gently squeeze out any excess moisture. Remove any stems. With a sharp knife, score an "X" shape on the top of the mushroom caps.

4. In a small bowl, whisk together the bone broth, tamari, coconut vinegar, gelatin, and sesame oil.

5. Heat the avocado oil in a large skillet over high heat. When the oil just begins to shimmer (but not smoke) add the garlic and ginger and sauté, stirring frequently for 30 seconds. Add the mushrooms and sauté 1 minute longer. Pour in the bone broth mixture and heat until boiling. Once the sauce boils, reduce the heat to a simmer. Cover the pan and cook until the mushrooms are completely tender and the sauce has thickened, about 20 minutes for overnight-soaked mushrooms and up to 40 minutes for quick-soaked mushrooms. While the mushrooms cook, move on to the next step. >>

6. Bring a large pot of water to boil and fill a large bowl with ice water. Once the water is boiling, place the bok choy in the boiling water for 2 minutes for smaller or 3 minutes for larger bok choy, until crisp-tender. Immediately drain the bok choy and submerge them in the ice water bath for 1 minute to stop the cooking process. Shake off excess water and place in a colander to drain.

7. To serve, slice the drained bok choy into halves lengthwise. Arrange them in a circle on a round serving plate with the root ends facing outward. Mound the mushrooms in the center of the circle and pour the sauce over top. Serve immediately.

MACRONUTRIENTS PER SERVING
CALORIES: 104 KCAL FAT: 7 G, 59 KCAL CARBOHYDRATE: 9 G (7 G NET), 34 KCAL PROTEIN: 5 G, 19 KCAL

34   KETO PASSPORT

KETO-FRIENDLY SRIRACHA

MAKES ABOUT 1½ CUPS

INGREDIENTS

2 pounds red jalapeño peppers, stems trimmed off (see Note)

¼ cup filtered water

8 cloves garlic

2 teaspoons fine sea salt

2 teaspoons plain yogurt or brine (optional, see Note)

½ cup apple cider or white vinegar

¼ cup coconut vinegar, or use additional apple cider or white vinegar

2 tablespoons fish sauce (optional)

Equipment

1 quart-size jar or 2 pint-size jars

1 or 2 glass fermentation weight(s) (optional but recommended)

Food preparation gloves (optional but recommended)

1. Before beginning, wash and sterilize all equipment that will come in contact with your peppers such as the fermentation jars and utensils. We recommend wearing food preparation gloves while handling the chilis and fermented chili puree.

2. Place the peppers, water, garlic, and salt in a high-powered blender or food processor. Blend until it forms a purée, stopping to scrape down the sides of the bowl as needed. If using, add the yogurt and pulse until combined.

3. Use a silicone spatula to transfer the pepper purée into the jar(s), pressing down to release air pockets and leaving at least an inch of headspace. Place the jar weight(s) on top of the peppers and press down to squeeze brine from the purée to cover the peppers. Cover the jar loosely with a sterilized lid (do not tighten) or lay an overturned plate over top. Place the jar(s) inside a dish in case the fermentation pushes brine over the top of the jar. Leave to ferment in a temperature-stable room away from any fresh fruit, vegetables, or trash receptacles.

4. After 3 days, check the peppers. You should see tiny bubbles forming. Use a sterilized non-metal utensil to stir the purée, then replace the jar weight, press down, and cover. If you see any mold forming on the surface, you must discard this batch and start again.

5. After 7 to 10 days, the peppers will be ready (they will be slightly tangy, but it can be hard to detect over the spiciness—anywhere in this time range will be fine). Place them back in the blender along with the vinegars and the fish sauce if using. Blend until the purée is very smooth. >>

6. Place a fine mesh strainer over a saucepan on the stove. Pour the purée through the strainer, stirring and pressing the mixture through the strainer with a spatula. This takes several minutes. When the mixture is fully strained, discard the solids. Bring the liquid in the saucepan to a boil and boil gently for 5 minutes to thicken. Allow to cool, then transfer to an airtight container and store in the refrigerator.

NOTES: *You can substitute serrano or the even spicier cayenne for some of the red peppers in this recipe if you are a fan of heat.*

The yogurt or brine is not necessary in this recipe, but it provides a dose of lactobacilli that can aid in the fermentation. You may use brine from any fermentation, including the Sauerkraut (page 211), Kimchi (page 45), Polish Dill Pickles (page 193), or even Beet Kvass (page 175) from this book. The flavor of the brine might subtly impact the flavor of the sriracha.

It is impossible to get accurate nutritional information for home-fermented vegetables. We researched a variety of brands of sriracha sauces and determined that the majority of the carbs in commercially available options come from added sugars. The amount of carbohydrate per serving in homemade sugar-free sriracha should be negligible. These values are provided as an estimate. Read the "Fermenting" section on page xiv before fermenting for the first time.

MACRONUTRIENTS PER SERVING (1 TABLESPOON)
CALORIES: 1 KCAL FAT: 0 G, 0 KCAL CARBOHYDRATE: <1 G (<1 G NET), 1 KCAL PROTEIN: 0 G, 0 KCAL

EAST ASIA   37

BULGOGI

MAKES 6 SERVINGS

Customarily, bulgogi recipes do not include vegetables beyond onions, scallions, and carrots, but we enthusiastically support experimenting with Layla's family recipe. Try adding a cup or two of sliced cremini mushrooms, bell peppers, broccoli, or any other vegetable you enjoy; simply add them in step 4 below. This recipe can also be made with sliced chicken thigh meat or portabella mushroom caps in place of the beef. Leftover bulgogi tastes excellent and is a good option if you want to prepare meals ahead of time.

INGREDIENTS

2 pounds well-marbled beef such as ribeye or chuck roast

$\frac{1}{4}$ medium Asian pear, peeled (See Note)

2 cloves garlic, smashed

$\frac{1}{2}$-inch knob of fresh ginger, peeled and roughly sliced

2 tablespoons tamari or coconut aminos

6 to 9 drops liquid stevia or the equivalent keto-friendly sweetener of choice

1 large carrot, julienned

2 scallions, white and green parts, thinly sliced

$\frac{1}{2}$ medium yellow onion, thinly sliced

1 tablespoon sesame oil

1 tablespoon light olive oil

1. Optional but recommended: Place the beef in the freezer for 30 minutes to an hour to make it easier to slice.

2. Slice the beef across the grain into pieces approximately $\frac{1}{8}$-inch thick and 1 to 2 inches long. Do not be concerned if the pieces are ragged-looking or not quite uniform. Place the sliced meat into a large bowl and set aside.

3. Place the pear, garlic, ginger, tamari, and stevia into the bowl of a food processor or blender. Purée until smooth.

4. Add the pear purée, carrot, scallion, onions, and sesame oil to the bowl of meat. Using your hands, mix well for 2 or 3 minutes, until the ingredients are thoroughly coated. Once mixed, pack down the meat and allow to marinate at room temperature for 30 minutes, or place in the refrigerator and marinate it up to overnight.

5. Heat a large skillet over medium-high heat and add the olive oil to the pan. Working in small batches, stir-fry the marinated beef and vegetables until cooked through, about 5 to 7 minutes per batch. Serve immediately with any pan juices.

NOTE: *If you are unable to find an Asian pear, you may also use $\frac{1}{2}$ of a peeled and seeded Bosc pear.*

MACRONUTRIENTS PER SERVING
CALORIES: 284 KCAL FAT: 15 G, 133 KCAL CARBOHYDRATE: 4 G (3 G NET), 18 KCAL PROTEIN: 34 G, 134 KCAL

CHASU PORK BELLY

MAKES 10 SERVINGS

This adaptation of chasu pork belly uses a small quantity of bourbon whiskey instead of the typical granulated sugar or honey in order to create the sweet caramel flavor that makes this dish so well-loved. We recommend using a non-GMO Bourbon such as Four Roses or Buffalo Trace, but feel free to exclude the bourbon entirely if you would prefer a more savory pork belly.

INGREDIENTS

2 pounds pork belly (select the widest piece possible, thin strips will not work)

2 cups chicken bone broth, stock, or water

¼ cup non-GMO bourbon whiskey

¼ cup tamari

2 tablespoons mirin (see Note)

1 shallot, roughly chopped

6 scallions, white and green parts roughly chopped

6 cloves garlic, crushed and halved

1 2-inch knob of ginger, sliced

Equipment: Cooking twine

1. Preheat the oven to 275°F. Tightly roll the pork belly "jelly (or sushi) roll" style so that the skin is on the outside. Slide several pieces of cooking twine beneath the rolled pork belly in 1-inch intervals and tie securely. This will allow the pork belly to maintain its rolled shape while cooking. Set aside.

2. In a medium saucepan, combine the bone broth, bourbon, tamari, mirin, shallot, scallions, garlic, and ginger. Bring to a rolling boil, then remove from heat.

3. Place the pork belly roll seam-side down in a deep roasting dish or casserole with a lid. (A small chicken roasting dish with a lid is ideal.) Pour the hot bone broth mixture around the pork and cover with the lid slightly ajar. Roast the pork in the oven until it is fully tender, about 3 to 3 ½ hours depending on the width of the pork. The pork is done when the skin is soft and semi-translucent and a skewer can be driven through the entire roast with little resistance.

4. Remove the pork from the oven and allow to cool until safe to handle. Slice and serve immediately, or chill in the refrigerator before reheating (the pork will have a firmer shape if chilled). Slice thinly before reheating.

NOTE: *Mirin is sweet Japanese rice wine. Although you might be inclined to omit it, we recommend using it in this recipe. Properly made, it is a traditional fermented food. Look for one with only rice and koji (aspirgillius) as ingredients, such as Eden Foods brand, which is also non-GMO and organic. You can substitute a tablespoon of sherry or vermouth plus 1 to 2 drops stevia if you wish..*

MACRONUTRIENTS PER SERVING
CALORIES: 510 KCAL FAT: 49 G, 438 KCAL CARBOHYDRATE: 4 G (3 G NET), 15 KCAL PROTEIN: 11 G, 42 KCAL

DO CHUA
(VIETNAMESE PICKLED VEGETABLES)

MAKES 4 SERVINGS

Do Chua is a common Vietnamese side dish, perhaps best known as a topping for banh mi sandwiches. The traditional preparation includes carrots and daikon radish, but do chua is also delicious with other vegetables. To fill your plate with color, try adding zucchini, red radish, cucumber, shredded red cabbage, or any other firm vegetable.

INGREDIENTS

2 tablespoons coconut vinegar, plus more to taste

½ teaspoon fish sauce

1 tablespoon mirin (see Note)

½ cup carrots, cut into matchsticks or thin noodles

½ cup daikon radish, cut into matchsticks or thin noodles

1. Mix together the coconut vinegar, fish sauce, and mirin in a medium-sized bowl.

2. Place the carrots and daikon radish into the bowl and mix well, using your hands to squeeze the vegetables together with the vinegar. Cover and refrigerate for 30 minutes. Stir well before serving.

NOTE: *Mirin is sweet Japanese rice wine, which perhaps makes it an unusual ingredient in a keto recipe. Although you might be inclined to skip it, we recommend against doing so to preserve the flavor of the dish. Properly made Mirin is a traditional fermented food. Look for one with only rice and koji (aspirgillius) as ingredients. Eden Foods brand makes a mass-market traditional mirin that is non-GMO and organic. You can substitute a tablespoon of sherry or vermouth plus 1 to 2 drops stevia if you wish.*

MACRONUTRIENTS PER SERVING
CALORIES: 16 KCAL FAT: 0 G, 1 KCAL CARBOHYDRATE: 4 G (3 G NET), 16 KCAL PROTEIN: 0 G, 1 KCAL

KIMCHI

Baechu kimchi made with napa cabbage is perhaps one of the most famous of all Korea's many banchan (side dishes). Making kimchi is often a community social affair, with many families gathering together to share the work of preparing several crates' worth of cabbage at once. This recipe, straight from Layla McGowan's mother Chong Ye (who was born and raised in Chungcheongnam-do, on the western coast of South Korea), allows you to make a smaller quantity of this gut-nourishing fermented dish.

INGREDIENTS

1 medium head Napa cabbage (about 3 to 4 pounds total)

1 cup or more Korean brining salt or coarse sea salt, plus more to taste

2 tablespoons fish sauce

1½ medium heads garlic, peeled

1 1-inch piece fresh ginger, peeled

5 to 6 tablespoons gochugaru chili flakes, also known as Korean red pepper powder (see Note)

1 tablespoon filtered water, as needed

½ medium Korean Joeson radish (mu) or daikon radish, peeled, cut into 2" long matchsticks

6 large scallions, white and green parts sliced into 1-inch pieces

Equipment

1 wide-mouth quart-size jar

Non-metal tamper (optional)

1 glass fermentation weight (see page xv)

Food preparation gloves (optional but recommended)

1. Remove any protruding core from the bottom of the cabbage and slice the head in half lengthwise. Chop the halves crosswise into 2" wide strips, then rinse the cabbage and shake off any excess water.

2. In a large nonmetallic bowl, arrange a large handful of the cabbage strips into a single layer. Sprinkle the cabbage with a generous pinch of salt so that the entire surface is lightly coated. Continue to add layers of cabbage and salt until all the cabbage has been used. Once the cabbage has been salted, use your hands to press down on the leaves with gentle pressure to help release water. As the cabbage wilts, water will accumulate in the bowl.

3. Leave the cabbage on a countertop for about 3 or 4 hours. After each hour, gently flip the cabbage so that the bottom layer is now on the top. This prevents the bottom layers >>

from becoming overly wilted and soft. Once the cabbage has wilted through, gently rinse the leaves with fresh water 2 to 3 times to remove excess salt from the leaves. Drain well.

4. While the cabbage drains, prepare the gochugaru paste. Place the fish sauce, garlic, ginger, and gochugaru chili flakes into the bowl of a food processor or blender and process into a paste. If the mixture is too thick to blend well, add a tablespoon or more of water as needed. We recommend wearing food preparation gloves while handling the gochugaru puree and prepared kimchi.

5. Place the drained cabbage, Korean radish, scallions, and gochugaru paste into a large bowl. Toss well to coat. Taste the cabbage for saltiness and add more salt to your taste if necessary. Good kimchi should be pleasantly salty, not overpoweringly so. Once the taste is to your liking, tightly pack the prepared cabbage into a large glass jar, tamping down the contents with your hands or a non-metal tamper so that there are no air bubbles.

6. Freshly-prepared kimchi can be eaten immediately or left to ferment. To ferment your kimchi, cover the mouth of the jar with an overturned plate and leave the jar in an area of the house that is dark, maintains stable slightly cool temperature, and is away from any plants, trash cans, or fresh fruits and vegetables for 3 or more days. Longer fermentation times will result in more pungently "tangy" kimchi. Store any uneaten kimchi in an airtight container in the fridge to prevent further fermentation.

NOTES: *Gochugaru is a distinctive Korean seasoning that consists of coarsely-ground sun-dried Korean chili peppers. It's readily available in most Asian markets, where it is most commonly sold in bags. It can also be purchased online at various retailers such as Amazon.com or the US-based Korean grocery store chain, HMart (www.hmart.com). Simply search for "red pepper powder."*

It is impossible to get accurate nutritional information for home-fermented vegetables. These values are provided as an estimate. Read the "Fermenting" section on page xv before fermenting for the first time.

MACRONUTRIENTS PER SERVING (½ CUP)
CALORIES: 15 KCAL FAT: 0 G, 3 KCAL CARBOHYDRATES: 2 G (2 G NET), 9 KCAL PROTEIN: 1 G, 6 KCAL

46   KETO PASSPORT

OMURICE

MAKES 4 INDIVIDUAL OMELETS

These Japanese omelets, aka omu-raisu, are usually made with fried rice, but—surprise!—the recipe here calls for cauliflower. It would also be wonderful with riced turnips, parsnips, rutabaga, or broccoli stems. We suggest making a double batch of Okonomiyaki to top your omurice if you love the flavor.

INGREDIENTS

1 cup cooked cauliflower rice

2 tablespoons unsalted butter or ghee

½ medium onion, diced

½ pound pork belly or boneless, skinless chicken thighs, diced into ½-inch pieces

½ small carrot, grated

1 scallion, white and green parts, thinly sliced

¼ cup Okonomiyaki (page 53) plus ¼ cup more for serving (optional)

2 tablespoons avocado oil or fat of choice

4 large eggs

1 teaspoon fine sea salt

1 tablespoon Japanese-style mayonnaise (page 53)

1 tablespoon no-sugar-added ketchup

1 tablespoon minced fresh chives or additional scallions

1. Place the cauliflower rice in a clean kitchen towel and squeeze out any excess water. Set aside.

2. Heat the butter in a large skillet over medium-high heat. Add the onions and sauté until softened, about 5 minutes. Add the pork belly and sauté until cooked through, 5 to 8 minutes. Add the carrot, cauliflower rice, scallion, and ¼ cup okonomiyaki, stirring well to combine. Cook for 2 minutes, then remove from heat.

3. To prepare the omelets, season an omelet pan or small skillet with 2 tablespoons of oil and heat over medium. Working one egg at a time, break the egg into a small bowl, season with a pinch of salt, and beat gently. Pour the beaten egg into the heated pan and tilt to coat the bottom. Cook briefly until the edges are just set but the egg is still raw on top, about 60 to 90 seconds.

4. Spoon ¼ of the meat and rice filling onto half of the egg, forming a line just to one side of the center. Avoid placing the filling directly in the middle of the omelet. Use a spatula to gently fold the edges of the omelet over the filling. The egg will not fully wrap the filling. Move the omelet to one end of the pan.

5. Place the plate over the pan and, holding the plate in place with one hand, simultaneously invert both the pan and plate, causing the omelet to gently fall onto the plate with its >>

folded sides tucked underneath (see Note). For a traditional presentation, cover the omelet with a paper towel or clean cloth and mold it into an oval or football shape while still warm. Repeat for the remaining ingredients.

6. Serve drizzled with Japanese-style mayonnaise, ketchup, okonomiyaki, and fresh chives.

NOTE: *This is the customary presentation. If you aren't familiar with omurice, before attempting it the first time it can be helpful to watch a video online to see how it's made. Instead of the method described here, you may instead drape the egg over top of the filling. To do this, follow the first two steps as written, then divide the filling between 4 serving plates and use your hands to form the filling into tight, oval mounds. Move on to step 3, but allow the egg to cook for 2 to 3 minutes, until just cooked but still very tender. Carefully use a spatula to remove the egg from the pan and drape it over top the mounded rice. Serve drizzled with Japanese-style mayonnaise, ketchup, okonomiyaki, and fresh chives.*

MACRONUTRIENTS PER SERVING (WITH PORK BELLY AND ADDITIONAL OKONOMIYAKI)
CALORIES: 543 KCAL FAT: 51 G, 456 KCAL CARBOHYDRATE: 8 G (5 G NET), 33 KCAL PROTEIN: 13 G, 54 KCAL

EAST ASIA   49

LARB LETTUCE CUPS

MAKES 4 SERVINGS

Larb is a simple ground meat dish that is a favorite in Thailand and Laos. It whips up quickly for a speedy and tasty weeknight dinner. Serve it alongside a simple green salad and sliced raw cucumbers for a complete meal.

INGREDIENTS

3 tablespoons coconut oil

4 scallions, white and light green parts thinly sliced

1 small jalapeño, ribs and seeds removed, finely minced

1-inch knob fresh ginger, grated or very finely minced

1½ pounds ground pork, ground turkey, or a mixture

1 small bunch fresh cilantro, leaves finely chopped, stems discarded

1 small bunch fresh mint, leaves finely chopped, stems discarded

Zest and juice of 1 lime

Zest and juice of 1 lemon

2 teaspoons fish sauce

½ teaspoon fine sea salt

¼ teaspoon ground black pepper

1 head butter lettuce, leaves separated

Optional accompaniments

1 batch Spicy Mayo (page 63)

Keto-friendly Sriracha (page 35)

Shoyu Tamago (page 57)

1. Melt the coconut oil in a large skillet over medium heat. Add the scallions, jalapeño, and ginger. Sauté two minutes until just fragrant. Break up the meat with your hands and add it to the skillet. Stir to combine, then cook about 5 minutes until a little pink remains, breaking up the meat with a spoon or meat chopper as it cooks.

2. Scatter the chopped cilantro and mint over the meat and stir well to combine. Stir in the zest and juice of the lime and lemon, the fish sauce, salt, and pepper. Continue to cook until no pink remains, stirring occasionally. Turn the heat down to low and simmer about 10 minutes until most of the liquid has evaporated. Taste and adjust salt and pepper as needed.

3. Transfer to a serving bowl. Serve with lettuce leaves for wrapping and any desired accompaniments on the side.

MACRONUTRIENTS PER SERVING (no optional accompaniments)
CALORIES: 490 KCAL FAT: 40 G, 356 KCAL CARBOHYDRATE: 5 G (4 G NET), 20 KCAL PROTEIN: 28 G, 110 KCAL

OKONOMIYAKI SAUCE

MAKES ABOUT ½ CUP

A combination of okonomiyaki sauce, Japanese-style mayonnaise, and ketchup is the customary topping for omurice, the Japanese-style omelet featured on page 47, but don't feel limited to using these sauces only to top omelets! Try combining the okonomiyaki sauce with your meat of choice and a heap of tender vegetables for an incredible no-fuss stir-fry. Or use the Japanese-style mayonnaise in your next batch of deviled eggs along with a sprinkling of crispy roasted sea vegetables for an Asian twist.

INGREDIENTS
2 tablespoons Worcestershire sauce (see Note)

¼ cup no-sugar-added ketchup

2 tablespoons tamari or coconut aminos

2 teaspoons fermented mirin or dry sherry

In a small bowl, stir together the Worcestershire sauce, ketchup, tamari, and mirin until thoroughly combined.

NOTE: *You can substitute 2 teaspoons apple cider vinegar, 1 teaspoon coconut aminos, and ¼ teaspoon Dijon mustard for the Worcestershire sauce.*

MACRONUTRIENTS PER 1 TABLESPOON
CALORIES: 10 KCAL FAT: 0 G, 0 KCAL CARBOHYDRATE: 2 G (2 G NET), 9 KCAL PROTEIN: 0 G, 2 KCAL

. . . .

JAPANESE-STYLE MAYONNAISE

MAKES ABOUT ¼ CUP

INGREDIENTS
4 tablespoons avocado oil mayonnaise

1 teaspoon coconut vinegar

3 to 4 drops liquid stevia or 1 teaspoon erythritol

In a small bowl, stir together the mayonnaise, coconut vinegar, and stevia until thoroughly combined. Taste and adjust the level of sweetness as desired.

MACRONUTRIENTS PER 1 TABLESPOON
CALORIES: 100 KCAL FAT: 11 G, 99 KCAL CARBOHYDRATE: 0 G, 0 KCAL PROTEIN: 0 G, 0 KCAL

PORK SATAY

MAKES 4 SERVINGS

For pork satay, using a fattier cut of meat like a butt roast makes a much tastier dish, compared to leaner chops. It's the lemongrass that really makes this dish, though.

INGREDIENTS

1 stalk lemongrass, bottom stem and woody outer leaves removed, finely chopped

2 cloves garlic, minced

¼ teaspoon ground ginger

5 tablespoons full-fat coconut milk

1 tablespoon red curry paste

½ tablespoon fresh lime juice

½ teaspoon fish sauce

½ tablespoon ground turmeric

½ teaspoon ground cumin

2 drops stevia, 1 teaspoon erythritol or ¼ tablespoon unsweetened marmalade

1 pound pork butt or shoulder roast

Almond Satay Sauce

½ cup full-fat coconut milk

¼ cup chicken bone broth or stock

¼ cup almond butter (no sugar added)

1 tablespoon red curry paste

1 to 2 drops stevia, ½ teaspoon erythritol or ¼ tablespoon unsweetened marmalade

¼ teaspoon lime juice

1 tablespoon coconut vinegar

¼ teaspoon fish sauce

Fine sea salt, to taste

Equipment: 12 short or 6 long skewers, metal or bamboo (see Note)

1. In a large bowl, mix together the lemongrass, garlic, ginger, coconut milk, curry paste, lime juice, fish sauce, turmeric, cumin, and stevia.

2. Cut the pork into strips 1 inch wide by ¼ inch thick. Toss the pork with the mixture in the bowl. Cover and refrigerate for 1 hour, or up to 8 hours.

3. While the pork marinates, prepare the almond satay sauce. In a small saucepan over medium heat, gently warm the coconut milk. Next, add the bone broth, almond butter, curry paste, and stevia. Simmer for about 5 minutes stirring constantly until the marinade becomes smooth. Once smooth, stir in the lime juice, vinegar, and fish sauce. Remove from heat. Season with salt to taste. Transfer to a bowl and set aside.

4. If grilling, brush the grill well with oil and heat it to medium-high heat. If broiling, preheat the broiler to high. Shake any excess marinade and larger pieces of lemongrass from the pork and thread the pork onto the skewers.

5. Grill or broil at a distance of about 4 inches from the heating element for 3 to 5 minutes per side, until cooked through. Serve with individual dishes of satay sauce for dipping.

NOTE: *If you are using wooden skewers, soak them in warm water for a minimum of 30 minutes prior to cooking in order to prevent them from burning.*

MACRONUTRIENTS PER SERVING
CALORIES: 414 KCAL FAT: 31 G, 282 KCAL CARB: 8 G (5 G NET), 31 KCAL PROTEIN: 25 G, 100 KCAL

SHOYU TAMAGO

MAKES 4 SERVINGS

Shoyu tamago, aka soy sauce eggs or ramen eggs, are hard-boiled eggs marinated in a mixture of soy sauce and, usually, mirin. Our version uses gluten-free tamari and coconut vinegar instead. Enjoy these as a snack, or serve them with Zoodle Ramen (page 72), Larb Lettuce Cups (page 51), or use them to create a unique twist on deviled eggs (page 265).

INGREDIENTS

4 hard-boiled large eggs, peeled (see Note)

¾ cup tamari

2 tablespoons coconut vinegar

1 teaspoon sesame oil

1. Combine the tamari, vinegar, and sesame oil in a jar or other airtight glass container that will fit your eggs. Add the eggs, seal the jar, and place in the refrigerator.

2. Allow to marinate for at least an hour, but up to 24 hours or even longer depending on your preferences. The longer the marinating time, the stronger the flavor. If desired, remove from the marinade and store in an airtight container in the refrigerator.

. . . .

VARIATION: QUAIL SHOYU TAMAGO

Quail eggs are delightfully bite-sized, creamy, and downright wonderful.

INGREDIENTS

¾ cup tamari

2 tablespoons coconut vinegar

1 teaspoon sesame oil

Water

10 quail eggs

1. Combine the tamari, vinegar, and sesame oil in a jar or other airtight glass container that will fit your eggs. Set aside.

2. Place a steamer basket inside a medium saucepan. Add water just to the bottom of the basket and bring it to a boil. Place the eggs in the basket, cover the pan, and steam the eggs for 3½ minutes. (For softer yolks, steam for 3 minutes; for harder yolks, 4 minutes.) Meanwhile, prepare an ice bath. >>

3. When the eggs are cooked, transfer them immediately to the ice bath. When cool, carefully peel them under running water. Place the eggs in the marinade, seal the jar, and place in the refrigerator.

4. Allow to marinate for at least an hour, or longer. (The first time you make these, test an egg every hour or so to find your personal sweet spot.) Remove the eggs from the marinade and store in an airtight container in the refrigerator.

NOTES: *The amount of marinade that actually gets absorbed into each egg is small. A conservative estimate, which we used to calculate the macronutrients, would be that 20% of the marinade is absorbed (much less for eggs marinated only an hour or two).*

MACRONUTRIENTS PER SERVING (1 EGG)
CALORIES: 90 KCAL FAT: 6 G, 54 KCAL CARBOHYDRATE: 1 G (1 G NET), 5 KCAL PROTEIN: 7 G, 30 KCAL

MACRONUTRIENTS PER SERVING (5 QUAIL EGGS)
CALORIES: 96 FAT: 6 G, 58 CALORIES CARBOHYDRATE: 1 G (1 G NET), 6 CALORIES PROTEIN: 8 G, 32 CALORIES

SOKKORI GOMTANG (OXTAIL SOUP)

MAKES 6 SERVINGS

Layla likes to call this highly nourishing Oxtail Soup "Original Korean Bone Broth." This recipe was passed down to her from her mother. A clear (or even milky-colored) broth is prized, so the meat is rinsed several times during cooking to wash away any of the water-soluble proteins that cause foam, metallic flavors, or a dark coloration. Like any bone broth, you will have the best results if the bones are from healthy animals and have been simmered patiently in order to maximize the release of minerals and collagen.

INGREDIENTS

2½ pounds oxtails

Water

4 cloves garlic, halved

1 tablespoon fine sea salt, to taste

1 teaspoon black peppercorns

1 pound Korean white radish (mu) or Daikon radish, peeled and chopped into ¼-inch thick half-moons

4 green onions, white and green parts thinly sliced

Freshly ground black pepper for serving

1. Rinse the oxtails under running water and trim away any excess fat, leaving the silver membrane intact. You may save this fat for another use (such as rendering for tallow) or discard. Fill a large bowl with cold water and allow the oxtails to soak for 20 minutes to an hour. The water in the bowl will turn pink as the oxtails rest. Discard the water and rinse the oxtails.

2. Place the oxtails in a large pot and fill with enough water to cover the oxtails by 1 to 2 inches. Bring to a rolling boil and allow to boil for 10 minutes. A large quantity of beige-colored foam should rise to the surface of the water. Drain the water and rinse the oxtails. This parboiling step is optional but highly recommended for a clear, mild-tasting broth.

3. Fill a clean pot with approximately 3 liters (12 cups) of water, then add the rinsed oxtails, garlic, sea salt, and black peppercorns. Bring to a boil, then reduce to a simmer. Simmer for 3 to 4 hours uncovered, until the meat on the oxtails is fork-tender. While the oxtails simmer, periodically skim off any foam that accumulates on the surface. If the water reduces by more than half during cooking, pour in an additional 3 to 4 cups of water as needed.

4. Once the meat is fork-tender, skim off the peppercorns and discard. If there is an excessive quantity of liquified fat on top of the broth, you may skim this off the surface as well.

5. Add the sliced radish to the broth and allow to simmer until translucent and tender throughout, about 20 to 30 minutes. If necessary, you may also add another 1 or 2 cups of water to the broth if it has reduced below half. Add salt to taste. >>

6. Sokkori Gomtang is traditionally served with the meat left on the bone, but you may shred the meat off the bones prior to serving if desired. In either instance, fill individual bowls with 1 to 3 joints of meat (depending on size) and a generous quantity of mu radish and broth. Immediately before serving, sprinkle each bowl with sliced green onion and freshly ground pepper. Serve piping hot, preferably with a side of kimchi (page 45).

MACRONUTRIENTS PER SERVING
CALORIES: 510 KCAL FAT: 29 G, 258 KCAL CARBOHYDRATE: 5 G (3 G NET), 18 KCAL PROTEIN: 56 G, 224 KCAL

SPICY MAYO

MAKES ABOUT 2/3 CUP

Spicy mayo is a sushi restaurant staple, but you can (and should!) use it on everything from sashimi to burgers to Brussels sprouts. It makes an excellent dip for Churrasco Chicken Hearts (page 298).

INGREDIENTS

½ cup avocado oil mayonnaise or Japanese-style Mayonnaise (page 53)

1 to 2 tablespoons Keto-friendly Sriracha (page 35), to taste, or substitute store-bought

1 to 2 tablespoons fresh lime juice, to taste

1. In a small bowl, whisk together the mayonnaise, 1 tablespoon sriracha, and 1 tablespoon lime juice. Taste and adjust the sriracha and lime juice to suit your palate.

2. Use immediately, or transfer to an airtight container and store in the refrigerator.

MACRONUTRIENTS PER SERVING (1 TABLESPOON)
CALORIES: 105 KCAL   FAT: 11 G, 101 KCAL   CARBOHYDRATE: 0 G, 1 KCAL   PROTEIN: 0 G, 0 KCAL

TAK BOKKEUM TANG

MAKES 4 SERVINGS

This spicy braised chicken dish is one of the many Korean dishes that Layla learned to cook from her mother. It contains gochujang, a fermented red chili paste whose flavor will be familiar to anyone who loves Korean food (see the Note). Ask the butcher at your grocery store to cut your chicken for you to save time.

INGREDIENTS

1 3- to 4-pound chicken

2 tablespoons Korean gochujang (see Note)

1 tablespoon tamari or coconut aminos

1 tablespoon coconut vinegar

1 teaspoon sesame oil

1 teaspoon grated fresh ginger

2 cloves garlic, grated

2 tablespoons Korean gochu chili flakes or dried red chili flakes

½ medium onion, chopped

1 cup chicken bone broth or water

1 medium carrot, roll cut or diced large

1½ cups peeled daikon radish, cut into 1-inch pieces

1 jalapeño, seeds and ribs removed, diced

1 scallion, white and green parts cut into 1-inch pieces, plus more for garnish if desired

Fine sea salt, to taste

1. Cut the chicken into 10 pieces (drumsticks, thighs, wings, and breasts), splitting each breast into 2 equal-sized pieces. Whisk the gochujang, tamari, vinegar, sesame oil, ginger, garlic, and chili flakes together in a large bowl. Toss the cut chicken and onion in the gochujang mixture until coated.

2. Transfer the chicken and onions to a deep skillet or braising pot and pour in the bone broth. Bring to a boil over medium-high heat, then reduce to a vigorous simmer. Cook for 10 minutes, stirring occasionally.

3. Stir in the carrot, radish, and jalapeño and cook for an additional 8 to 10 minutes, until the carrots are tender and the chicken is cooked through. Add the scallions cook for 1 minute longer, then remove from heat. Season with salt to taste.

4. To serve, transfer the chicken and vegetables to a large serving platter. Spoon the pan sauce over the chicken. Optionally garnish with scallion slices.

NOTE: *Be sure to find a brand of gochujang that does not contain corn syrup (it can be found online if not locally). If you object strongly to rice in the ingredients (which we do not mind in this quantity and because it is fermented), you can always make your own substitute. Nothing will perfectly approximate the distinct flavor of gochujang, but you can get some of the heat and the salty sweetness with red pepper flakes and coconut aminos, perhaps with a dollop of sambal oelek or harissa.*

MACRONUTRIENTS PER SERVING
CALORIES: 375 KCAL FAT: 21 G, 185 KCAL CARBOHYDRATE: 11 G (9 G NET), 43 KCAL PROTEIN: 34 G, 138 KCAL

THIT HEO NUONG XA (VIETNAMESE-STYLE PORK CHOPS)

MAKES 4 SERVINGS

The secret to not drying out these pork chops is a quick cook in a hot pan. Serve the chops with cold zucchini noodles lightly dressed in sesame oil for a quick and easy meal.

INGREDIENTS

¼ cup onion, finely minced

1 clove garlic, minced

12 drops liquid stevia (recommended) or 1½ teaspoons unsweetened marmalade

2 tablespoons coconut vinegar

2 tablespoons fish sauce

½ teaspoon lime juice

2 pounds thin-cut pork chops (boneless or bone-in)

Generous pinches of fine sea salt and pepper

2 tablespoons avocado oil

1. To prepare the marinade, in a small bowl whisk together the onion, garlic, stevia, coconut vinegar, fish sauce, and lime juice. Pour half the marinade into a shallow dish and lay the pork chops on top. Pour the remaining marinade on top and turn the pork chops a few times to coat. Allow to marinate at room temperature for 30 minutes.

2. Remove the pork chops from the marinade, shaking off any excess. Reserve the remaining marinade. Season the pork chops with salt and pepper. Heat the oil in a large skillet over medium-high heat and cook the chops 2 to 4 minutes per side depending on thickness, until cooked through. Move the pork chops to a covered dish and set aside to rest.

3. Bring the reserved marinade to a boil in a small saucepan. Boil for about a minute to thicken.

4. Serve the pork chops with the marinade drizzled over top.

MACRONUTRIENTS PER SERVING
CALORIES: 555 KCAL FAT: 30 G, 268 KCAL CARBOHYDRATE: 2 G (2 G NET), 7 KCAL PROTEIN: 66 G, 264 KCAL

TOM YUM GOONG

MAKES 4 SERVINGS

Besides pad thai, tom yum soup might be the dish most associated with Thai food, at least to Americans. Spicy, tangy, and surprisingly complex, it is no wonder its popularity has spread across the globe! The best part is that it cooks up in less than 20 minutes start to finish, even though the flavor feels like it should take much longer.

INGREDIENTS

4 cups chicken bone broth or seafood stock

2 tablespoons red curry paste, or to taste

1 stalk lemongrass, roughly chopped, pounded until bruised

12 ounces large shrimp, peeled and deveined

4 ounces button mushrooms, sliced

2 tablespoons lime juice

1 tablespoon fish sauce

½ cup sliced cherry tomatoes

1 scallion, white and green parts, thinly sliced

1 tablespoon fresh cilantro leaves, to garnish

2 Thai chilis or serrano peppers, seeded and sliced (optional but recommended)

Lime wedges, to garnish

1. In a large pot, bring the seafood stock to a gentle boil. Add the red chili paste and lemongrass and cook for 6 minutes.

2. Strain the soup to remove the lemongrass pieces and return the stock to the pot. Add the mushrooms and shrimp and cook for 2 to 3 minutes, until the shrimp are just opaque and begin to curl into a loose C-shape (if they curl into tight Os, they are overcooked). Remove from heat.

3. Add the lime juice, fish sauce, and cherry tomatoes and stir to combine. Ladle the soup into serving bowls top with the scallions, cilantro, sliced chilis, and lime wedges.

MACRONUTRIENTS PER SERVING
CALORIES: 162 KCAL FAT: 3 G, 31 KCAL CARBOHYDRATE: 6 G (4 G NET), 23 KCAL PROTEIN: 27 G, 109 KCAL

YOGURT PROBIOTIC SHOTS

MAKES ABOUT 8 1-OZ SERVINGS

This recipe is inspired by the popular Japanese probiotic yogurt drink, Yakult. Layla has fond memories of the sweet and tangy "Yakuruto" (Yakult's Korean name) drink her mother used to serve her after dinner. Often this treat was followed with the puzzling warning that she shouldn't drink too many of them because "Yakuruto is medicine." Unfortunately, Yakult-type drinks are usually made with skim milk powder and other objectionable ingredients. These probiotic shots, however, are free from any objectionable additives and make use of the leftover acid whey that results from straining yogurt.

INGREDIENTS
1 cup acid whey (see the Yogurt recipe, page 115)

¼ teaspoon vanilla extract

4 to 6 drops liquid stevia, or equivalent quantity keto-friendly sweetener of choice

1. In a small bowl, mix together the acid whey, vanilla extract, and stevia. The mixture should taste pleasantly tangy. Adjust the level of sweetness to your preference by adjusting either the vanilla or stevia.

2. Store the shots in the refrigerator portioned into individual miniature jars or in a single air-tight container. Like other probiotic supplements, you will derive the most benefit from the yogurt shots if they are consumed on an empty stomach. A 1-ounce serving equals 2 tablespoons.

NOTE: *It is impossible to get accurate nutritional information for home-fermented recipes. These values are provided as an estimate. Read the "Fermenting" section on page xiv before fermenting for the first time.*

MACRONUTRIENTS PER SERVING
CALORIES: 8 KCAL FAT: 0 G, 0 KCAL CARBOHYDRATE: 2 G (2 G NET), 6 KCAL PROTEIN: <1 G, 1 KCAL

ZOODLE RAMEN

MAKES 6 SERVINGS

This is a keto-friendly adaptation of shoyu ramen. Here, the traditional three-day cooking time has been shortened significantly and the wheat-based noodles substituted with spiralized zucchini.

INGREDIENTS

1½ pounds pork ribs

8 cups filtered water

¼ cup bonito flakes

2 cups chicken bone broth

6 cloves garlic, smashed

½-inch piece of fresh ginger, sliced and bruised

1 4- to 6-inch piece dried kombu, or 1 knot if tied

1 whole leek, chopped roughly

1 tablespoon mirin (see Note)

¼ cup tamari

For serving

2 large zucchinis, cut into noodles

3 peeled hard-boiled medium eggs, halved

6 1-ounce slices leftover Chasu Pork Belly (page 41, or substitute pancetta, sliced or cubed, fried)

2 scallions, white and green parts thinly sliced

1 cup mung bean sprouts

Chili and sesame oils (optional)

1. Place the ribs in a large pot and cover completely with water. Bring the water to a boil and allow the ribs to boil for 20 minutes. A raft of brownish froth will collect at the top of the pot. Remove the ribs and rinse well, making sure to wash away any dark scum. Discard the water.

2. Pour 8 cups of water into a clean soup pot and add the ribs, bonito flakes, bone broth, garlic, ginger, kombu, leek, mirin, and tamari. Bring to a boil and simmer for 2 ½ hours, adding more water to the pot as needed.

3. Strain the broth and discard any cooked vegetables. You may reserve the cooked pork and bones for another use. Alternatively, you may chop the pork and added to the ramen if desired.

4. Divide the raw zucchini noodles evenly between 6 bowls and top the noodles with the egg halves and pork slices. Carefully pour the ramen broth over top of the noodles, then sprinkle with scallions and mung bean sprouts. Serve immediately with chili and sesame oils for topping.

NOTE: *Mirin is sweet Japanese rice wine, which perhaps makes it an unusual ingredient in a keto recipe. Although you might be inclined to skip it, we recommend against doing so to preserve the flavor of the dish. The quantity used is very small per serving, and properly made mirin is a traditional fermented food. Look for one with only rice and koji (aspirgillius) as ingredients. Eden Foods brand makes a mass-market traditional mirin that is non-GMO and organic. You can substitute a tablespoon of sherry or vermouth plus 1 to 2 drops stevia if you wish.*

MACRONUTRIENTS PER SERVING (WITH 1 TEASPOON SESAME OIL)
CALORIES: 197 KCAL FAT: 14 G, 129 KCAL CARBOHYDRATE: 6 G (4 G NET), 22 KCAL PROTEIN: 13 G, 52 KCAL

BHINDI PYAZ (OKRA WITH ONIONS)

MAKES 4 SERVINGS

This simple version of Bhindi Pyaz (okra with onions) is sautéed with red bell pepper for a little extra color. A quick stir fry prevents the okra from becoming slimy. Okra is a bit higher carb than other vegetables, so it's not an everyday food for us, but we love this dish when okra is in season at the local farmer's markets.

INGREDIENTS

3 tablespoons avocado oil or ghee

½ teaspoon cumin seeds

1 teaspoon dark mustard seeds (brown or black, see Note)

3 cloves garlic, smashed and chopped

12 ounces fresh okra, stem cap removed, halved on the diagonal

1 small red bell pepper, cut into 2-inch strips

1 small yellow onion, sliced

½ teaspoon chili powder

½ teaspoon garam masala

½ teaspoon fine sea salt, plus more to taste

1. Heat the avocado oil in a large skillet over medium-high heat. When the oil just begins to shimmer, add the cumin seeds and mustard seeds. Immediately remove the pan from the heat and stir continuously with a spatula. After about 30 seconds the seeds should begin to pop.

2. Turn the heat to low and return the skillet to the burner. Add the garlic and cook for about 1 minute, stirring frequently, until just golden. Avoid over-browning the garlic or it will become bitter.

3. Add the okra, bell pepper, and onion and increase the heat to medium-high. Sauté, stirring frequently for 2 to 3 minutes, until the vegetables are tender-crisp. Add the chili powder, garam masala, and sea salt and stir to coat the vegetables. Cook for 2 minutes longer until the okra is soft but not mushy. Taste the okra and add more salt if needed. Transfer to a serving dish and serve immediately.

NOTE: *Brown and black mustard seeds are sometimes difficult to find at standard grocery stores, but they are readily available at both Indian and Middle Eastern markets. If you wish, you may also substitute white (yellow) mustard seeds; this will result in a less spicy dish.*

MACRONUTRIENTS PER SERVING
CALORIES: 139 KCAL FAT: 11 G, 97 KCAL CARBOHYDRATE: 10 G (7 G NET), 41 KCAL PROTEIN: 2 G, 10 KCAL

CHICKEN BIRYANI

MAKES 6 SERVINGS

Biryani is a popular Indian dish with Persian roots, apparently brought to India by invaders many centuries ago. Like so many traditional dishes with long roots, there are myriad ways to prepare biryani, but they share in common a base of richly spiced rice. This version calls for chicken, but biryani can be made with almost any meat or seafood, or it can be made vegetarian.

INGREDIENTS

1½ cup prepared Indian-Style Cauliflower Rice (page 91)

1½ teaspoons garam masala

1 teaspoon fine sea salt

½ teaspoon chili powder

Pinch of ground cardamom

1½ pounds boneless, skinless chicken thighs, cut into 1½-inch cubes

¼ cup heavy whipping cream, or substitute full-fat coconut milk

Scant ½ teaspoon saffron threads

4 tablespoons ghee or butter

½ medium onion, thinly sliced

1 serrano pepper, ribs and seeds removed, thinly sliced

1 tablespoon minced fresh ginger

2 medium tomatoes, cut into wedges

1. If you haven't already done so, prepare the cauliflower rice according to the directions on page 91. Set aside.

2. Mix together the garam masala, salt, chili powder, and cardamom in a large bowl. Add the chicken and toss to coat well with the spices. Set aside.

3. Pour the cream into a small bowl. Crush the saffron threads between your index finger and thumb and sprinkle into the cream. Set aside to soak.

4. While the saffron soaks, heat a large skillet (see Note) over medium-high heat and melt the ghee. Fry the onions in the ghee for about 5 minutes until they begin to caramelize, stirring frequently. Add the serrano pepper, and ginger and fry for 1 to 2 minutes longer. The onions will become richly aromatic and take on a deep golden color. Use tongs to remove the onion mixture from the pan, leaving as much ghee in the bottom as possible. Set the onion mixture aside.

5. Preheat the oven to 375°F.

6. Working in batches if necessary, add the chicken to the pan in which the onions cooked, taking care not to overcrowd. Cook the chicken for 3 to 4 minutes per side until golden brown. When all of the chicken has been browned, return all the chicken to the pan along with the onion mixture. Add the tomato wedges and 2 tablespoons of the saffron cream. Allow to simmer for 2 or 3 minutes, leaving the tomatoes undisturbed. During this time, you may add a tablespoon or more of water as needed to the pan to prevent it from drying out.

7. Transfer the cooked chicken mixture to a baking dish. Layer the prepared cauliflower rice on top. Drizzle the remaining saffron milk over the top and bake uncovered for 10 minutes until the chicken is cooked through. Allow to rest for 5 to 10 minutes before serving.

NOTE: *This dish can also be cooked in a single oven-proof cast iron skillet for a one-pan preparation.*

MACRONUTRIENTS PER SERVING
CALORIES: 305 KCAL FAT: 21 G, 186 KCAL CARBOHYDRATE: 6 G (4 G NET), 25 KCAL PROTEIN: 25 G, 99 KCAL

CHICKEN KORMA

MAKES 6 SERVINGS

Korma is a dish most associated with India in which meat is braised in a spiced yogurt sauce—perfect for keto enthusiasts. You can control the spiciness by using more or fewer peppers.

INGREDIENTS

½ cup full-fat plain Greek yogurt or coconut milk yogurt

⅓ cup full-fat coconut milk

2 serrano peppers, ribs and seeds removed, minced

1 tablespoon almond flour

2 teaspoons ground cumin

1 teaspoon coriander seed

1 teaspoon garam masala

1 teaspoon fine sea salt

½ teaspoon ground cayenne pepper

¼ teaspoon ground cardamom

Pinch ground cinnamon

1 clove garlic, grated or very finely minced

½ teaspoon grated fresh ginger

½ tablespoon tomato paste

2 tablespoons ghee or butter

½ medium onion, chopped

2 pounds boneless, skinless chicken thighs, cut into 1½-inch cubes

1. Stir the yogurt and coconut milk together in a medium bowl. Whisk in the chilis, almond flour, cumin, coriander, garam masala, salt, cayenne, cardamom, cinnamon, garlic, ginger, and tomato paste. Set aside.

2. Heat the ghee in a large skillet over medium-high heat. Sauté the onions for about 5 minutes, stirring frequently, until soft and fragrant. Add the chicken and brown for about 2 minutes, continuing to stir frequently.

3. Pour the yogurt sauce over the chicken and mix well. Cover and reduce heat to low. Simmer for 15 minutes, stirring occasionally.

4. If you want a thicker sauce, uncover the skillet and turn the heat up to high. Cook for 2 to 3 minutes, stirring continuously. Transfer the chicken and sauce to a serving bowl and serve warm.

MACRONUTRIENTS PER SERVING
CALORIES: 291 KCAL FAT: 16 G, 146 KCAL CARBOHYDRATE: 4 G (3 G NET), 15 KCAL PROTEIN: 32 G, 130 KCAL

MADRAS CURRY SPICE BLEND

MAKES ABOUT ½ CUP

INGREDIENTS

2 tablespoons black peppercorns

½ tablespoon whole cardamom pods

4 tablespoons coriander seed

2 tablespoons cumin seeds

2 tablespoons whole fenugreek seeds
(see Note on page 5)

2-inch cinnamon stick

2 whole cloves

½ tablespoon ground ginger

2 tablespoons ground turmeric

½ tablespoon cayenne pepper

1. Heat a dry skillet over low heat and add the peppercorns, cardamom pods, coriander, cumin, and fenugreek seeds. Toast for 1 or 2 minutes, until the seeds begin to pop. While toasting, stir the spices and shake the pan regularly to help them cook evenly. Add the cinnamon and cloves and toast for 1 to 2 minutes longer, until the mixture becomes very fragrant and is warmed through.

2. Using a spice grinder or small food processor, grind the warmed spice mix until it becomes a fine powder. Add the ginger, turmeric, and cayenne pepper and pulse to combine.

3. Allow to cool, then store in an airtight container at room temperature.

MACRONUTRIENTS PER SERVING (1 TEASPOON)
CALORIES: 10 KCAL · FAT: 0 G, 0 KCAL · CARBOHYDRATE: 2 G (2 G NET), 10 KCAL · PROTEIN: 0 G, 0 KCAL

CURRIED FISH

MAKES 4 SERVINGS

Tamarind paste is derived from the pods of the tamarind tree. It is used in a huge variety of regional cuisines across Asia, Africa, and the Americas. A little goes a long way in this simple curry, which is delicious served with riced veggies (cauliflower, broccoli, turnip, or kohlrabi are all great) and roasted eggplant.

INGREDIENTS

2 tablespoons coconut oil

½ teaspoon mustard seeds

½ medium onion, diced

1 serrano pepper, ribs and seeds removed (optional), sliced

3 garlic cloves, chopped

1-inch knob fresh ginger, minced

1 teaspoon coarse sea salt, plus more to season the fish

1 teaspoon ground coriander

½ teaspoon garam masala

½ teaspoon ground turmeric

½ teaspoon paprika

¼ teaspoon ground black pepper, plus more to season the fish

1 cup full-fat coconut milk

½ teaspoon tamarind paste

1¼ pounds cod, haddock, or similar mild white fish), cut into 4 filets

¼ cup fresh cilantro leaves, chopped

1. In a small saucepan, melt 1 tablespoon of oil over medium-low heat. Add the mustard seeds. When they start to pop, add the onion and serrano pepper and turn the heat up to medium. Sauté until the onion just starts to brown, 5 to 6 minutes. Add the garlic and ginger and cook stirring constantly until fragrant, about 1 minute more.

2. Add the salt, coriander, garam masala, turmeric, paprika, and black pepper. Stir well to coat the onions in the spices. Stir in the coconut milk and allow it to come to a simmer. Turn down the heat to maintain the simmer and stir in the tamarind paste until fully dissolved. Allow to the mixture to simmer for 2 minutes, then remove from the heat.

3. Use an immersion blender to blend the sauce until mostly smooth. (You can instead carefully transfer the mixture to a stand blender.)

4. Season both sides of the fish with a pinch of salt and pepper. Heat the remaining 1 tablespoon coconut oil in a skillet over medium heat. Add the fish in a single layer and pour the sauce over top. Spoon the sauce over the fish to coat. When the sauce starts to bubble, cover the skillet and turn the heat down to medium-low. Simmer covered for 5 minutes, then uncover and continue cooking until the fish is cooked through, another 1 to 3 minutes depending on the thickness of the fish.

5. Carefully transfer the fish to serving plates. Spoon the sauce from the skillet over top and sprinkle with cilantro. Serve immediately.

MACRONUTRIENTS PER SERVING
CALORIES: 290 KCAL FAT: 18 G, 164 KCAL CARBOHYDRATE: 4 G (4 G NET), 17 KCAL PROTEIN: 26 G, 106 KCAL

GHEE

Ghee, or clarified butter, is an important source of dietary fat in many cuisines around the world. The process of making ghee removes the milk solids from the butter, so it is often tolerated by individuals with dairy sensitivities, making it a great staple in any keto kitchen.

INGREDIENTS
1 pound unsalted butter, preferably
   pastured

1. Melt the butter in a deep saucepan over medium heat, stirring occasionally. As soon as the butter has melted fully, reduce the heat to a simmer and cook for 10 to 15 minutes. As the butter cooks, the water will evaporate, causing it to bubble and foam. After the initial bubbling stops, you will begin to see light-colored whey solids floating to the top of the butter in the form of a thin foam. Skim the whey from the top with a spoon and reserve for another use, such as seasoning vegetables, if desired.

2. Soon after the whey solids stop rising to the top, the butter will become very fragrant and turn a bright translucent yellow color. Flakes of light-colored milk solids will collect at the bottom and sides of the pot. If you prefer light-colored, milder ghee, you may remove the ghee from the heat at this point and continue to the next step. If you prefer nuttier, richer ghee, allow the milk solids to brown slightly by cooking for an additional 2 to 3 minutes. Remove from heat.

3. Allow the ghee to cool slightly for a couple minutes, then strain through a fine mesh strainer lined with cheesecloth or a coffee filter to remove the milk solids. Repeat this process if necessary until only the liquid ghee remains. Store finished ghee in an airtight container. Although ghee does not require refrigeration, it will stay fresh longer if kept cool.

MACRONUTRIENTS PER SERVING (1 TABLESPOON)
CALORIES: 37 KCAL FAT: 4 G, 38 KCAL CARBOHYDRATE: 0 G, 0 KCAL PROTEIN: 0G, 0 KCAL

INDIAN-SPICED ROASTED BRUSSELS SPROUTS

MAKES 4 SERVINGS

Brussels sprouts aren't a vegetable that typically appears in Indian cuisine, but we think they pair beautifully with piquant spiciness of curry seasonings. If you have any leftovers, consider adding them to your next salad.

INGREDIENTS

1 pound Brussels sprouts, halved or quartered if large

4 tablespoons coconut oil, melted

1 teaspoon brown or black mustard seeds

¼ teaspoon cumin seeds

2 cloves garlic, minced

1 jalapeño, ribs and seeds removed, minced (or more or less to taste)

½ small onion, diced

1 teaspoon ground cumin

½ teaspoon fine sea salt

¼ teaspoon ground cayenne pepper

¼ teaspoon ground coriander

¼ teaspoon ground turmeric

2 tablespoons filtered water

2 tablespoons full-fat coconut milk

1. Preheat the oven to 425°F. In a large bowl, toss the Brussels sprouts with 2 tablespoons of the coconut oil, the mustard seeds, and the cumin seeds. Arrange the Brussels sprouts in a single layer on a baking sheet and roast in the oven for 15 minutes, shaking the pan and stirring the Brussels sprouts once or twice during cooking to ensure even browning.

2. While Brussels sprouts roast, heat the remaining 2 tablespoons of oil in a large skillet over medium high heat. Add the garlic and jalapeño to the oil and saute for 1 minute to soften the garlic, stirring frequently.

3. Add the onion to the pan and cook until soft and golden, about 7 to 8 minutes. Add the cumin, salt, cayenne, coriander, and turmeric to the onions and stir well to coat. Cook the spiced onions stirring frequently until fragrant, about 1 minute. Deglaze the pan by pouring in the water followed by the coconut milk, scraping up any browned bits at the bottom. Remove from the heat and set aside until the Brussels sprouts are done cooking.

4. Remove the Brussels sprouts from the oven and carefully transfer them to the pan with the onion mixture. Stir well to thoroughly combine. Serve immediately.

MACRONUTRIENTS PER SERVING
CALORIES: 196 KCAL FAT: 16 G, 140 KCAL CARBOHYDRATE: 12 G (7 G NET), 49 KCAL PROTEIN: 4 G, 18 KCAL

INDIAN-STYLE CAULIFLOWER RICE

MAKES 4 SERVINGS

We know that it's easy to tire of cauliflower rice, but this one is far from boring. You might even find yourself craving cauliflower rice, for real!

INGREDIENTS

2 tablespoons ghee or butter

3 whole cardamom pods or
⅛ teaspoon ground cardamom

2-inch cinnamon stick

¼ teaspoon cumin seed

¼ teaspoon ground turmeric

⅛ teaspoon ground cloves

½ medium onion, diced

1 clove grated garlic

1 teaspoon grated fresh ginger

2 cups riced cauliflower, fresh or frozen
and thawed

1 teaspoon fine sea salt

1 tablespoon dried cilantro

2 tablespoons fresh cilantro leaves, minced
(optional, for garnish)

1. Melt the ghee in a skillet over medium heat. Add the cardamom, cinnamon, cumin, turmeric, and cloves to the pan and gently fry for 3 minutes, stirring constantly. As the spices cook, they will become sweetly fragrant.

2. Add the onion and stir well to coat with the spices. Cook for 1 minute, stirring constantly. If the pan begins to look dry, add an additional ½ tablespoon of ghee. Add the garlic and ginger and cook one minute more, continuing to stir frequently.

3. Add the cauliflower rice, salt, and dried cilantro. Stir until everything is thoroughly combined. The rice will become a rich golden-yellow color. Continue to cook for 2 to 4 minutes, until the rice is completely heated through. Taste the rice. If you want rice that is more tender, cook for an additional 2 minutes and test again.

4. If desired, remove the cinnamon stick and any whole cardamom pods. Transfer the rice to a serving dish and optionally sprinkle with the fresh cilantro. Serve hot or at room temperature.

NOTE: *For a fluffier, drier rice, instead of cooking the cauliflower in the skillet, roast it in the oven. Preheat the oven to 400°F. Follow the first two steps above, then remove the pan from the heat. Stir in the rice, salt, and dried cilantro, then spread the spiced cauliflower onto a baking sheet. Roast for 5 minutes. Remove the pan from the oven and taste the rice. If you want it cooked more, stir it, spread it out on the baking sheet again, and return it to the oven for 3 to 5 minutes more. If desired, remove the cinnamon stick and any whole cardamom pods. Transfer the rice to a serving bowl, stir it well, and optionally garnish it with fresh cilantro.*

MACRONUTRIENTS PER SERVING
CALORIES: 51 KCAL FAT: 4 G, 39 KCAL CARBOHYDRATE: 3 G (2 G NET), 12 KCAL PROTEIN: 0 G, 0 KCAL

LASSI (3 WAYS)

EACH RECIPE MAKES 2 SERVINGS

If you are only familiar with sweet lassi like the mango variety so popular in Indian restaurants in America, you are in for a treat. Savory lassi are fantastically refreshing, allowing the delectable tanginess of yogurt to shine through. With each of these recipes, we recommend trying them without sweetener first, and then slowly adding sweetener only as needed.

Mint Lassi

INGREDIENTS

1½ cup plain full-fat yogurt or dahi, or use coconut or almond milk yogurt

¼ cup fresh mint leaves

1 tablespoon fresh lemon juice

¼ teaspoon ground cumin or coriander (choose one)

Scant ¼ teaspoon fine sea salt

½ to 1 cup cold filtered water as needed

Keto friendly sweetener to taste (optional)

Crushed ice (optional)

1. Use a high-powered blender to blend the yogurt, mint, lemon juice, cumin (or coriander), and salt until smooth.

2. Add water ¼ cup at a time until the lassi reaches the desired consistency. Taste the lassi and optionally sweeten to taste.

3. Pour into glasses (with crushed ice if desired) and drink immediately or cover and transfer to the refrigerator to chill for 30 minutes or longer.

MACRONUTRIENTS PER SERVING (NO SWEETENER)
CALORIES 120 KCAL FAT: 6 G, 55 KCAL CARBOHYDRATE: 10 G (9 G NET), 41 KCAL PROTEIN: 7 G, 27 KCAL

Saffron Avocado Lassi

INGREDIENTS

Small pinch saffron threads (optional)

2 tablespoons warm water

1 cup plain full-fat yogurt or dahi, or use coconut or almond milk yogurt

1 small avocado

½ teaspoon ground cardamom

½ to 1 cup cold filtered water as needed

Keto friendly sweetener to taste (optional)

Crushed ice (optional)

1. If using, soak the saffron threads in the warm water for 15 minutes.

2. Use a high-powered blender to blend the yogurt, avocado, and cardamom, along with the saffron and its soaking liquid, until smooth.

3. Add water ¼ cup at a time until the lassi reaches the desired consistency. Taste the lassi and optionally sweeten to taste.

4. Pour into glasses (with crushed ice if desired) and drink immediately or cover and transfer to the refrigerator to chill for 30 minute or longer.

MACRONUTRIENTS PER SERVING (NO SWEETENER)
CALORIES:191 KCAL FAT: 15 G, 131 KCAL CARBOHYDRATE: 12 G (7 G NET), 48 KCAL PROTEIN: 6 G, 23 KCAL

Salted Margarita Lassi

INGREDIENTS

1 cup plain full-fat yogurt or dahi, or use coconut or almond milk yogurt

1 small avocado or additional ½ cup yogurt

½ small cucumber, peeled, seeded, and chopped

Zested peel and juice of 1 small lime

¼ cup loosely packed fresh cilantro leaves

¼ teaspoon fine sea salt

½ to 1 cup cold filtered water as needed

Keto friendly sweetener to taste (optional)

Crushed ice (optional)

1. Use a high-powered blender to blend the yogurt, avocado (if using), cucumber, lime zest and juice, cilantro, and salt until smooth.

2. Add water ¼ cup at a time until the lassi reaches the desired consistency. Taste the lassi and optionally sweeten to taste.

3. Pour into glasses (with crushed ice if desired) and drink immediately or cover and transfer to the refrigerator to chill for 30 minute or longer.

MACRONUTRIENTS PER SERVING (NO SWEETENER)
CALORIES: 199 KCAL FAT: 15 G, 131 KCAL CARBOHYDRATE: 14 G (9 G NET), 58 KCAL PROTEIN: 6 G, 23 KCAL

PALAK PANEER

MAKES 6 SERVINGS

Saag paneer is a popular North Indian curry made of stewed greens—such as kale, mustard greens, or turnip greens—and cubes of paneer cheese. When made entirely with spinach (palak), it is known as palak paneer. If you've ever eaten in an Indian restaurant, chances are you've experienced this dish; and once you see how easy it is to make at home, chances are you'll be eating it more often!

INGREDIENTS

14 ounces fresh spinach

½ cup chicken bone broth, vegetable broth, or water

1 1-inch knob fresh ginger, chopped

1 serrano pepper, ribs and seeds removed

3 tablespoons ghee or unsalted butter

1 teaspoon ground turmeric

½ teaspoon ground cayenne pepper

12 ounces paneer cheese (page 99 or store-bought)

½ medium onion, diced

4 cloves garlic, smashed and minced

1 teaspoon ground cumin powder

½ teaspoon ground coriander

½ teaspoon fine sea salt

½ cup heavy whipping cream

1. Place the spinach, bone broth, ginger, and serrano pepper in a high-powered blender or food processor and blend until smooth. Set aside.

2. Warm a skillet over medium-high heat and melt 2 tablespoons of ghee. Add the turmeric and cayenne pepper to the ghee and allow the spices to cook for about 30 seconds to 1 minute, stirring constantly. Once the spices have become fragrant, add the paneer to the ghee and toss gently to coat. Fry the paneer in the spiced ghee for about 6 to 8 minutes, until richly golden on all sides. Remove the paneer from pan and set aside.

3. Add the remaining 1 tablespoon of ghee and the onion to the pan. Sauté the onion for 5 minutes, stirring frequently, until softened. Lower the heat to medium-low and add the garlic, cumin, coriander, and salt. Cook the onion for an additional 10 minutes, stirring occasionally. If the pan begins to dry out and the onions stick as they cook, add in 1 or 2 tablespoons of water to release the spices from the bottom of the pan.

4. Add the spinach puree and cream to the pan and stir gently until well mixed. Add the fried paneer and stir until the paneer is coated, taking care not to break the cubes apart. Cover and lower the heat to a simmer. Simmer for 15 minutes, stirring occasionally.

5. Serve immediately.

MACRONUTRIENTS PER SERVING
CALORIES: 365 KCAL FAT: 32 G, 284 KCAL CARBOHYDRATE: 7 G (5 G NET), 26 KCAL PROTEIN: 16 G, 62 KCAL

PANEER

MAKES ABOUT 8 OUNCES

Paneer is a popular fresh-milk cheese often featured in Indian cuisine. Because it does not require aging or cultures, it's easy to make at home. Not only is making your own cheese satisfying, it gives you the ability to enjoy fresh, two-ingredient paneer that is free of food starches, stabilizers, and any possible cross-contamination by allergens. You may find that due to the lack of binders, homemade paneer is more delicate in texture than store-bought. If you are using this paneer in a recipe such as Palak Paneer (page 97), stir with care to prevent the cheese from crumbling.

INGREDIENTS

8 cups whole milk (See Note)

2 cups lukewarm filtered water

½ teaspoon citric acid (check the canning section of your grocery store)

1. Pour the milk into a large saucepan with the tip of a candy thermometer or instant-read thermometer submerged in the milk but not touching the bottom of the pan. Slowly heat the milk to 190°F, stirring constantly. When the milk reaches 190°F, allow it to simmer between 185°F and 195°F for 20 minutes, stirring frequently.

2. Remove the pan from the heat and allow the milk to cool to 175°F.

3. When the milk has cooled, dissolve the citric acid in the water and very slowly stir the mixture into the milk. You should see milk curds begin to coagulate at the top of the pot, separating from the liquid whey. Leave the pot undisturbed for 15 minutes.

4. Strain the curds through very fine muslin or a nut milk bag. Reserve the nutritious whey (the liquid that comes off the curds) for another use if desired. Gather up the ends of the muslin and twist to form a ball, squeezing out any excess whey from the curds. At this stage the paneer will be crumbly. If you want firmer paneer that can be sliced, place the muslin-wrapped paneer in a fine mesh strainer set over a bowl. Set a weight (such as a heavy pot) on the paneer and allow it to sit for 15 to 20 minutes. Store the paneer in an airtight container in the refrigerator.

NOTE: *Avoid Ultra-Heat Treated (UHT), Ultra Pasteurized (UP), or High-Temperature Short-Time (HTST) treated milk. The extreme temperatures used in high-temperature pasteurization processes partially denature the whey and casein proteins present in the milk, preventing it from curdling properly. Paneer made with UP/UHT milk may not set into a block.*

MACRONUTRIENTS PER SERVING (1 OUNCE)
CALORIES: 105 KCAL FAT: 9 G, 78 KCAL CARBOHYDRATE: 1 G (1 G NET), 2 KCAL PROTEIN: 6 G, 24 KCAL

POL SAMBOL (COCONUT SAMBAL)

MAKES ABOUT 1½ CUPS

There are many, many variations on sambol (or sambal), chili pastes that are staple condiments in South Asia. Pol Sambol is most commonly attributed to Sri Lanka. Usually it is ground by hand using a tool called a miris gala. Assuming most readers will not have one of these at home, this recipe calls for making the sambol in a food processor, but it can also be made using a large mortar and pestle. Use it as a condiment for baked fish or grilled chicken, eat it with Paneer (page 99) and Blini (page 179—pretend they are naan!), or anywhere else you want some sweet heat!

INGREDIENTS

6 dried red Thai chilis (or more if you prefer spicier sambal)

½ teaspoon fine sea salt

1 teaspoon granulated monkfruit sweetener

1 tablespoon Maldive fish chips (optional, see Note)

8 ounces grated coconut, fresh or frozen and thawed

1 small red onion, diced

Juice from 1 lime

1. Place the chilis, salt, and sweetener (if using) in a small food processor. Pulse until finely chopped. Optionally add the fish chips and pulse 5 times to combine.

2. If using frozen coconut, drain the coconut in a sieve and use a spatula to press out any extra liquid. Add the coconut to the blender and pulse until thoroughly incorporated.

3. Scrape down the sides of the bowl. Add the red onion and pulse until the onions are finely chopped.

4. Scrape down the sides of the bowl again, then add the lime juice. Allow the food processor to run until the mixture is a uniform texture, to desired smoothness. Taste and adjust the salt. Store in an airtight container in the refrigerator.

NOTE: *Maldive fish chips are a traditional Sri Lankan ingredient made from cured, dried fish. It is used as a flavor additive. You can find them in Asian food marts. Feel free to omit for a vegetarian sambol.*

MACRONUTRIENTS PER 2 TABLESPOON SERVING (NO FISH CHIPS)
CALORIES: 71 KCAL FAT: 6 G, 58 KCAL CARBOHYDRATE: 4 G (2 G NET), 17 KCAL PROTEIN: 1 G, 3 KCAL

TANDOORI CHICKEN

MAKES 4 SERVINGS

Tandoori chicken is a classic Indian dish that is popular worldwide. It gets its name from the tandoor—a clay oven—in which it is traditionally cooked. Serve this with Indian-Style Cauliflower Rice (page 91) and Palak Paneer (page 97) for a delicious and aromatic meal.

INGREDIENTS

2 pounds chicken leg quarters

1 tablespoon unsalted butter or ghee

½ teaspoon chili powder

1 teaspoon ground coriander

½ teaspoon garam masala

½ teaspoon ground turmeric

½ teaspoon coconut flour

3 cloves garlic, microplaned or finely grated

1 tablespoon grated fresh ginger

½ cup full-fat Greek yogurt or strained coconut yogurt

1 tablespoon fresh lemon juice

For serving (optional)

8 cups chopped lettuce or spring mix

2 medium tomatoes, cut into wedges

1. Prepare the chicken by making several hash-mark slices completely through the skin and partially through the meat. Place in a large shallow dish and set aside.

2. Heat a skillet over medium-high heat. Once hot, melt the butter. When the butter stops foaming, stir in the chili powder, coriander, garam masala, and turmeric. Cook the spices until richly fragrant, about 1 minute, stirring constantly. Remove from heat and allow to cool slightly.

3. Transfer the spice mixture to a bowl and add the coconut flour, garlic, ginger, yogurt, and lemon juice. Stir well. Pour the yogurt mixture over the chicken and toss until thoroughly coated. Cover and marinate for 3 hours.

4. Preheat the oven to 475°F. Shake any excess marinade off of the chicken pieces and place the chicken on wire rack set on a rimmed baking sheet. Discard the remaining marinade. Bake for 20 to 25 minutes, until cooked through.

5. Serve hot atop fresh salad greens with tomato slices.

NOTE: *The macronutrient values provided include all of the marinade to be conservative. If you want more precise values, you will need to weigh your marinade before and after marinating the meat to determine how much is being discarded.*

MACRONUTRIENTS PER SERVING (CHICKEN AND MARINADE ONLY)
CALORIES: 532 KCAL FAT: 38 G, 344 KCAL CARBOHYDRATE: 3 G (3 G NET), 12 KCAL PROTEIN: 42 G, 166 KCAL
MACRONUTRIENTS PER SERVING (WITH SERVING ACCOMPANIMENTS)
CALORIES: 561 KCAL FAT: 38 G, 344 KCAL CARBOHYDRATE: 9 G (6 G NET), 36 KCAL PROTEIN: 44 G, 174 KCAL

(Denmark)

ICELAND

CANADA

UNITED STATES

North Atlantic Ocean

MEXICO

THE BAHAMAS

CUBA

BELIZE

HONDURAS

JAMAICA

PUERTO RICO (U.S.)

GUATEMALA

EL SALVADOR

NICARAGUA

COSTA RICA

PANAMA

GAMBIA

GUINEA BISSAU

SENEGAL

VENEZUELA

COLOMBIA

GUYANA

SURINAME

FRENCH GUIANA

ECUADOR

PERU

BRAZIL

BOLIVIA

BAKED COD WITH TAHINI SAUCE

MAKES 6 SERVINGS

This light, easy dish is delicious served with tabbouleh (such as on page 111). If you use store-bought tahini, make sure it does not have objectional oils such as canola. It is also incredibly easy to make your own (see the recipe on page 129).

INGREDIENTS

6 6-ounce fillets of cod, or substitute any firm white fish

2 tablespoons lemon juice

4 tablespoons extra-virgin olive oil

2 tablespoons unsalted butter

Coarse sea salt and ground black pepper

1 medium onion, thinly sliced

½ cup tahini (page 129 or store-bought)

1 teaspoon ground cumin

1 clove garlic, smashed

1 tablespoon minced fresh parsley leaves

3 tablespoons hot water

1. Preheat the oven to 350°F. Place the cod on a rimmed baking sheet or in a shallow casserole dish. Drizzle the cod with the 1 tablespoon of the lemon juice and 2 tablespoons of the olive oil. Season generously with salt and pepper. Top each fillet with 1 teaspoon of butter. Bake for 15 minutes.

2. Meanwhile, heat the remaining olive oil in a large skillet over medium-high heat. Sauté the onions in the oil until caramelized, stirring frequently, about 15 minutes. Set aside.

3. Pour the tahini into a small bowl and stir in the cumin, garlic, and parsley. Slowly whisk in the remaining 1 tablespoon lemon juice and the hot water until a light emulsion is formed. If your emulsion breaks, you may try re-mixing it while very gently heating the tahini sauce over the stove or gradually adding more hot water.

4. Scatter the caramelized onions over the fish and top with a dollop of the tahini sauce. Return the fish to the oven and bake for 15 to 20 minutes until the fish is cooked through and the tahini sauce begins to bubble. Serve immediately.

MACRONUTRIENTS PER SERVING
CALORIES: 362 KCAL FAT: 24 G, 216 KCAL CARBOHYDRATE: 6 G (4 G NET), 24 KCAL PROTEIN: 34 G, 134 KCAL

BEEF KHORESH

MAKES 4 SERVINGS

This is a version of the popular Iranian dish known as khoresh-e ghormeh sabzi, a deliciously tangy stew made with an abundance of sautéed herbs that give it a vibrant green color. Traditionally gormeh sabzi is prepared with beans, which have been omitted for this keto- and ancestral-eating-friendly adaptation.

INGREDIENTS

3 tablespoons olive oil or avocado oil

½ large onion, diced

1 pound beef stew meat, cut into 1½-inch cubes

1 teaspoon kosher salt

½ teaspoon ground cinnamon

1 teaspoon ground fenugreek (see Note on page 5)

2 teaspoons ground turmeric

2½ cups bone broth (beef or chicken) or water

1 ounce (about ½ cup) chopped fresh chives

1 ounce (about ½ cup) chopped fresh parsley leaves

2 tablespoons lime juice (See Note)

1. Heat 2 tablespoons of the oil in a large pot over medium-high heat. Add the onions and gently sauté until golden, about 3 to 4 minutes. Salt the beef and add to the pot. Cook stirring occasionally until thoroughly browned, about 10 minutes.

2. Add the cinnamon, fenugreek, and turmeric to the pot, and stir well to coat. Cook stirring frequently until richly aromatic, about 2 to 3 minutes.

3. Pour in the bone broth and reduce the heat. Simmer covered for 45 minutes, stirring occasionally.

4. Once the meat is done simmering, heat the remaining tablespoon of oil in a skillet over medium heat. Fry the chives and parsley in the oil for 2 to 3 minutes.

5. Stir the fried herbs and lime juice into the meat and simmer uncovered for 30 to 35 minutes longer until the meat is tender and the stew has a reached a thick, chili-like consistency.

NOTE: *This recipe uses lime juice as a convenience. For a more traditional preparation, omit the lime juice and substitute with 2 dried Persian limes (limoo omani) that have been pierced with a fork.*

MACRONUTRIENTS PER SERVING
CALORIES: 275 KCAL FAT: 16 G, 140 KCAL CARBOHYDRATE: 7 G (5 G NET), 26 KCAL PROTEIN: 29 G, 116 KCAL

MIDDLE EAST   109

CAULIFLOWER TABBOULEH

MAKES 6 SERVINGS

Tabbouleh (aka tabbouli) is typically made with bulgur, which is a cereal grain, or sometimes couscous, neither of which is keto-friendly. No problem, parsley is really the star of this Middle Eastern salad anyway, and cauliflower easily swaps in for the high-carb grains.

INGREDIENTS

1 medium head cauliflower, riced (about 1 pound)

6 tablespoons avocado oil

1 tablespoon apple cider vinegar

2 cloves garlic

2 tablespoons lemon juice

1 teaspoon grated lemon zest

Leaves from 1 sprig fresh mint

2 scallions, white and green parts roughly chopped

2 cups packed fresh parsley leaves

½ medium English cucumber, diced

8 ounces tomatoes, any variety, seeded (if large) and diced

½ teaspoon fine sea salt

½ teaspoon red pepper flakes (optional)

1. Preheat the oven to 400°F. Mix the cauliflower with 2 tablespoons of oil until well coated. Spread the cauliflower evenly on a rimmed baking sheet and bake for 12 minutes, stirring halfway through the cooking time. Set aside and allow to cool.

2. While the cauliflower cools, put the apple cider vinegar, the remaining 4 tablespoons of avocado oil, garlic, lemon juice, lemon zest, mint, scallions, and parsley into the bowl of a food processor. Pulse until thoroughly combined, scraping down the sides of the bowl as needed. Transfer the mixture to a large mixing bowl.

3. When the cauliflower is cool, add it to the mixing bowl along with the cucumber, tomato, salt, and red pepper flakes if using. Stir gently to combine. Taste and adjust salt. Serve immediately or cover and refrigerate until ready to serve.

NOTE: *We recommend baking the cauliflower because it helps dry it out. If you cook your cauliflower using a different method, you might want to squeeze it out in a clean kitchen towel and then fluff it with a fork before adding it in the third step.*

MACRONUTRIENTS PER SERVING
CALORIES: 161 KCAL FAT: 14 G, 127 KCAL CARBOHYDRATE: 8 G (5 G NET), 33 KCAL PROTEIN: 3 G, 11 KCAL

CHICKEN KEBABS

MAKES 4 SERVINGS

This simple preparation is perfect for doubling or tripling to serve to a larger group. You can choose to use skinless chicken if you wish, or substitute chicken breasts, but using skin-on thighs yields the juiciest, most flavorful kebabs.

INGREDIENTS

Pinch saffron threads

2 tablespoons warm water

2 pounds boneless, skin-on chicken leg quarters or thighs (see Notes)

3 cloves garlic, smashed

2 tablespoons lemon juice

½ cup extra-virgin olive oil

½ medium onion

2 teaspoons paprika

For serving

1 head butter lettuce, leaves separated

½ cup Toum (page 133)

½ cup Cucumber Yogurt Sauce (page 119)

Equipment: 4 long or 8 short skewers, metal or bamboo (see Notes)

1. Crush the saffron threads by rolling them between your index finger and thumb and sprinkle into a small bowl of warm water. Allow to soak for 5 minutes or longer.

2. Cut the chicken into 1½-inch to 2-inch pieces, leaving the skin intact. Place the cut chicken pieces in a shallow dish and set aside.

3. Put the garlic, lemon juice, olive oil, onion, and paprika into the bowl of a food processor or blender. Process until smooth, about 1 minute.

4. Pour the onion purée over the chicken and toss gently to coat. Place the dish in the refrigerator and allow the chicken to marinate for 1 to 2 hours.

5. Slide the chicken onto kebab skewers (or pre-soaked bamboo skewers) with the skin facing in the same direction. Discard any leftover marinade.

6. TO BROIL: Set the broiler to high heat and place a rack about 6 inches from the heating element. (If using an under-oven broiler, set heat to low.) Broil the chicken for 10 to 15 minutes, until cooked through, turning once about halfway through.

   TO GRILL: Heat the grill to high. Grill until cooked through, about 15 to 20 minutes, turning occasionally. >>

7. Serve warm with lettuce leaves for wrapping. Top each serving with generous dollops of Toum and Cucumber Yogurt Sauce.

NOTES: *If you can only find bone-in skin-on chicken, ask your butcher to remove the bones for you; or debone the chicken yourself and freeze the bones to use in your next batch of homemade bone broth.*

If you are using bamboo skewers, soak them in warm water for a minimum of 30 minutes prior to cooking in order to prevent them from burning.

The macronutrient values provided include all of the marinade to be conservative. If you want more precise values, you will need to weigh your marinade before and after marinating the meat to determine how much is being discarded.

MACRONUTRIENTS PER SERVING (KEBABS AND MARINADE ONLY)
CALORIES: 512 KCAL FAT: 35 G, 318 KCAL CARBOHYDRATE: 3 G (2 G NET), 10 KCAL PROTEIN: 46 G, 185 KCAL

MACRONUTRIENTS PER SERVING (WITH SERVING ACCOMPANIMENTS)
CALORIES: 728 KCAL FAT: 58 G, 518 KCAL CARBOHYDRATE: 6 G (5G NET), 24 KCAL PROTEIN: 48 G, 192 KCAL

YOGURT

MAKES ABOUT 4 CUPS

Anthropological records show evidence of yogurt production all the way back to the 5th century B.C.E. The neolithic herding people of the Middle East and Central Asia were among the first to use fermentation to preserve milk to make the tangy, creamy food we know today as yogurt. This simple recipe allows you to make yogurt at home with no special equipment required. All you will need is a well-sealed oven, a small Dutch oven, some dish towels, and a food thermometer.

INGREDIENTS

1 quart whole milk (see Note) or 2 14-ounce cans full-fat coconut milk

1 packet dairy or vegan yogurt starter culture

1 tablespoon gelatin (optional, for thickening coconut milk yogurt only)

1. Wash and sanitize all of the equipment that will come into contact with your yogurt, including any stirring utensils, the Dutch oven and its lid, and the thermometer.

2. Pour the milk or coconut milk into the Dutch oven. Place an instant read or candy thermometer in the liquid so the tip is not touching the bottom of the pan. Gently heat the milk until the temperature reads 140°F, taking care not to exceed this temperature or heat too rapidly. Stir frequently as it heats to ensure that it does not scorch at the bottom of the pot. At no point should the milk boil. Once the desired temperature has been reached, immediately remove the pot from the heat.

3. If you are making coconut milk and wish to use gelatin as a thickener (recommended): Pour about 1 cup of the coconut milk from the Dutch Oven into a shallow bowl and sprinkle the gelatin over top. Allow the gelatin to "bloom" for 1 minute, then stir well until completely dissolved. Pour the gelatin-mixed coconut milk back into the Dutch oven and stir to incorporate.

4. Allow the milk to cool to a temperature between 115°F and 110°F. If you wish to speed up the process, place the Dutch oven in a basin filled with ice water. Take care not to allow any water to enter the pot. Stir the milk periodically and check the temperature in several spots to ensure the milk is evenly cooled. Once the temperature falls within the 115°F to 110°F range, sprinkle the starter culture over top and stir.

5. Cover the Dutch oven with the lid and wrap tightly in two or more layers of dish towels for insulation. Set the oven to the lowest possible temperature (usually 125°F or less) and preheat for 5 minutes. Turn the oven off and turn on the oven light to provide some additional warmth. The interior of the oven should be just toasty warm and not hot. Place the wrapped Dutch oven onto the center oven rack and close the door. >>

6. Leave the milk to incubate for a minimum of 6 hours for dairy yogurt or 8 hours for coconut yogurt. During this time, it is essential that the oven door not be opened for any reason. If you are making dairy yogurt, you may check the yogurt after 6 hours to test the consistency and taste. If you prefer thicker and tangier yogurt, leave the yogurt to incubate for 1 or 2 additional hours. If you are making coconut yogurt, your yogurt will not fully thicken until it has been completely chilled. Check the taste after 8 hours and ensure that it is tangy enough for your liking. If it is too mild, incubate it for an additional 1 or 2 hours. Once the yogurt has reached your desired taste and consistency, transfer the finished yogurt into an airtight container and store in the refrigerator.

7. If you wish to make strained "Greek-style" yogurt using dairy yogurt, layer one to two squares of cheesecloth or a coffee filter inside of a fine-mesh strainer set over a bowl. Spoon the yogurt into the strainer and allow the liquid (known as acid whey) to drip from the yogurt for 1 to 2 hours or until the desired consistency is reached. After straining dairy yogurt about 2 hours, you should have about 3 cups of Greek-style yogurt and 1 cup of acid whey. You may reserve this nutritious acid whey for other uses, such as mixing into smoothies or making Yogurt Probiotic Shots (page 71). If desired, coconut yogurt may also be strained using the method above, but it tends not to thicken as well. The best way to thicken coconut yogurt is to slightly increase the quantity of gelatin used during pasteurization.

NOTES: *If you are using dairy milk, avoid ultra-pasteurized (UP) or ultra-high temperature pasteurized (UHT) milk, as the high heat treatment denatures the milk proteins and may prevent the yogurt from sufficiently thickening.*

It is impossible to get accurate nutritional information for home-fermented recipes. These values are provided as an estimate. Read the "Fermenting" section on page xiv before fermenting for the first time.

MACRONUTRIENTS PER SERVING (½ CUP)
CALORIES: 75 KCAL FAT: 4 G, 39 KCAL CARBOHYDRATE: 6 G (6 G NET), 23 KCAL PROTEIN: 4 G, 16 KCAL

CUCUMBER YOGURT SAUCE

MAKES A GENEROUS 1½ CUPS

This basic, versatile sauce is a great way to add some flavor to grilled meats, veggies, and salads. Experiment with adding chopped fresh herbs like dill, oregano, or tarragon for yummy variations.

INGREDIENTS

¼ English cucumber with skin, diced small

1 cup Greek-style yogurt or strained coconut yogurt

3 tablespoons finely-minced onion

⅛ teaspoon paprika

1 tablespoon fresh parsley, minced

Combine the cucumber, yogurt, onion, paprika, and parsley in a bowl and mix well. Serve with kebabs or roasted lamb. Store any leftovers in an airtight container inside the refrigerator. Consume promptly.

MACRONUTRIENTS PER SERVING (2 TABLESPOONS)
CALORIES: 26 KCAL FAT: 2 G, 18 KCAL CARBOHYDRATE: 1 G (1 G NET), 5 KCAL PROTEIN: 1 G, 3 KCAL

FRIED HALLOUMI WITH ZA'ATAR

MAKES 4 SERVINGS

Halloumi is a sort-of-tangy, sort-of-chewy cheese from the Levant. We considered putting this recipe in the Western Europe section on the book though, because it turns out that Brits are mad for halloumi! In summer, 2018, the UK's demand for halloumi outpaced supply, leading to a shortage and whipping the British media into a tizzy. Any cheese that is good enough to create a national crisis is good enough for us!

INGREDIENTS

¼ cup coconut flour

1 tablespoon Za'atar Spice Blend (page 135 or store-bought, see Note)

¼ cup coconut oil

1 pound halloumi cheese, cut into 1-inch cubes

1. Mix the coconut flour and za'atar in a small bowl. A few pieces at a time, dredge the halloumi with the spiced coconut flour, turning to thoroughly coat, and place on a plate.

2. Heat ¼ cup of coconut oil in a skillet over medium heat. Gently place the cheese into the hot oil in batches. Do not overcrowd the pan. The cheese will fry quickly, so be attentive here. Fry 20 to 30 seconds per side until browned on all sides. Transfer to a clean plate (lined with a clean kitchen towel if desired). Allow to cool for a minute or two, then serve hot.

NOTE: *Za'atar is just one option here, but almost any seasoning blend would work in this recipe. Cajun seasoning blend is another favorite of ours.*

MACRONUTRIENTS PER SERVING
CALORIES: 526 KCAL FAT: 44 G, 399 KCAL CARBOHYDRATE: 7 G (4 G NET), 26 KCAL PROTEIN: 25 G, 100 KCAL

ISRAELI SALAD

MAKES 6 SERVINGS

Parsley is a champion when it comes to helping remove toxins such as heavy metals from the body. This refreshing Israeli Salad is the perfect accompaniment to kebabs. It can be enjoyed at any meal of the day and is an important component of the traditional Israeli breakfast.

INGREDIENTS

1 pound English (or hothouse) cucumber with skin and seeds, diced (see Note)

1 pound tomatoes, seeded and diced (See Note)

⅓ cup onion, diced

½ cup fresh parsley leaves, minced

1 sprig mint leaves, minced

3 tablespoons extra-virgin olive oil

3 tablespoons fresh lemon juice

½ teaspoon of fine sea salt, or more to taste

1. Place the cucumbers, tomato, onion, parsley and mint into a large bowl and mix well.

2. Drizzle the olive oil and lemon juice over the vegetables and sprinkle with salt. Toss or mix until evenly coated. Serve chilled or at room temperature.

NOTE: *The tomato is the star of the salad, so seek out the least-acidic, ripest tomato you can find. Heirloom varieties such as Brandywine and the dramatically-colored Black Cherry are excellent choices. Alternatively, you may choose to use 1 pound of grape or cherry tomatoes. If you can't find English cucumber, substitute regular hothouse cucumber, but stripe (lightly peel) and seed the cucumber or else the salad will be bitter.*

MACRONUTRIENTS PER SERVING
CALORIES: 89 KCAL FAT: 7 G, 63 KCAL CARBOHYDRATE: 6 G (4 G NET), 26 KCAL PROTEIN: 2 G, 7 KCAL

JEWELED CAULIFLOWER RICE

MAKES 4 SERVINGS

Fragrant and richly spiced jeweled rice is usually served at weddings and other festive celebrations. You might have ordered it at your favorite Persian or Iranian restaurant, where it might have been called morausa polo or jahaver polow. This adaptation uses—you guessed it—cauliflower. If you can find barberries, which are traditional to the recipe, use them in place of the cherries.

INGREDIENTS

1 small orange, preferably organic

1 small carrot, shredded

2 cups plus 2 tablespoons filtered water

¼ teaspoon saffron strands

1 to 3 drops stevia (optional)

6 tablespoons unsalted butter or ghee

3 tablespoons slivered blanched almonds

3 tablespoons pistachios, chopped

Pinch ground allspice

Pinch ground cardamom

Pinch cinnamon

Pinch ground cumin

Pinch ground black pepper

1 medium onion, diced

2 cups riced cauliflower

2 tablespoons unsweetened dried cherries, minced (can substitute cranberries)

1. Peel the orange using a vegetable peeler, removing the rind as well as some of the pith. Slice the rind into very thin strips. Save the flesh for another use.

2. Place the shredded carrot and orange rind in a small saucepan with 2 cups of water. Bring the water to a boil, then reduce the heat to low and simmer for 15 minutes. Meanwhile, crumble the saffron in a small bowl. Add 2 tablespoons of water and the stevia. Mix well and set aside to infuse.

3. Drain the carrots and orange peel and set aside.

4. Heat 2 tablespoons of the butter in a large skillet over medium heat. Roast the almonds and pistachios for 1 to 2 minutes until just starting to brown. Use a slotted spoon to remove the nuts to a bowl.

5. Melt the remaining butter in the same skillet and increase the heat to medium-high. Add the allspice, cardamom, cinnamon, cumin, and pepper to the butter. Cook for 1 minute, stirring constantly. Add the onions to the pan and sauté, stirring frequently, until they begin to caramelize, 10 to 15 minutes.

6. Stir in the riced cauliflower, carrots, orange rind, saffron threads and water, almonds, pistachios, and cherries. Cook for 5, stirring occasionally. Test the cauliflower. If you want tenderer rice, cook another 2 to 5 minutes until the desired tenderness is reached.

7. Transfer the rice to a serving bowl. Serve hot or at room temperature.

MACRONUTRIENTS PER SERVING
CALORIES: 261 KCAL FAT: 23 G, 207 KCAL CARBOHYDRATE: 12 G (9 G NET), 50 KCAL PROTEIN: 4 G, 16 KCAL

KEBAB-E BARG

MAKES 4 SERVINGS

These lamb kebabs are delicious served with a side of cauliflower rice and lettuce wraps in place of bread. Make sure you have plenty of extra sauce for topping!

INGREDIENTS

2 cloves garlic

2 tablespoons fresh lime juice

2 tablespoon extra-virgin olive oil

1 large onion, roughly chopped

Pinch saffron threads

1 pound lamb rump or leg roast, cut into 1-inch cubes

2 medium tomatoes, cut into wedges

For serving (optional)

12 large leaves from a head of red lettuce

½ cup Toum (page 133)

½ cup Cucumber Yogurt Sauce (page 119)

Equipment: 4 long or 8 short skewers, metal or bamboo (see Note)

1. In a blender or food processor, process the garlic, lime juice, olive oil, and onion until puréed. Pour the mixture into a large bowl or shallow dish. Crumble the saffron threads between your fingers and stir it in.

2. Toss the lamb with the onion mixture until thoroughly coated. Cover and place in the refrigerator to marinate for several hours, preferably overnight.

3. Thread the lamb and tomato wedges onto separate skewers and brush the tomatoes with any leftover marinade.

4. TO BROIL: Heat the broiler to high. (If using an under-oven broiler, set heat to low.) Place the skewers 6 to 8 inches from the heating element. Broil the tomatoes for 4 to 5 minutes and the lamb for 10 to 12 minutes, turning frequently, until cooked to the desired doneness.

   TO GRILL: Heat the grill over high heat. Grill the tomatoes for 4 to 5 minutes and the lamb for 10 to 15 minutes, turning frequently, until cooked to the desired doneness.

5. Serve with leaves of red lettuce for wrapping, with Toum and/or Cucumber Yogurt Sauce on the side.

NOTES: *If you are using bamboo skewers, soak them in warm water for a minimum of 30 minutes prior to cooking in order to prevent them from burning.*

The macronutrient values provided include all of the marinade to be conservative. If you want more precise values, you will need to weigh your marinade before and after marinating the meat to determine how much is being discarded.

MACRONUTRIENTS PER SERVING (KEBABS AND MARINADE ONLY)
CALORIES: 353 KCAL FAT: 22 G, 198 KCAL CARBOHYDRATE: 7 G (6 G NET), 28 KCAL PROTEIN: 31 G, 123 KCAL

MACRONUTRIENTS PER SERVING (WITH SERVING ACCOMPANIMENTS)
CALORIES: 572 KCAL FAT: 44 G, 400 KCAL CARBOHYDRATE: 11 G (9 G NET), 44 KCAL PROTEIN: 33 G, 130 KCAL

TAHINI

MAKES ABOUT ½ CUP

Tahini is a paste made from sesame seeds that is a staple in Middle Eastern and Mediterranean cuisine. It can form the base of endless delicious sauces, dressings, and dips. Tahini is actually pretty easy to get at a store, but if you're a kitchen do-it-yourselfer, you can also make it easily at home.

INGREDIENTS

1 cup hulled sesame seeds (raw, not toasted)

2 to 4 tablespoons avocado oil

1. Heat a large, flat-bottomed skillet over medium-low heat. When hot, add the sesame seeds and cook stirring constantly for about 3 minutes. When the seeds are fragrant and just starting to turn light brown, remove the pan from the heat. Transfer the seeds to a plate or pie pan and spread them out to cool.

2. When cool, place the seeds in a small food processor. Process for 30 seconds until coarsely ground. Add 2 tablespoons of avocado oil and process for 30 seconds. Scrape down the sides of the bowl and process 30 seconds more. Scrape down the sides again. If the mixture is dry, add another tablespoon of oil and blend for 1 minute more. Add the other tablespoon of oil if needed and blend until totally smooth (3 tablespoons is usually the right amount).

3. Transfer the tahini to a jar with a tight-fitting lid. Store in the refrigerator for up to a month. Before using the tahini, stir it well, as tahini tends to separate.

MACRONUTRIENTS PER SERVING
CALORIES: 164 KCAL FAT: 17 G, 149 KCAL CARBOHYDRATE: 2 G (0 G NET), 9 KCAL PROTEIN: 4 G, 15 KCAL

TAHINI TURMERIC DRESSING

MAKES ABOUT ²/₃ CUP

This sauce is excellent as a dip for Souvlaki (page 151) or other grilled meats or raw veggies. Toss raw broccoli or cauliflower in it before roasting in a hot oven. Mix with yogurt and marinate chicken thighs before grilling (see the recipe Note). There are so many possibilities!

INGREDIENTS

½ cup tahini (store-bought or homemade, page 129)

¼ cup extra-virgin olive oil

2 tablespoons, plus 2 teaspoons fresh lemon juice

2 cloves garlic, pressed

2 teaspoons ground turmeric

½ teaspoon curry powder

¼ teaspoon ground black pepper

Fine sea salt to taste, if desired

In a small bowl, thoroughly mix the tahini, olive oil, lemon juice, garlic, turmeric, curry powder, and black pepper. Taste and add salt if desired. Store in an airtight container in the refrigerator.

NOTE: *Depending on how you want to use this—as a dipping sauce, marinade, salad dressing, or recipe ingredient—you might want to thin out the sauce. You can do so by adding warm water 1 tablespoon at a time. For creamier options, whisk this paste into coconut milk or plain yogurt. A good rule of thumb is to start with 2 parts Tahini Turmeric Sauce to 1 part coconut milk or yogurt.*

MACRONUTRIENTS PER SERVING (1 TABLESPOON)
CALORIES: 123 KCAL FAT: 12 G, 107 KCAL CARBOHYDRATE: 4 G (2 G NET), 14 KCAL PROTEIN: 2 G, 9 KCAL

TOUM

MAKES ABOUT 4 CUPS

Toum is a tangy, garlic-based condiment that is frequently served with shawarma or kebabs. It has a creamy texture similar to mayonnaise and packs a spicy punch when fresh. Although its fireiness mellows as it ages, its addictiveness does not. Try it in marinades, dressings, and sauces, or drop a spoonful onto a buttered ribeye for a savory, garlicky kick.

INGREDIENTS

4½ ounces garlic cloves (the yield from about 2 or 3 heads)

2 teaspoons kosher salt

6 tablespoons lemon juice

5 tablespoons ice water

3 cups olive oil (see Note)

1. Remove the germs from garlic cloves. To do this, cut the root end off of each clove and slice in half lengthwise. If a pale yellow or green sprout is present in the center of the clove, use the tip of your knife to pry it out. Discard the sprouts. This step is optional but highly recommended. Toum made with garlic germs may not emulsify well and tends to have a bitter taste.

2. Place the garlic cloves and salt in the bowl of a food processor. This recipe works best with smaller volume (4- to 6-cup) food processor bowls. If your food processor has a small bowl insert, use it here. Process until the garlic is very finely minced and forms a lumpy paste, stopping regularly to scrape down the sides.

3. While the food processor is running, slowly pour in 1 tablespoon of lemon juice. Process until the garlic paste becomes fluffy and bright in color. Stop and scrape down the sides of the bowl.

4. From this point on, you will leave the food processor running until the toum is finished. Drizzle in ½ cup of olive oil as slowly as possible. Aim to pour the oil in a very thin but constant stream. Once the olive oil has been incorporated, slowly pour in 1 tablespoon of lemon juice followed by 1 tablespoon of ice water. Repeat this process—½ cup olive oil followed by a tablespoon each of lemon and ice water in that order—until all of the olive oil has been used. Continue to process the toum until it has an airy, slightly springy texture like beaten egg whites. Store refrigerated in an airtight container.

NOTE: *Using extra-virgin olive oil results in toum with a bit of a "bite" because good EVOO is pleasantly piquant. Using light olive oil results in a lighter tasting toum that is a bit like mayonnaise. Both are excellent, so which you use is a matter of personal preference.*

MACRONUTRIENTS PER SERVING (2 TABLESPOONS)
CALORIES: 186 KCAL FAT: 20 G, 183 KCAL CARBOHYDRATE: 2 G (1 G NET), 6 KCAL PROTEIN: 0 G, 1 KCAL

ZA'ATAR SPICE BLEND

MAKES ABOUT 3 TABLESPOONS

INGREDIENTS

1 tablespoon ground sumac (see Note)

1 tablespoon dried thyme

1 tablespoon toasted sesame seeds

1 teaspoon kosher salt

Combine all the ingredients in a spice grinder (a clean coffee grinder works well) or use a mortar and pestle. Grind until the sesame seeds are completely blended with the other ingredients. Store in an airtight jar.

NOTE: *If you have difficulty locating sumac, it is often sold in Middle Eastern and Mediterranean markets. Alternatively, you may purchase it online.*

MACRONUTRIENTS PER SERVING (1 TEASPOON)
CALORIES: 6 KCAL FAT: <1 G, 4 KCAL CARBOHYDRATE: <1 G (<1 G NET), 2 KCAL PROTEIN: <1 G, 1 KCAL

NITED STATES

CANADA

UNITED STATES

MEXICO

THE BAHAMAS

CUBA

BELIZE

HONDURAS

GUATEMALA

JAMAICA

PUERTO RICO (U.S.)

EL SALVADOR

NICARAGUA

North

VENEZUELA

COLOMBIA

GUYANA

ISLANDS (U.S.)

Pacific Ocean

CALDO VERDE

Portugal's famous green soup is usually made with potatoes, but daikon radishes are featured in this low-carb version. When cooked in soup, they are almost indistinguishable from potatoes. Find them with the other root vegetables in most grocery stores. They look like fat, white carrots.

INGREDIENTS

3 tablespoons bacon fat or fat of choice

1 leek, white part thinly sliced

1 bunch curly kale or collard greens, stems and leaves separated

2 cloves garlic, chopped

1 medium daikon radish, peeled and thinly sliced

1 bunch radishes, trimmed and quartered

4 cups chicken bone broth or stock

4 cups filtered water

1 teaspoon kosher salt

16 ounces linguiça

6 teaspoons good quality extra-virgin olive oil

1. Melt the fat in a large stockpot over medium-high heat. When it is hot, add the leeks. Dice the kale stems only (not the leaves, save them for later in the recipe) and add them to the leeks. Sauté for 5 minutes. Stir in the garlic and cook 1 minute more.

2. Add both types of radishes and the bone broth. Turn the heat up to high and heat until the broth boils, then reduce the heat to a simmer. Cover the pot, set a timer for 20 minutes, and move on to the next step.

3. In a large saucepan, bring the water and salt to a boil. Prick the linguiça with a fork and add it to the boiling water. Boil it for 5 minutes, then use tongs remove it to a plate or cutting board. Carefully pour the water into the soup.

4. Roughly chop the kale leaves into bite-sized pieces. When the timer goes off, stir them into the soup. Slice the linguiça ¼-inch thick and add it to the soup. Cook for about 5 minutes more, until the radishes are very soft. Optionally, use a potato masher to break up the radishes. Taste and adjust the salt.

5. Ladle the soup into individual serving bowls. Drizzle each with 1 teaspoon olive oil. Serve hot.

MACRONUTRIENTS PER SERVING
CALORIES: 338 KCAL FAT: 27 G, 239 KCAL CARBOHYDRATE: 9 G (6 G NET), 36 KCAL PROTEIN: 17 G, 68 KCAL

MEDITERRANEAN

CAPRESE SALAD (INSALATA CAPRESE)

This is perhaps our favorite way to eat garden-fresh tomatoes when they ripen in the summer! (Yes, you can have tomatoes on a ketogenic diet.) Select high-quality olive oil for this recipe, as the flavor really makes a difference.

INGREDIENTS

1 pound tomatoes (heirloom if possible), seeded and cubed

1 pound whole milk fresh mozzarella, cubed

16 fresh basil leaves, chiffonade (see Note)

6 tablespoons extra-virgin olive oil

½ teaspoon freshly ground black pepper, or to taste

½ teaspoon coarse or flaked sea salt

1½ tablespoons good balsamic vinegar (optional)

1. Combine the tomatoes, mozzarella, basil, olive oil, and black pepper in a large bowl and toss gently to coat. Transfer to a serving platter and sprinkle with the salt.

2. Optionally drizzle the balsamic over the top. Serve immediately.

NOTE: *To chiffonade basil, place several leaves on top of each other and roll them tightly to create a long cigar (roll them side to side, not tip to stem). Use a sharp knife to cut the cigar into narrow strips.*

MACRONUTRIENTS PER SERVING (WITH BALSAMIC VINEGAR)
CALORIES: 378 KCAL FAT: 32 G, 291 KCAL CARBOHYDRATE: 6 G (5 G NET), 22 KCAL PROTEIN: 17 G, 68 KCAL

MEDITERRANEAN   141

CHICKEN CACCIATORE, UMBRIAN STYLE

MAKES 4 SERVINGS

Umbria is a region of central Italy. Unlike familiar chicken cacciatore recipes that call for tomatoes, the Umbrian version does not; and the Umbrian version calls for olives, a great source of natural fats for keto eaters. We not-so-secretly prefer the flavors and aromas of this version, and it's more keto-friendly!

INGREDIENTS

2 tablespoon avocado oil

¼ teaspoon fine sea salt, plus more for seasoning chicken

¼ teaspoon ground black pepper, plus more for seasoning chicken

Generous pinch salt and pepper

4 bone-in skin-on chicken thighs

4 skin-on chicken drumsticks

1 small onion, thinly sliced

8 ounces cremini mushrooms, sliced

½ cup pitted olives, black, green, or a mix

3 cloves garlic, minced

1 tablespoon capers, drained

1 cup chicken broth or stock

Juice of 1 lemon

1 tablespoon balsamic vinegar

1 sprig rosemary

6 fresh sage leaves

1. Heat 1 tablespoon olive oil in a large, deep skillet over medium heat. Season the chicken on all sides with salt and pepper. Working in batches, brown the chicken about 4 minutes per side until golden-brown. Remove to a plate.

2. Heat the remaining 1 tablespoon oil in the same skillet. Add the onions and mushrooms. Season with ¼ teaspoon each salt and pepper. Sauté until soft, 5 to 7 minutes. Add the olives, garlic, and capers. Sauté 2 minutes more to cook the garlic.

3. Pour in about half the chicken stock and use a wooden spoon to scrape up any browned bits from the bottom of the pan. Stir in the lemon juice and vinegar.

4. Add the chicken and any juices that collected on the plate back to the skillet. Turn the chicken to coat it in sauce and place the thighs skin side up. Nestle the rosemary and sage around the chicken. Pour in the rest of the stock. Turn the heat to high and bring the liquid to a boil, then reduce the heat to a simmer. Cover and simmer 20 minutes. Remove the cover, flip the chicken, and simmer 15 minutes more. Check that the internal temperature of the chicken has reached 165°F. Add more cooking time if necessary.

5. To serve, use tongs to move the chicken to a serving platter. Remove and discard the rosemary sprig and (optionally) the sage leaves. Spoon the pan sauce and vegetables over the chicken. Serve hot.

MACRONUTRIENTS PER SERVING
CALORIES: 450 KCAL FAT: 28 G, 248 KCAL CARBOHYDRATE: 8 G (6 G NET), 32 KCAL PROTEIN: 42 G, 170 KCAL

COQUILLES ST. JACQUES
(SCALLOPS IN MUSHROOM CREAM SAUCE)

MAKES 4 SERVINGS

If you want to impress your dinner guests, this decadent but easy-to-prepare dish is what you need. Even the name is impressive! Maybe don't tell your guests about the pork rinds at first. It does feel a tad incongruous topping scallops with pork rinds, but they make an excellent substitute for breadcrumbs. Don't omit the tarragon as it imparts a unique flavor.

INGREDIENTS

6 tablespoons unsalted butter or ghee

3 shallots, diced

8 ounces small cremini mushrooms, sliced

½ teaspoon fine sea salt

¼ teaspoon ground black pepper

¼ cup chicken or fish stock

2 tablespoons red wine vinegar

2 teaspoons minced fresh tarragon leaves

½ cup heavy whipping cream, or substitute full-fat coconut milk

1 large egg yolk

¼ teaspoon paprika

Pinch cayenne pepper

1 pound bay scallops, or sea scallops cut in half, or quartered if large (see Note)

½ cup shredded Gruyère cheese, or substitute Jarlsberg cheese

½ cup plain pork rind crumbs (see Note) or additional cheese

2 tablespoons extra-virgin olive oil

¼ cup fresh parsley leaves, finely chopped

1. Preheat the oven to 400°F. Use 2 tablespoons of butter to grease an oval gratin or casserole dish around 10 inches long.

2. Melt the remaining 4 tablespoons of butter in a skillet over medium heat. Sauté the shallots for about 2 minutes, until they start to soften and brown. Stir in the mushrooms and season with ¼ teaspoon each salt and pepper. Turn the heat to medium-low and sauté about 10 minutes, until the mushrooms are very soft.

3. Deglaze the pan by adding the stock and using a wooden spoon to scrape up any browned bits stuck to the bottom of the pan. Add the vinegar and the tarragon and stir well. Allow the liquid to come to a boil, then reduce the heat to low.

4. In a small saucepan, gently heat the cream over medium-low heat. While it warms, lightly beat the egg yolk in a small bowl. When the cream just starts to steam, temper the egg yolk by spooning a few spoonfuls of warm cream into the egg, whisking constantly. Then, slowly pour the egg yolk mixture back into the cream, whisking vigorously. Remove from heat and whisk in the remaining ¼ teaspoon salt, the paprika, and cayenne.

5. Return the mushroom mixture to medium heat. Whisk the cream mixture into the mushrooms. Allow it to simmer for a few minutes until the cream sauce has thickened, stirring frequently.

6. Place the scallops in an even layer in the bottom of the prepared baking dish. Carefully pour the mushroom mixture evenly over the scallops. In a small bowl, mix together the Gruyere, pork rind crumbs, olive oil, and half the parsley. Sprinkle this mixture evenly over the top of the mushrooms. Place the dish in the oven. Bake for 15 to 20 minutes until the sauce is hot and bubbling and the top is crisped.

7. Remove from the oven and sprinkle with the remaining parsley. Allow to cool for a few minutes before serving.

NOTES: *If using sea scallops, make sure you pull off and discard the foot before using.*

Pork rind crumbs can sometimes be found in stores, but it is also easy to make your own by crushing chicharrones in a food processor or using a rolling pin.

MACRONUTRIENTS PER SERVING
CALORIES: 572 KCAL FAT: 47 G, 426 KCAL CARBOHYDRATE: 8 G (7 G NET), 33 KCAL PROTEIN: 29 G, 116 KCAL

DOLMAS

Dolmas are made by wrapping herbed rice (with or without meat) in grape leaves and cooking them in water. The rice absorbs the water and cooks while the grape leaves soften and the flavors all meld together. Because we use turnips here instead of rice, these dolmas are steamed and the filling pre-cooked. Feel free to experiment with adding cooked ground lamb to this recipe, too!

INGREDIENTS

2 tablespoons pine nuts

2 tablespoons avocado oil

1 medium onion, diced small

3 medium turnips, peeled and shredded

6 fresh mint leaves, finely chopped

1/2 cup fresh parsley leaves, finely chopped

1/4 teaspoon ground allspice

1/4 teaspoon fine sea salt

3 teaspoons lemon juice

8-ounce jar grape leaves, rinsed and patted dry (see Note)

Filtered water

2 teaspoons extra-virgin olive oil

1. Heat a small, dry skillet over medium-low heat. Add the pine nuts and cook stirring constantly until they are lightly browned, about 3 minutes. Transfer to a plate to cool and set aside.

2. In a medium skillet, heat the avocado oil over medium heat. Add the onion and sauté about 3 minutes until just starting to become translucent. Stir in the turnip, mint, parsley, allspice, and salt. Sauté for 5 minutes stirring frequently. Taste test the turnip. It should be soft but not mushy. If it is still crunchy, cook a few minutes longer. Test again and adjust salt as needed. Remove the skillet from the heat and stir in the pine nuts and 1 teaspoon lemon juice. Allow the mixture to cool for a few minutes.

3. Working one at a time, place a grape leaf shiny side down on a cutting board with the stem end facing toward you. Spoon a heaping spoonful (about 1½ tablespoons depending on the size of the leaf) onto the middle of the leaf. Fold the stem end over the mixture, then fold in the two sides and roll it up like a little burrito. Place the rolled grape leaf seam side down on a plate. Repeat until you run out of turnip mixture.

4. Place a steamer basket in a pot or deep skillet. Fill the pot with water to the bottom of the basket and bring the water to a boil. Whisk together the remaining 2 teaspoons lemon juice and the olive oil. Place the dolmas seam side down in the steamer basket and brush the top with the olive oil mixture. (Make a second layer if necessary to fit them.) Cover the pot and steam the dolmas for 40 minutes, keeping an eye on the water level and adding more if it gets low.

5. Use tongs to carefully transfer the dolmas to a plate. Allow to cool before serving or refrigerate until ready to serve and serve cold.

NOTE: *You might not use the whole 8-ounce jar of grape leaves.*

MACRONUTRIENTS PER SERVING
CALORIES: 153 KCAL FAT: 12 G, 112 KCAL CARBOHYDRATE: 10 G (6 G NET), 40 KCAL PROTEIN: 2 G, 10 KCAL

GREEK SALAD

This classic Greek salad makes a great accompaniment to souvlaki or any other grilled meat. The oregano is what gives it its distinctive flavor, so don't skimp on that. Choose feta cheese packed in brine (as opposed to crumbled feta) for extra tangy deliciousness.

INGREDIENTS

¼ cup extra-virgin olive oil

1 tablespoon red wine vinegar

1 teaspoon dried oregano

1 medium tomato, diced

1 small red onion, very thinly sliced

1 medium cucumber, seeded and sliced ¼-inch thick

1 small green bell pepper, thinly sliced

20 pitted kalamata olives

1 cup fresh feta cheese, cubed or crumbled

4 cups packed spinach leaves, chopped

Ground black pepper (optional)

1. Place the olive oil, vinegar, and oregano in a jar with a tight-fitting lid. Shake well to combine.

2. In a large bowl, combine the tomato, onion, cucumber, bell pepper, olives, and feta. Pour in the dressing and toss to coat. This can be done a little ahead, and the veggies placed in the refrigerator to marinate in the dressing.

3. Just before serving, toss the spinach into the salad. Optionally top the salad with freshly ground black pepper. Serve.

MACRONUTRIENTS PER SERVING
CALORIES: 359 KCAL FAT: 31 G, 283 KCAL CARBOHYDRATE: 10 G (8 G NET), 42 KCAL PROTEIN: 11 G, 44 KCAL

LAMB SOUVLAKI

Souvlakia are spiced meat kabobs made with chicken, beef, goat, or lamb. Souvlaki is one of the most recognizable dishes from Greece, where it is ubiquitous. Serve it with Cucumber Yogurt Sauce (page 119) on top and Greek Salad (page 149) and Dolmas (page 146) for a complete Greek feast.

INGREDIENTS

1 cup olive oil or avocado oil

1 small red onion, cut into large pieces

2 cloves of garlic, pressed or very finely minced

Juice of 1 lemon

1 teaspoon dried oregano, crushed between your palms

1 teaspoon dried thyme

½ teaspoon ground cumin

½ teaspoon sweet paprika

¼ teaspoon ground black pepper

3 pounds lamb leg or shoulder, cut into chunks

Equipment: 8 long metal or bamboo skewers

1. In a large glass bowl, whisk together the oil, onion, garlic, lemon juice, oregano, thyme, cumin, paprika, and pepper. Add the lamb and toss very well to coat. Marinate at least 3 hours, but up to overnight. Stir the meat a few times during the marinating process.

2. Thread the meat onto the skewers. Discard any leftover marinade.

3. TO BROIL: Heat the broiler to high and place a rack about 6 inches from the heating element. (If using an under-oven broiler, heat to low.) Broil the lamb for 8 to 10 minutes, turning once about halfway through, until cooked through.

   TO GRILL: Heat a grill over high heat. Grill for 15 minutes, turning every 4 to 5 minutes, until cooked through

4. Serve hot.

NOTES: *If you are using bamboo skewers, soak them in warm water for a minimum of 30 minutes prior to cooking in order to prevent them from burning.*

The macronutrient values provided include all of the marinade to be conservative. If you want more precise values, you will need to weigh your marinade before and after marinating the meat to determine how much is being discarded.

MACRONUTRIENTS PER SERVING
CALORIES: 716 KCAL FAT: 61 G, 550 KCAL CARBOHYDRATE: 2 G (2 G NET), 7 KCAL PROTEIN: 39 G, 154 KCAL

LEMON GARLIC SARDINES

MAKES 4 SERVINGS

If you've only eaten canned sardines, look for fresh in fish markets during summer months and try this simple, flavorful preparation. Sardines are high in omega-3 fatty acids and boast an impressive nutrient profile that puts them alongside other powerhouse foods such as liver. Because sardines are forage fish and occupy a lower spot on the food chain, they are considered a more sustainable option than larger and slower-growing "game" fish. No wonder sardine consumption is so lauded by keto folks!

INGREDIENTS

2 pounds (about 6 to 14 fish depending on size) fresh sardines, cleaned (see Note)

½ cup unsalted butter or ghee, melted

1 tablespoon fine sea salt

½ teaspoon freshly ground black pepper

3 cloves garlic, crushed and minced

Flesh of 1 large lemon, pith and seeds removed, minced

2 tablespoons fresh parsley, minced

1. Preheat the broiler or a barbeque grill to the highest heat setting. Brush the sides and inner cavities of the sardines with ¼ cup of the melted butter and season the fish with salt and pepper.

2. If grilling, clean and oil the grates well and cook the fish directly atop the grates. If broiling, place the fish on a broiling or sheet pan and cook 6 to 8 inches beneath the heating element. Cook for 4 to 6 minutes (depending on size), carefully turning the fish once during cooking. Place the sardines on a serving plate.

3. Bring the remaining ¼ cup of butter to a simmer in a small saucepan over medium-low heat. Add the garlic and gently heat for 1 or 2 minutes, until fragrant. Do not allow the garlic to brown or the butter will taste bitter. Remove the pan from heat and stir in the chopped lemon pulp.

4. Drizzle the sardines with the garlic lemon butter. Sprinkle the chopped parsley over top and serve immediately.

NOTE: *Depending on where you buy them, your sardines might come prepared. If not, to clean the sardines, use a knife to scrape from tail to head to remove the scales. Rinse the fish under running water. Cut open the belly and remove the innards. Removing the heads is optional. Rinse the sardines again inside and out, then pat dry.*

MACRONUTRIENTS PER SERVING
CALORIES: 570 KCAL FAT: 44 G, 400 KCAL CARBOHYDRATE: 3 G (2 G NET), 12 KCAL PROTEIN: 40 G, 158 KCAL

MOUSSAKA

Although it looks like a lot of ingredients and steps, this moussaka is actually incredibly easy to put together and so delicious! Double the recipe and cook it in a small lasagna dish if you want leftovers, which reheat well.

INGREDIENTS

1 large (approximately 14 ounces) eggplant, sliced crosswise into rounds about ⅛-inch thick

6 tablespoons extra-virgin olive oil

2 tablespoons avocado or coconut oil

½ small yellow onion, diced

1 pound ground lamb

3 cloves garlic, chopped

1 teaspoon dried oregano

½ teaspoon ground cinnamon

½ teaspoon ground nutmeg

½ teaspoon fine sea salt

¼ teaspoon ground cloves

¼ cup dry red wine (see Note)

3 tablespoons tomato paste

½ cup grated Parmesan cheese

For the béchamel

3 tablespoons salted butter

8 ounces whole milk ricotta cheese

4 ounces soft goat cheese

2 egg yolks, lightly beaten

⅛ teaspoon grated nutmeg

1. Heat the oven to 400°F.

2. Place the eggplant slices in a single layer on a large baking sheet. Use two sheets if necessary. Brush the tops generously with 3 tablespoons of olive oil. Flip the eggplant and brush the other side with the remaining 3 tablespoons olive oil. Place the eggplant in the oven for 15 minutes (meanwhile, move on to Step 3). Flip the eggplant and bake another 10 minutes. The eggplant should be very tender, not chewy. If needed, add an additional 5 minutes cooking time. Remove from the oven and set aside.

3. While the eggplant cooks, make the meat sauce: Heat the avocado oil in a large skillet over medium heat. Sauté the onions for 5 minutes until soft. Crumble in the ground lamb and cook about 6 minutes, breaking up the meat as it cooks, until just a little pink remains. Clear a space in the center of the meat and add the garlic. Sauté the garlic for 1 minute, then stir into the meat. Season the meat with the oregano, cinnamon, nutmeg, salt, and cloves, and stir well to thoroughly combine.

4. In a small bowl, whisk together the red wine and tomato paste, then stir this mixture into the meat. Reduce the heat to low and simmer for 10 minutes. Meanwhile, move on to Step 5.

5. While the meat sauce simmers, make the béchamel: Melt the butter in a small saucepan over medium heat. Add the ricotta and goat cheese and stir until just melted. Whisking constantly, slowly pour in the egg yolks. Stir in the nutmeg and remove from heat.

6. Assemble the moussaka: Use half the eggplant to line the bottom of a 6x6-inch glass baking dish (8x8-inch will also work). Spoon half the meat mixture in an even layer over the top and smooth to cover the eggplant. Layer the remaining eggplant over the meat mixture and cover with the remaining meat mixture. Pour the béchamel evenly over the top, using a spatula or spoon to spread it so it completely covers the meat. Sprinkle the Parmesan cheese over the entire surface.

7. Place the pan in the oven and bake for 30 minutes until hot and bubbling. Remove from the oven and let sit for 10 minutes before serving.

NOTE: *If you choose not to cook with red wine, you can substitute ¼ cup beef stock and ¾ teaspoon red wine vinegar or apple cider vinegar.*

MACRONUTRIENTS PER SERVING
CALORIES: 648 KCAL FAT: 55 G, 497 KCAL CARBOHYDRATE: 13 G (9 G NET), 53 KCAL PROTEIN: 25 G, 98 KCAL

PORCINI MUSHROOM BEEF STEW

MAKES 8 SERVINGS

Italian-style porcini mushroom beef stew is such a crowd-pleaser! If your grocery store does not stock dried porcini mushrooms, check an Italian deli, or they can be purchased online. In a pinch, shiitake or other dried mushrooms will make a fine substitute.

INGREDIENTS

1½ ounces dried porcini mushrooms

2½ cups filtered water, boiling

2½ pounds beef round or chuck roast, cut into 1½-inch pieces

2 tablespoons avocado oil

2 ounces diced pancetta

2 teaspoons of coarse grain salt, plus more to taste

1 large carrot, cut into 1-inch pieces

2 medium stalks celery, cut into 1-inch pieces

1 medium onion, chopped

4 cloves garlic, smashed and chopped

1 sundried tomato, minced (about 2 tablespoons) or 1 tablespoon tomato paste

1 bay leaf

1 tablespoon fresh rosemary leaves, minced

1 cup dry red wine (see Note)

28-ounce can crushed San Marzano tomatoes

¼ cup basil, chiffonade (see Note on page 141)

Equipment: Unbleached parchment paper

1. Place the porcini mushrooms in a medium heat-proof bowl and pour the water over top. Allow to soak for 30 minutes. While the mushrooms soak, pat the beef dry and allow to rest at room temperature, then prepare and chop the vegetables.

2. Preheat the oven to 325°F. When the mushrooms have finished soaking, Use a slotted spoon to remove them from the liquid and chop them into 1-inch slices. Carefully pour the soaking liquid through a very fine strainer into a clean bowl, leaving behind as much sediment as possible. Set the mushrooms and strained liquid aside.

3. Heat a large oven-safe Dutch oven or casserole over medium-high heat. Add the oil. Once hot, add the pancetta and cook until just browned, 2 to 3 minutes. Remove the pancetta with a slotted spoon and reserve in a large bowl.

4. Season the beef well with coarse salt and sear in the same Dutch oven, working in batches so as not to crowd the pan. Allow the beef to cook undisturbed for 2 minutes per side so a deep golden-brown crust forms. Add more oil if the pan becomes too dry. Place the cooked beef in the bowl with the pancetta.

5. Add the carrot, celery, and onion to the pot and sauté 5 minutes, stirring frequently. Add the garlic, sundried tomato, mushrooms, bay leaf, and rosemary. Sauté for an additional 1 to 2 minutes until fragrant.

6. Deglaze the pot by pouring in the wine and using a spatula or wooden spoon to scrape up any browned bits on the bottom of the pot. Allow the wine to come to a boil. Cook until the liquid has reduced by half, 5 to 10 minutes depending on the diameter of your pot. Stir in the reserved mushroom liquid and allow to come to a boil.

7. Add the beef, pancetta, any juices from their bowl, and the crushed tomatoes to the pot. Stir well and remove from heat.

8. Cut a piece of parchment paper cut slightly larger than the diameter of your pot. Press the paper down so it lays on top of the stew and comes up the sides of the pot. Cover the pot with the lid and return to the oven. Cook for 1½ to 2 hours, until the beef is fork-tender.

9. Stir in the basil just before serving. Taste and adjust the salt as needed. Serve hot.

NOTE: *If you choose not to cook with red wine, you can substitute 1 cup beef stock and 1 tablespoon red wine vinegar or apple cider vinegar, but it will change the flavor somewhat.*

MACRONUTRIENTS PER SERVING
CALORIES: 477 KCAL FAT: 31 G, 283 KCAL CARBOHYDRATE: 12 G (9 G NET), 48 KCAL PROTEIN: 30 G, 121 KCAL

SPINACH RICOTTA DUMPLINGS

This is our take on gnocchi verde, a classic Italian dish. Normally they are made with flour and gently simmered, but without the flour these fall apart in the water, so this version is baked instead.

INGREDIENTS

10 ounces frozen spinach, thawed

1½ cups shredded mozzarella cheese

¼ cup coconut flour

½ teaspoon fine sea salt

¼ teaspoon ground black pepper

¼ teaspoon ground nutmeg

½ cup whole milk ricotta cheese

2 large eggs, lightly beaten

For serving

4 tablespoons unsalted butter

1 clove garlic, chopped

8 sage leaves

½ cup grated Parmesan cheese

1. Preheat the oven to 350°F. Line a baking sheet with parchment paper. Place the spinach in a sieve over a bowl and use a spatula or wooden spoon to press the liquid out of it. Set aside to drain.

2. Mix the mozzarella cheese, coconut flour, salt, pepper, and nutmeg in a microwavable glass bowl. Microwave on high for 1 minute. Remove from the microwave, add the ricotta, and stir well. Microwave on high another 30 seconds. Stir well again. If the cheese is melted and the dough has come together in a uniform ball, add the eggs. Otherwise, continue to microwave in 15 second increments until fully melted, then add the eggs.

3. Mix the eggs into the dough until fully incorporated. Press any remaining liquid out of the spinach and stir it into the dough until well combined.

4. Scoop out about 1 tablespoon of dough at a time and roll it into a ball. If the dough is too soft to handle, place it in the freezer for a few minutes to firm. Place the ball on the prepared baking sheet. Repeat until all the dough has been used. You should end up with about 24 gnocchi.

5. Bake in the oven for 20 to 25 minutes until browned on the bottom and lightly brown on top. A longer cooking time will result in drier gnocchi, whereas a shorter time will result in moister gnocchi; cook to your preference. Remove from the oven.

6. Heat the butter in a medium skillet over medium-low heat. Add the garlic and sage leaves. Cook, stirring, for 3 minutes. Remove and discard the sage leaves.

7. Place the gnocchi in a shallow serving bowl. Pour the sage butter over top and stir gently to coat. Sprinkle with the Parmesan cheese. Serve immediately.

MACRONUTRIENTS PER SERVING
CALORIES: 424 KCAL FAT: 32 G, 284 KCAL CARBOHYDRATE: 13 G (8 G NET), 51 KCAL PROTEIN: 24 G, 96 KCAL

TAPAS ASSORTMENT

We love the tradition of tapas—small plates, often shared, that when made into a meal allow diners to sample a variety of hot and cold Spanish dishes. It's the ultimate sampler platter! Note that the servings are small on these dishes because they are meant to be eaten together. If standing alone, consider doubling the recipes.

Champinones al Ajillo (Garlic Mushrooms)
MAKES 4 SERVINGS

These are best when made with small mushrooms that can be popped in your mouth in a single bite!

INGREDIENTS

1 pound button or cremini mushrooms (smaller is better)

2 tablespoons salted butter

3 tablespoons avocado oil

3 cloves garlic, thinly sliced

3 cloves garlic, pressed or ground into a paste

2 tablespoons fresh lemon juice

½ teaspoon smoked paprika

¼ teaspoon fine sea salt

¼ teaspoon ground black pepper

¼ teaspoon red chili flakes, or to taste

¼ cup fresh parsley, finely chopped

1. If the mushrooms are large, halve or quarter them. You want the pieces to be about the size of a large marble.

2. Heat the butter and 2 tablespoons of avocado oil in a large skillet over medium heat. When the butter stops foaming, adjust the heat down a bit and add the mushrooms and sliced garlic. Sauté 6 to 8 minutes, until the mushrooms are softer but still a bit firm. While they cook, in a small bowl mix together the remaining 1 tablespoon avocado oil, the pressed garlic, lemon juice, paprika, sea salt, pepper, and chili flakes.

3. Pour the lemon juice mixture over the mushrooms and stir well to coat. Cook another 3 minutes or so, until the mushrooms are soft and the garlic is no longer raw.

4. Transfer the mushrooms to a serving dish and sprinkle with the parsley. Serve warm.

MACRONUTRIENTS PER SERVING
CALORIES: 162 KCAL FAT: 16 G, 145 KCAL CARBOHYDRATE: 4 G (4 G NET), 17 KCAL PROTEIN: 2 G, 7 KCAL

Aioli
MAKES A GENEROUS ¾ CUP

A dipping sauce for everything! Use with each of the tapas dishes here.

INGREDIENTS

¾ cup avocado oil mayonnaise

2 to 3 cloves garlic to taste, pressed or ground into a paste

1 tablespoon fresh lemon juice

Whisk all the ingredients together. Store in an airtight container in the refrigerator.

MACRONUTRIENTS PER SERVING (1 TABLESPOON)
CALORIES: 101 KCAL FAT: 11 G, 99 KCAL CARBOHYDRATE: <1 G (<1 G NET), 1 KCAL PROTEIN: 0 G, 0 KCAL

Asparagus and Serrano Ham
MAKES 4 SERVINGS

Omit the cheese if you do not eat dairy. These will still be great!

INGREDIENTS

24 thin or 12 thick asparagus spears (thin preferred), trimmed to about 6-inches long

4 ounces manchego cheese, cut into matchsticks

12 slices serrano ham (aka jambon serrano), or substitute prosciutto

1. Two spears at a time (1 if using thick spears), place the asparagus at one end of a slice of ham so the ham is just below the asparagus tips. Place a few matchsticks of cheese atop the asparagus and start to roll the cheese and asparagus together in the ham. (Place the cheese so it is covered by the ham—sticking out a little bit is ok.) If the ham starts to tear, simply pinch it together and keep rolling—it will stick to itself.

2. Place the asparagus roll-up seam side down on a broiler-safe pan. Repeat for the rest of the ingredients, leaving space between the roll-ups.

3. Place a rack about 4 inches below the oven broiler and heat the broiler to low. Place the pan under the broiler and broil about 2 to 3 minutes on the first side. Watch carefully so the ham crisps but does not burn. Flip the asparagus and cook another 2 or so minutes on the second side until crisp.

4. Remove from the oven and allow to cool for 5 to 10 minutes before serving, until they can be safely handled. These are meant to be finger food.

MACRONUTRIENTS PER SERVING
CALORIES: 248 KCAL FAT: 17 G, 149 KCAL CARBOHYDRATE: 3 G (1 G NET), 11 KCAL PROTEIN: 24 G, 95 KCAL

Faux Patatas Bravas
MAKES 4 SERVINGS

Patatas bravas is one of the classic tapas dishes—fried potatoes. Obviously that won't fly on a keto diet, so here is an alternative.

INGREDIENTS

1 quart water

½ tablespoon kosher salt

3 kohlrabi bulbs, peeled and cut into ¾-inch cubes

¼ cup duck fat

¾ teaspoon smoked paprika

¼ teaspoon chipotle chili powder

¼ teaspoon ground cayenne pepper

Flaky sea salt like Maldon for serving

1. Bring the water and kosher salt to a rolling boil in a large saucepan. Add the kohlrabi and boil 10 minutes, until the kohlrabi is easily pierced with a fork but not mushy. Drain thoroughly. Place to kohlrabi on a clean kitchen towel to dry a bit. Let sit 5 minutes.

2. Heat the duck fat in a large skillet over medium heat. When very hot, add the kohlrabi and fry about 5 minutes, stirring frequently, until browned on all sides and tender. Use a slotted spoon to remove to a plate lined with paper towel.

3. Mix the paprika, chili powder, and cayenne in a medium bowl. Toss the kohlrabi in the spices. Transfer to a serving plate and sprinkle with a pinch of flaky salt. Serve with aioli.

MACRONUTRIENTS PER SERVING
CALORIES: 138 KCAL FAT: 13 G, 116 KCAL CARBOHYDRATE: 6 G (5 G NET), 23 KCAL PROTEIN: 2 G, 6 KCAL

Gildas

Olives and anchovies are keto superstars! These no-bake goodies can be made a couple days ahead and are perfect for lunchboxes and picnics.

INGREDIENTS

32 medium pitted green olives (such as Manzanilla)

16 anchovies packed in olive oil, drained

32 guindilla peppers, or use 16 pepperoncini or banana peppers

Equipment: 16 cocktail toothpicks

1. One at a time, skewer an olive on a toothpick. Hold 2 peppers together and wrap an anchovy around them like a belt (or wrap an anchovy around 1 pepper if using pepperoncini or banana peppers). Carefully skewer the toothpick through the anchovies and peppers, making sure the toothpick goes through both peppers and holds the anchovy in place. Thread another olive onto the toothpick. Place on a serving plate.

2. Repeat for the remaining ingredients. Refrigerate until ready to serve.

MACRONUTRIENTS PER SERVING
CALORIES: 100 KCAL FAT: 6 G, 51 KCAL CARBOHYDRATE: 4 G (3 G NET), 15 KCAL PROTEIN: 5 G, 20 KCAL

TONNATO SAUCE

MAKES ABOUT 1½ CUPS

Taste-wise, tonnato is reminiscent of Caesar dressing, but with a more interesting depth of flavor. Thanks to the tuna, it is jam-packed with healthy omega-3s and is an excellent option for people who struggle to consume enough protein. You can use it on practically anything!

INGREDIENTS

½ cup avocado oil mayonnaise

¼ cup extra-virgin olive oil, plus more if needed

1 5-ounce can tuna packed in olive oil, oil reserved (see Notes)

1 2-ounce tin anchovy fillets packed in olive oil, oil reserved (see Notes)

2 tablespoons capers, drained

Juice from 1 lemon

⅛ teaspoon ground black pepper

Salt to taste

1. Place the mayonnaise, olive oil, tuna and its oil, anchovies and their oil, capers, lemon juice, and pepper in a blender or small food processor. Blend on high until smooth, scraping down the sides of the blender if needed.

2. Taste the sauce and add salt and pepper as needed. If the sauce is too thick (it should be the consistency of Caesar salad dressing), blend in more olive oil, 1 tablespoon at a time.

3. Store in an airtight container in the refrigerator.

NOTES: *Our favorite brands for sustainably caught tuna, Safe Catch and Wild Planet, both offer canned tuna packed with nothing but tuna and salt. In this case, simply add the tuna and whatever oil is in the can (this will be oil that came out of the fish during canning), then add additional tablespoons of olive oil as needed in the second step.*

Often tonnato recipes call for only a couple anchovy fillets, but we love anchovies! If you aren't as keen on anchovies as we are, start with 2 fillets and none of the anchovy oil, then add more as desired.

MACRONUTRIENTS PER 2 TABLESPOON SERVING
CALORIES: 132 KCAL FAT: 13 G, 114 KCAL CARBOHYDRATE: <1 G (<1 G NET), 2 KCAL PROTEIN: 4 G, 16 KCAL

VITELLO TONNATO
(BEEF TONGUE WITH TONNATO SAUCE)

MAKES 6 TO 8 SERVINGS

If you didn't grow up eating tongue (lingua), preparing it at home might be a bit outside your comfort zone. We understand, it isn't the most attractive part of the cow. Once cooked, however, the meat could easily be mistaken for pot roast.

INGREDIENTS

1 beef tongue (about 3 pounds)

1 tablespoon kosher salt

5 peppercorns

3 cloves garlic, smashed

1 dried bay leaf

Filtered water

2 tablespoons tallow, lard, or fat of choice (optional)

For serving

1 batch Tonnato (page 167)

3 tablespoons capers, drained (optional)

3 tablespoons chopped fresh parsley leaves (optional)

1. Place the beef tongue, salt, peppercorns, garlic, and bay leaf in your countertop pressure cooker and cover completely with filtered water. Secure the lid and cook on high pressure for 60 minutes. Allow the pressure to release naturally for 20 minutes, then manually release the pressure and open the lid.

2. Use tongs to transfer the tongue to a cutting board and discard the other contents of the pressure cooker. Allow it to rest 5 to 10 minutes until it is cool enough to handle.

3. Use a sharp paring knife to score the skin, then peel it away from the meat and discard. Trim or scrape off any bits that do not look like something you would want to eat and discard those bits.

4. OPTION 1: Cover the tongue and place it in the refrigerator to chill at least 20 minutes. When it is completely chilled, slice the tongue against the grain into thin medallions. Arrange the medallions on a serving plate.

   OPTION 2: Slice the warm tongue against the grain into thin medallions. Heat the fat in a skillet over medium-high heat. Working in batches, sear the outside of the tongue until crispy. Optionally cut the slices into strips or bite-sized pieces. Arrange the tongue on a serving plate.

   OPTION 3: Shred the warm tongue using 2 forks. If desired, heat the fat in a skillet over medium-high heat and quickly sauté the meat until crispy. Transfer to a serving bowl.

5. Spoon the tonnato over the tongue, placing any extra tonnato in a ramekin for dipping. Sprinkle the capers and parsley over top. Serve immediately.

NOTES: *If you don't have a pressure cooker, you can simmer the tongue on your stovetop for about 3 hours until it is easily pierced with a knife (the rule of thumb is 1 hour per pound). Make sure you keep an eye on the water level and add more as needed. Alternatively, you can cook it in a slow cooker on low for 6 to 8 hours. In either case, you want the tongue to be completely covered by liquid while cooking.*

It is difficult to predict exactly how much meat a cooked tongue will yield. Macronutrient values are calculated using 4 ounces of tongue. We suggest weighing your portion before eating if you are tracking your macros.

MACRONUTRIENTS PER SERVING (FOR 6 SERVINGS WITH 4 OUNCES OF TONGUE EACH)
CALORIES: 587 KCAL FAT: 51 G, 457 KCAL CARBOHYDRATE: 1 G (1 G NET), 4 KCAL PROTEIN: 30 G, 120 KCAL

BACON BORSCHT

Borscht is a soup that's popular all over Eastern Europe and comes in many different varieties. This version pairs the sour-sweet flavor of the beets and kvass with smoky bacon.

INGREDIENTS

6 ounces thick sliced bacon, cut into ½-inch squares

4 cups bone broth or stock (any type, fish or vegetable recommended)

4 medium beets, peeled and halved

½ ounce dried mushrooms (any variety)

1 small carrot, chopped

3 cloves garlic, smashed and minced

1 medium onion, thinly sliced

1 tablespoon unsalted butter or ghee

½ tablespoon fine sea salt

¼ cup fresh parsley, chopped

3 tablespoons fresh dill weed, plus more to garnish, chopped

2 cups beet kvass (page 175 or store-bought)

Pinch white or black pepper

8 tablespoons sour cream (or coconut yogurt for dairy-free), to garnish

1. Heat a large stockpot or Dutch oven over medium-high heat. Sauté the bacon pieces until just crisp and the fat begins to render out, about 2 to 3 minutes. Remove the bacon from the pot with a slotted spoon and set aside, leaving the fat in the pan.

2. Pour the bone broth into the same stock pot, then add the beets, dried mushrooms, carrot, garlic, and half of the sliced onion. Bring to a low boil and cook for 30 to 45 minutes until the beets are tender. Once the beets are tender, use a slotted spoon to remove them to a bowl. Set aside to cool. Place a fine mesh strainer over a large heatproof bowl and strain the broth. Discard the solids and reserve the broth.

3. While the beets cool, brown the remaining sliced onions. Wipe down the inside of the stockpot if necessary, then return the pot to medium-high heat. Melt the butter and add the onions. Sauté stirring frequently until the onions become soft and turn golden, about 5 minutes. Pour in the reserved broth and bring to a boil.

4. Chop the beets into half-moon slices or bite-sized cubes and add to the broth, then stir in the reserved bacon, sea salt, parsley, and dill. Remove the pot from the heat and stir in the kvass and pepper. Taste and adjust the salt and pepper as needed. Serve hot or cold, topped with a sprinkling of fresh dill and a tablespoon of sour cream.

MACRONUTRIENTS PER SERVING
CALORIES: 181 KCAL FAT: 13 G, 114 KCAL CARBOHYDRATE: 6 G (5 G NET), 24 KCAL PROTEIN: 11 G, 44 KCAL

BEET KVASS

MAKES 8 CUPS

Kvass is a traditional Slavic fermented drink that is a great source of enzymes, gut-boosting bacteria, and minerals. We like to think of it more as a nourishing health-promoting tonic than a sipping beverage—a couple ounces goes a long way!

INGREDIENTS

2 large beets (preferably organic), washed and cut into 1-inch cubes

8 cups non-chlorinated filtered water (see Note)

1 tablespoon fine sea salt

2 tablespoons brine from a recent batch of lacto-fermented vegetables, such as sauerkraut (optional, see Note)

Equipment: 1 half-gallon jar or fermentation crock, sterilized

1. Place the beets into the jar and pour the filtered water over top, leaving at least an inch or two of headspace at the top. Stir in the salt and brine (if using).

2. Cover the mouth of the jar with a clean dish towel, coffee filter, or paper towel secured with a rubber band. You may also use an airlock fermentation lid, if available.

3. Ferment the kvass in a dark, temperature-stable area away from any plants, trashcans, or fresh fruits and vegetables at room temperature for 3 to 5 days, until the desired taste has been achieved. Finished beet kvass typically has an earthy, mineral taste that is slightly tangy and sweet. In colder months, it may take upwards of 5 to 7 days for the kvass to fully ferment. Once fermented, store in the refrigerator in an airtight container.

4. To serve the kvass as a health tonic, pour a few ounces of the liquid into a glass and drink, preferably on an empty stomach and away from any meals. You may also use kvass as an add-in to unheated dressings, sauces, and smoothies for an extra probiotic boost.

NOTES: *Using more brine will enable a shorter fermentation time. It is important to use filtered water when making kvass because the presence of chlorine in water such as that from a municipal tap may cause the beneficial bacteria present on the beet skins to die en masse before they have the opportunity to reproduce. Dead bacteria cannot ferment carbohydrates, so this will result in a jar of wet, rotten beets instead of a delicious batch of kvass.*

It is impossible to get accurate nutritional information for home-fermented recipes. These values are provided as an estimate. Read the "Fermenting" section on page xiv before fermenting for the first time.

MACRONUTRIENTS PER SERVING (½ CUP)
CALORIES: 8 KCAL FAT: 0 G, 0 KCAL CARBOHYDRATE: 2 G (2 G NET), 8 KCAL PROTEIN: 0 G, 0 KCAL

BIGOS

MAKES 6 GENEROUS SERVINGS

Bigos, aka Polish hunter's stew, is usually cooked low and slow on the stovetop for hours. This recipe cuts the cooking time by more than half without sacrificing any of the hearty, homey flavor by using a countertop pressure cooker. Bigos is even better after sitting in the refrigerator overnight.

INGREDIENTS

6 slices thick-cut bacon

1½ pounds country style pork ribs

3 allspice berries or 1½ teaspoons gin

1 cup chicken bone broth or stock

2 bay leaves

1 Parmesan cheese rind (optional, see Note)

12 ounces cremini mushrooms, sliced

1 small onion, sliced

1 medium head green cabbage, quartered, core removed, thinly sliced

1 teaspoon kosher salt

1 teaspoon ground black pepper

12 ounces kielbasa cut into 1-inch pieces

1 jar (16 ounces) sauerkraut and brine (store-bought or homemade, page 211)

1. Set your countertop pressure cooker to the Sauté function. Cook the bacon until just crisp. Use tongs to remove the bacon to a plate, leaving the rendered fat behind. Brown the ribs in the bacon fat for about 2 minutes per side, working in batches if necessary. Use tongs to remove the ribs. Press the Cancel button on your pressure cooker.

2. Carefully pour about half the reserved fat from your pressure cooker into a large, deep skillet or wok and set aside.

3. Place the ribs back in the pressure cooker. Add the allspice berries, chicken stock, and bay leaves, along with the Parmesan cheese rind if using. Secure the lid and cook under high pressure for 20 minutes; meanwhile move to the next steps.

4. Heat the skillet with the fat over medium heat. Add the mushrooms and onions. Sauté until soft, about 10 minutes. Add the cabbage a handful at a time, stirring until wilted. When all the cabbage is incorporated, season with salt and pepper and remove from heat.

5. When the pressure cooker time is up, manually release the pressure. Open the lid and remove and discard the Parmesan cheese rind. Use tongs to flip the ribs. Scatter the kielbasa on top of the ribs. Chop the bacon and add half to the pressure cooker; set the other half aside. Spoon the cabbage mixture from the skillet into the pressure cooker. Pour in the sauerkraut along with its brine and smooth over the top.

6. Seal the lid again. Cook under high pressure for 15 minutes. When the time is up, manually release the pressure. Use tongs to remove the ribs. Shred the rib meat and return the meat to the pressure cooker (optionally save the bones to use in a future batch

of bone broth). Stir the contents well. Carefully transfer the bigos to a serving bowl, removing and discarding the bay leaves. Sprinkle the remaining bacon over the top and serve hot or warm.

NOTE: *Bigos is often made with dried mushrooms, which add a nice umami element but also considerable carbs to this dish. Instead, we recommend a Parmesan cheese rind to impart umami. A good tip is to keep the spent rinds from Parmesan or other hard cheeses in a zip-top bag in your freezer to use in soups and stews. If you don't have one on hand, use a dash of tamari or coconut aminos instead.*

MACRONUTRIENTS PER SERVING
CALORIES: 518 KCAL FAT: 36 G, 322 KCAL CARBOHYDRATE: 15 G (9 G NET), 60 KCAL PROTEIN: 37 G, 148 KCAL

BLINI

Blini are little Russian pancakes usually made with buckwheat or wheat flour. In this recipe, the texture of the flax meal and the psyllium husk help give them the desired consistency while still remaining grain-free.

INGREDIENTS

¾ cup blanched almond flour

2 tablespoons finely ground flax meal

2 teaspoons psyllium husk

½ teaspoon aluminum-free baking powder

¼ teaspoon fine sea salt

¼ cup warm filtered water

1 large egg

¼ cup heavy whipping cream

1 tablespoon coconut oil, melted, plus 1 to 2 tablespoons more for cooking

1. In a medium bowl, mix together the almond flour, flax meal, psyllium husk, baking powder, and salt. Slowly stir in the warm water.

2. In a small bowl, lightly beat the egg, then stir in the cream. Pour this mixture into the batter and stir to incorporate. Add the coconut oil and stir until the batter is smooth.

3. Heat a flat-bottomed skillet or griddle pan over medium-low heat. Spoon one tablespoon of batter at a time into the pan and gently flatten with the back of the spoon. Cook about 2 minutes on the first side until golden. Flip and cook 2 minutes more on the second side. Remove to a plate. Repeat for the rest of the batter, adding more oil to the pan as needed. (Turn the heat down if the blini begin to brown too fast.)

4. Note that the batter will thicken the longer it sits. Serve immediately or refrigerate if not using promptly. These can be made a day or two ahead of assembling your final dish.

MACRONUTRIENTS PER SERVING (4 BLINI)
CALORIES: 279 KCAL FAT: 26 G, 230 KCAL CARBOHYDRATE: 7 G (3 G NET), 28 KCAL PROTEIN: 7 G, 29 KCAL

BLINI WITH SMOKED SALMON AND HERBED CRÈME FRAÎCHE

MAKES 4 SERVINGS

Smoked salmon and crème fraîche (or sour cream) are customary toppings for blini; we turn it up a notch here by making herbed crème fraîche. If you really want to get fancy, add a small dollop of caviar, also a traditional blini topping.

INGREDIENTS

1 batch Blini (see previous recipe)

6 tablespoons crème fraîche

1 tablespoon finely minced fresh chives

1 tablespoon finely minced fresh dill weed

8 ounces smoked salmon

Additional fresh dill weed to garnish (optional)

1. Make the blini according to the directions below. Allow them to cool to room temperature. While they cool, in a small bowl stir together the crème fraîche, chives, and dill. Place the bowl in the refrigerator until ready to assemble.

2. Cut the smoked salmon into 16 equal pieces (or as many blini as you made).

3. To assemble the dish, spoon about 1 teaspoon of the crème fraîche mixture on one of the blinis. Gently press one portion of the salmon into the crème fraîche, then place on a serving tray. Repeat for the remaining ingredients. Optionally garnish with additional dill before serving.

MACRONUTRIENTS PER SERVING
CALORIES: 418 KCAL FAT: 36 G, 322 KCAL CARBOHYDRATE: 8 G (3 G NET), 31 KCAL PROTEIN: 18 G, 73 KCAL

CHLODNIK

This refreshing beet and cucumber soup is popular in Lithuania and Poland. It is served chilled and features a base that is rich in both live probiotic cultures and fiber, making it an excellent choice for gut health.

INGREDIENTS

1 pound young beets with stems and leaves

Filtered water

½ teaspoon fine sea salt, plus more to taste

2 cups chilled chicken bone broth or stock

1¼ cups kefir or coconut kefir

1 cup full-fat yogurt or coconut yogurt

1 hothouse cucumber, grated

1 tablespoon fresh dill weed, chopped, plus more for garnish

For serving

2 radishes, very thinly sliced

1 green onion, white and green part finely chopped

4 tablespoons sour cream, or additional coconut yogurt

2 hard-boiled large eggs, peeled and quartered or sliced

1. Thoroughly wash the beets, along with their stems and leaves. Remove the stems from the beets and leaves from the stems. Dice both the leaves and stems. Peel the beets and discard the peel (wearing gloves prevents your hands from being stained).

2. Coarsely grate the beets and place in a large pot along with the stems and leaves. Fill the pot with just enough water to cover the grated beets and add the salt. Bring the water to a gentle simmer and cook for 15 minutes until the beets are just tender, then remove from heat.

3. Pour in the bone broth or stock. If desired, you may gently blend the soup with an immersion blender to further mince the beet greens and intensify the color of the soup. Pour into a large bowl and place in the refrigerator or freezer until thoroughly chilled, stirring occasionally to help dissipate heat.

4. Once the soup is cold, stir in the kefir, yogurt, grated cucumber, and dill. Taste and adjust salt to taste.

5. Serve chilled, garnished with radish slices, green onion, egg wedges, a small dollop of sour cream, and a sprinkling of fresh dill.

MACRONUTRIENTS PER SERVING
CALORIES: 158 KCAL FAT: 8 G, 71 KCAL CARBOHYDRATE: 13 G (10 G NET), 52 KCAL PROTEIN: 9 G, 35 KCAL

KAJMAK

Kajmak is a Serbian dairy spread made by heating raw milk, allowing it to cool, and skimming off the cream that solidifies on the surface. That creamy, fatty end product is mixed with salt and voilà: kajmak. Although simple to make at home, it also takes time and attention. This method makes a very passable substitute in minutes.

INGREDIENTS

1 cup full-fat cream cheese, room temperature

1 cup sour cream

½ cup crumbled feta cheese

4 tablespoons unsalted butter, room temperature

1. Place all the ingredients in a large bowl. Blend with a hand mixer until very smooth.

2. Transfer to an airtight container and place in the refrigerator to chill. Store covered in the refrigerator.

MACRONUTRIENTS PER SERVING (¼ CUP)
CALORIES: 158 KCAL FAT: 15 G, 139 KCAL CARBOHYDRATE: 2 G (2 G NET), 8 KCAL PROTEIN: 3 G, 14 KCAL

KAPUSTA (CABBAGE AND MUSHROOMS)

MAKES 6 SERVINGS

Kapusta is simply the Polish word for cabbage. As a dish, "kapusta" can refer to a number of different preparations, some of which call for fresh cabbage, some for sauerkraut, and others still for a mixture of the two. Kapusta can also include meat (usually pork). This version uses fresh cabbage and mushrooms, as well as bacon for a pleasing hint of smokiness.

INGREDIENTS

6 pieces thick-sliced bacon, diced

½ to 2 tablespoons unsalted butter or ghee, as needed

1 medium onion, diced

8 ounces cremini or button mushrooms, sliced

1 pound green cabbage (about ½ of a small head), shredded

¼ teaspoon fine sea salt

Pinch freshly ground black pepper

3 tablespoons chicken or beef bone broth or stock

1. Preheat the oven to 375°F.

2. In a skillet over medium-high heat, sauté the bacon until crispy and the fat has rendered out, about 3 to 4 minutes. Remove the bacon with a slotted spoon and set aside, reserving the fat in the pan.

3. Add butter to the skillet until there is at approximately 3 tablespoons worth of fat in the bottom of the pan. Add the onions and sauté stirring frequently until just softened and slightly golden, about 3 to 4 minutes. Add the mushrooms to the onions and sauté stirring frequently until browned, about 3 minutes.

4. In a large bowl, combine the cabbage, mushroom and onion mixture, and bacon. Season with the salt and pepper. Transfer the mixture to a large baking dish. Pour the bone broth over top and drizzle with any leftover pan drippings.

5. Cover the baking dish and bake for 35 to 40 minutes, until the cabbage is tender. If desired, you may remove the lid for the last 10 minutes of cooking time to brown the cabbage slightly. Serve immediately or allow to cool a bit and serve warm. Kapusta is especially delicious after resting overnight in the refrigerator.

MACRONUTRIENTS PER SERVING
CALORIES: 109 KCAL FAT: 6 G, 58 KCAL CARBOHYDRATE: 8 G (6 G NET), 31 KCAL PROTEIN: 6 G, 26 KCAL

MUSHROOM JULIENNE

MAKES 4 SERVINGS

Mushroom Julienne is simple to make, yet the end results tastes surprising. This Russian dish generally includes thinly-sliced mushrooms and onions in béchamel sauce topped with a cap of bubbling, melted cheese. In order to keep our Mushroom Julienne grain-free, we substitute sour cream for the traditional béchamel in order to create thickness without the use of a flour-based roux.

INGREDIENTS

- 3 tablespoons unsalted butter or ghee
- 1 medium onion, diced
- 1 clove garlic, minced
- 1 pound white mushrooms, thinly sliced
- ¼ cup dry white wine, or substitute chicken bone broth or stock
- ½ tablespoon gelatin (optional, but recommended)
- 1 cup sour cream or crème fraîche
- Fine sea salt, to taste
- Freshly ground black pepper, to taste
- 1 cup shredded melting cheese such as Gruyère, mozzarella, or Fontina

1. Preheat the broiler to low and set the oven rack 8 to 10 inches below the heating element. Heat the butter in a large skillet over medium-high heat. Add the onions and garlic. Sauté stirring frequently until just softened, about 3 minutes. Add the mushrooms to the onions and sauté until the mushrooms have reduced in size by about half, about 5 minutes.

2. Pour in the white wine and stir well. Cook for 2 to 3 minutes until the liquid is reduced by two thirds, then remove from heat. Stir the sour cream into the mushroom mixture until the sauce is well blended and the mushrooms are coated. Sprinkle the gelatin over top of the sauce and whisk gently until fully dissolved. Taste the sauce and season with salt and pepper to your preference. If desired, you may further thicken the sauce by allowing it to simmer for 5 minutes or longer.

3. Pour the mushrooms and sauce into a baking dish or divide between four 6-ounce ramekins. Spread the cheese over top the mushrooms and broil for 5 to 10 minutes until a uniformly golden crust develops. Serve immediately.

MACRONUTRIENTS PER SERVING
CALORIES: 353 KCAL FAT: 29 G, 260 KCAL CARBOHYDRATE: 10 G (8 G NET), 38 KCAL PROTEIN: 14 G, 57 KCAL

PALAČINKE

These Serbo-Croatian crepes are usually made with a simple batter of flour, eggs, milk, and water. They can be made sweet or savory and filled with just about anything you can imagine (check out the next page for a couple delicious ideas). The secret to success when making these is to keep your pan on low to medium-low heat. Too hot and they dry out and tear.

INGREDIENTS

4 large eggs

4 ounces full-fat cream cheese, room temperature

4 teaspoons psyllium husk

¼ cup heavy whipping cream, or substitute full-fat coconut milk

½ to 1 teaspoon monk fruit sweetener or keto-friendly sweetener of choice, to taste (optional)

2 tablespoons unsalted butter or coconut oil

Filtered water as needed

1. Place the eggs, cream cheese, psyllium husk, cream (and sweetener if using) in a blender, and blend until smooth.

2. Heat a skillet or crepe pan over medium-low heat. Add a small pat of butter (about ¾ teaspoon) and swirl to coat the bottom of the pan as it melts. When it starts to foam, turn the heat down a bit. Add a scant ¼ cup batter using a swirling motion to pour it into a wide circle. Swirl the pan to help the crepe batter spread a bit. Cook for 2½ to 3 minutes on the first side. Loosen the crepe with a spatula and carefully flip. Cook 20 to 30 seconds on the second side, then slide the crepe onto a plate.

3. If the batter appears too thick after testing this first crepe, blend in water half a tablespoon at a time until it is the desired consistency. Repeat the above step for the remaining batter, adding more butter to the pan between each crepe.

4. One at a time, fill the crepes with your filling of choice (two ideas provided below) and roll them up with the filling inside. Optionally place them seam side down in the skillet, cover, and cook over low heat for about 2 minutes to warm the filling. Serve warm or at room temperature.

MACRONUTRIENTS PER SERVING (2 CREPES)
CALORIES: 288 KCAL FAT: 26 G, 236 KCAL CARBOHYDRATE: 5 G (3 G NET), 21 KCAL PROTEIN: 9 G, 34 KCAL

EASY PALAČINKE FILLING IDEAS

Spinach and cheese

Squeeze as much water as possible out of ¾ cup thawed frozen spinach. Stir in ¾ cup kajmak (page 185) and a pinch of nutmeg. Taste and adjust salt as needed. Spread about 3 tablespoons of the mixture on each crepe and roll up.

MACRONUTRIENTS PER SERVING (2 CREPES)
CALORIES: 415 KCAL FAT: 38 G, 341 KCAL CARBOHYDRATE: 8 G (5 G NET), 32 KCAL PROTEIN: 12 G, 48 KCAL

. . . .

Strawberry cheesecake

Mix ¾ cup softened cream cheese or kajmak (page 185), 8 diced strawberries, and 5 drops liquid stevia (or to taste). Spread about 2 tablespoons of the mixture on each crepe and roll up.

MACRONUTRIENTS PER SERVING (2 CREPES)
CALORIES: 414 KCAL FAT: 38 G, 341 KCAL CARBOHYDRATE: 9 G (6 G NET), 34 KCAL PROTEIN: 11 G, 45 KCAL

POLISH DILL PICKLES

MAKES 8 TO 10 PICKLES

This recipe for lacto-fermented cucumbers is prepared in a style that is traditional to both Poland and Germany and is similar to New York style "full sour" pickles. In Poland, these pickles are known as ogórek kwaszony. In Germany, they are called salzgurken. Choose the freshest pickling cucumbers (which are smaller and have less seeds than slicing cucumbers) available for the best results.

INGREDIENTS

1 quart non-chlorinated water (see Note)

2 tablespoons canning or fine sea salt

2 or 4 fresh bay leaves

2 large sprig of dill

4 cloves garlic, peeled and halved

2 thin strips of fresh horseradish, about 1 inch in length

4 teaspoons whole yellow mustard seeds

2 grape or oak leaf

8 to 10 very fresh and blemish-free pickling cucumbers, about 4 to 6-inches long each

Equipment

2 quart-size jars

2 glass fermentation weights (optional but recommended)

1. Before beginning, wash and sterilize all equipment that will come in contact with your pickles such as the mixing bowl, fermentation vessel, and utensils.

2. Pour the water into a clean mixing bowl and add the salt. Stir until dissolved and set aside.

3. Divide the spices between the two jars by placing 1 or 2 bay leaves, 1 sprig of dill, 2 cloves of garlic, 1 strip of horseradish, and 2 teaspoons of mustard seeds into the bottom of each. Place the grape or oak leaves on top of the spices to hold them at the bottom of the jar.

4. Slice the flower end (opposite the stem) off each cucumber. Pack the cucumbers into the jar as tightly as possible, pushing them to the bottom of the jar. There should be at least half an inch of headspace from the top of the cucumbers to the mouth of the jar.

5. Pour the salt water into the jar, leaving about quarter inch of headspace at the top. Be sure that the pickles are completely submerged. If desired, you may place a fermentation weight atop the pickles to prevent them from floating. Cover the jar loosely with a sterilized lid (do not tighten) or lay an overturned plate over top. Leave to ferment in a temperature-stable room away from any fresh fruit, vegetables, or trash receptacles. As the pickles ferment, the brine will turn cloudy and bubble will appear. The gas bubbles caused by active fermentation may push the brine over the top of the jar and down the sides, so you may wish to place the jar inside of a shallow dish. >>

6. The pickles will be ready to eat after 1 to 3 weeks, depending on your taste preference and the ambient temperature of the room in which your fermentation takes place. Properly fermented pickles should taste sour. Once you are satisfied with their taste and texture, seal the jar with an airtight lid and store in the refrigerator.

NOTES: *Municipal tap water is often treated with chlorine in order to prevent bacterial growth from occurring inside of water mains and tanks. Unfortunately, this chlorine may make it difficult for your lacto bacteria to survive long enough to properly ferment your cucumbers. Therefore, it's strongly recommended that you use unchlorinated water for this recipe.*

It is impossible to get accurate nutritional information for home-fermented vegetables. These values are provided as an estimate. Read the "Fermenting" section on page xiv before fermenting for the first time.

MACRONUTRIENTS PER SERVING (1 PICKLE)
CALORIES: 5 KCAL FAT: 0 G, 0 KCAL CARBOHYDRATE: 1 G (<1 G NET), 5 KCAL PROTEIN: 0 G, 0 KCAL

RUSSIAN MUSHROOM SOUP

MAKES 6 SERVINGS

Usually Russian mushroom soup has a potato base, but this recipe swaps in daikon radishes instead. You could also use an equivalent amount of cauliflower or turnips if you can't find daikon in the store. The mushrooms are the star here anyway. This hearty soup can be a meal by itself.

INGREDIENTS

2½ tablespoons unsalted butter or bacon fat

1 pound cremini mushrooms, sliced

2 leeks, white and light green parts sliced

2 medium daikon radishes, peeled and cubed about ¾-inch square

1 medium carrot, peeled and sliced

6 cups chicken bone broth or stock

2 teaspoons dried dill weed

2 teaspoons fine sea salt

¼ teaspoon black pepper

1 dried bay leaf

¼ cup heavy whipping cream

¼ cup sour cream, plus 3 tablespoons more for serving

Additional salt and pepper, to taste

1. Melt 2 tablespoons of butter in a large pot over medium heat. Add the mushrooms and sauté for 5 minutes until soft. Use a slotted spoon to remove the mushrooms to a bowl. Set aside.

2. Melt the remaining ½ tablespoon of butter in the same pot. Add the leeks, radishes, and carrot and sauté for 5 minutes until soft.

3. Pour the broth over the vegetables and use a wooden spoon to scrape any browned bits off the bottom of the pot. Stir in the dill, salt, pepper, and bay leaf. Turn the heat to high and bring the broth to a boil. Reduce the heat to a simmer.

4. Cover and simmer the soup for 15 minutes. Check the daikon; it should be soft. If not, cover and simmer for 5 minutes more.

5. Remove and discard the bay leaf. Carefully ladle about 2 cups of soup into a blender and blend until smooth, then stir this liquid back into the soup. Alternately, you can use an immersion blender to blend the soup right in the pot, but leave some texture to the soup.

6. Stir the cream and ¼ cup sour cream into the soup. Stir in the mushrooms along with any reserved juices. Turn the heat back to medium and heat until hot. Taste and adjust the salt and pepper. Serve hot topped with a dollop of sour cream.

MACRONUTRIENTS PER SERVING
CALORIES: 222 KCAL FAT: 15 G, 135 KCAL CARBOHYDRATE: 14 G (11 G NET), 58 KCAL PROTEIN: 10 G, 39 KCAL

SALATA OD HOBOTNICE (OCTOPUS SALAD)

MAKES 6 SERVINGS

Any region that touches the sea has its own version of octopus salad. This Croatian version is made with octopus and potatoes dressed in red wine vinaigrette with herbs. Here, braised radishes stand in for the potatoes. Once you know how to prepare the octopus, you can add almost any combination of herbs and vegetables to make different regional variations.

INGREDIENTS

1½ pounds steamed octopus legs (see Note)

1 small red onion, finely chopped

⅓ cup extra-virgin olive oil

3 tablespoons red wine vinegar

2 bunches radishes

3 tablespoons salted butter or ghee

Salt to taste, if needed

¼ cup fresh flat-leaf parsley, finely chopped

1 lemon, cut into wedges

1. Optionally, peel the purple skin off the octopus and discard (the skin is totally edible, but some people prefer octopus without it). Dice the legs into pieces about ½-inch square. Place in a medium bowl and mix with the onion.

2. Combine the olive oil and vinegar in a small jar with a tight-fitting lid. Shake very well to combine, then pour over the octopus and onion. Stir well to coat. Place in the refrigerator.

3. Dice the radishes into pieces approximately the same size as the octopus. Melt the butter in a skillet over medium heat. Add the radish and sauté for 5 minutes stirring occasionally until just browned. Turn the heat down to medium-low, place a lid on the pan, and cook for 5 minutes more, stirring once after about 2 minutes. If the radishes are browning too much, turn the heat down. Test a radish—it should be tender. If not, sauté a few minutes more until softer.

4. Remove the pan from the heat and allow the radishes to cool. Once cool, stir the radishes into the octopus and onion mixture. You can serve the salata at this point, but it is even better if allowed to marinate in the refrigerator for at least an hour or, even better, overnight.

5. Before serving, stir well. Taste and add salt if necessary. Stir in the parsley and serve with lemon wedges on the side.

NOTE: *If you can't find steamed octopus legs in the store, you can prepare a whole octopus at home. You will need one small octopus (about 2 pounds; ask your butcher or fishmonger to clean it for you). Bring a large pot of water to a boil and add the octopus, 2 bay leaves, and a teaspoon of peppercorns. Simmer the octopus for about an hour, until you can easily separate the legs from the head. Discard the head and run the legs under cold water to chill, then proceed with the recipe. You may wish to weigh the legs with a food scale and adjust the recipe accordingly.*

MACRONUTRIENTS PER SERVING
CALORIES: 352 KCAL FAT: 20 G, 180 KCAL CARBOHYDRATE: 7 G (7 G NET), 28 KCAL PROTEIN: 34 G, 137 KCAL

TARATOR

MAKES 4 SERVINGS

For how simple it is, there is a lot to love about this cold cucumber soup native to Bulgaria. The raw garlic imparts a surprising pungency, while the cucumber and walnuts give the soup interesting textural elements. It is wonderful served on a hot summer afternoon.

INGREDIENTS

2 cups full-fat plain Greek yogurt, or substitute coconut or almond milk yogurt

Juice of 1 lemon

2 tablespoons extra-virgin olive oil or walnut oil, or a mix

3 cloves garlic, pressed or ground into a paste

2 tablespoons fresh dill weed, minced, plus more for garnish

½ teaspoon fine sea salt, or to taste

¼ teaspoon ground black pepper

Filtered water as needed

1 pound cucumbers, lightly peeled, cut into small dice

½ cup + 2 tablespoons chopped raw walnuts

1. In a medium bowl, combine the yogurt, lemon juice, oil, garlic, dill, salt, and pepper. Optionally add water 1 tablespoon at a time until the mixture reaches the desired consistency.

2. Stir in the cucumbers and ½ cup walnuts. Place the soup in the refrigerator to chill for at least 30 minutes.

3. Remove the soup from the fridge and stir. Taste and adjust the salt and pepper as needed. Divide between 4 serving bowls. Garnish with the remaining 2 tablespoons of walnuts and additional dill if desired. Serve cold.

MACRONUTRIENTS PER SERVING
CALORIES: 342 KCAL FAT: 31 G, 276 KCAL CARBOHYDRATE: 12 G (9 G NET), 48 KCAL PROTEIN: 8 G, 32 KCAL

ZRAZY

MAKES 6 SERVINGS

Zrazy is a popular Polish beef roulade that can be made with a number of different stuffings. Here, we use a mixture of onions, pickles (page 193), and bacon. Also experiment with fillings that include wild mushrooms, sauerkraut, hard-boiled egg, or other ingredients once you have the preparation method mastered.

INGREDIENTS

1 medium onion, halved and thinly sliced

6 thinly-sliced beef steaks (round, rump, or top sirloin), about 4-ounces each, pounded into rectangles ¼-inch thick

Fine sea salt

Ground black pepper

1 large or 2 small pickles (page 193), sliced lengthwise into 4 or 8 wedges

3 slices thick-cut bacon, halved crosswise then halved lengthwise

2 tablespoons avocado oil

1 tablespoon unsalted butter or ghee

½ cup beef bone broth or stock, plus more as needed

⅓ cup sour cream or full-fat coconut yogurt

Fresh dill weed or other herbs, chopped, for garnish

1. Set aside about ¾ of the onion to use in step 4. Lay a slice of steak on a flat surface. Sprinkle lightly with salt and pepper, then scatter a few slices of the remaining onion on top of the meat. Lay a pickle slice and piece of bacon parallel to one of the short ends of the steak, then tightly roll the steak around the pickle and bacon jelly-roll style. Secure the ends with a toothpick or tie with butcher's twine. Repeat this process with the remaining steaks.

2. Heat a deep skillet with a lid over high heat and add the avocado oil. When the oil just begins to shimmer, add the steak rolls and brown the exteriors, rotating the rolls every 30 seconds or longer until they are evenly browned on all sides. Once browned, remove the rolls to a dish and set aside.

3. Reduce the heat to medium-high and add the butter to the pan. Once the butter stops foaming (ghee will not foam), add the reserved onion slices and sauté, stirring frequently, until soft and browned, about 5 to 7 minutes. Remove the onions to a bowl.

4. Deglaze the pan by pouring in the bone broth and scraping up any browned bits off the bottom. Allow the bone broth to come to a boil, then reduce the heat to a simmer. Place the steak rolls inside the pan seam-side down and scatter the onions around and on top of the rolls. Spoon some of the broth on top of the steak and cover with the lid. Reduce the heat to a low simmer and simmer gently for 45 minutes to 1 hour until the rolls are tender, adding more broth to the pan as needed to prevent the pan from cooking dry.

5. To serve, use tongs to transfer the rolls to a serving platter. Remove and discard the toothpicks or string. Remove the skillet from the heat and gently whisk the sour cream or coconut yogurt into the pan juices. Spoon the sauce over top of the rolls and garnish with chopped dill.

MACRONUTRIENTS PER SERVING
CALORIES: 364 KCAL FAT: 27 G, 246 KCAL CARBOHYDRATE: 3 G (2 G NET), 12 KCAL PROTEIN: 26 G, 103 KCAL

ED STATES

CANADA

UNITED STATES

North A

MEXICO

THE BAHAMAS

CUBA

BELIZE

HONDURAS

JAMAICA

PUERTO RICO
(U.S.)

GUATEMALA

NICARAGUA

EL SALVADOR

COSTA
RICA

PANAMA

VENEZUELA

GUYANA

SURINAME

COLOMBIA

ECUADOR

PERU

BRAZ

Pacific Ocean

BOLIVIA

PARAGUAY

N

NW

NE

CHILE

WESTERN EUROPE

ASPARAGUS AND CELERY ROOT VICHYSSOISE

MAKES 4 SERVINGS

Vichyssoise is a simple soup made from potato, leek, cream, and chicken stock, blended and eaten cold. This particular recipe is based on a delightful variation from the Bon Appétit Test Kitchen with our own keto-friendly adjustments.

INGREDIENTS

2 tablespoons unsalted butter or ghee

1 leek, white and light green parts thinly sliced

1 celery root, peeled and cubed

2½ cups chicken stock or vegetable broth

10 ounces asparagus, trimmed and cut into 1-inch pieces (about 3 cups)

½ cup heavy whipping cream, or substitute full-fat coconut milk

5 large fresh mint leaves, finely chopped

¼ teaspoon fine sea salt

1. In a medium pot, heat the butter over medium heat. Add the leeks and celery root and sauté for 2 minutes.

2. Pour in the chicken stock, stir and cover. Reduce the heat to medium-low and simmer covered for 10 minutes.

3. Add the asparagus and simmer uncovered for 5 minutes. Remove from heat.

4. Pull out 8 asparagus tips and run them under cold water to stop the cooking. Set aside. Use an immersion blender to carefully blend the soup until smooth. You can also use a stand blender for this, working in batches.

5. Transfer the soup to a glass bowl. Cover and place in the refrigerator for several hours to chill. If you are in a hurry, you can place it in 4 individual serving bowls and place them in the freezer for 15 minutes instead.

6. Stir ¼ cup cream into the chilled soup (or 1 tablespoon per bowl). Whisk together the remaining ¼ cup cream with the mint and the salt until slightly thickened.

7. If you haven't already done so, divide the soup between 4 serving bowls. Drizzle the soup with the minted cream and garnish each bowl with 2 asparagus tips. Serve cool.

MACRONUTRIENTS PER SERVING
CALORIES: 230 KCAL FAT: 19 G, 167 KCAL CARBOHYDRATE: 11 G (8 G NET), 44 KCAL PROTEIN: 7 G, 27 KCAL

COQ AU VIN

MAKES 6 SERVINGS

Coq au Vin is a classic French dish that is traditionally made with the meat from a rooster (the "coq") slow braised in wine (the "vin"). The braising process helps to break down the connective tissue in the rooster meat, which is tougher than chicken. The same slow braising process also helps to release the collagen and minerals from the chicken into the sauce. Coq au vin can be made in advance and refrigerated up to three days. Reheat in a 350°F oven; to crisp the skin, pass the chicken briefly under a hot broiler.

INGREDIENTS

10 ounces thick-cut bacon, cut into ½ inch pieces

5 bone-in skin-on chicken quarters (about 3 pounds worth)

Generous pinches fine sea salt and freshly ground black pepper

1 medium carrot, chopped thick

3 stalks celery, diced

1 medium onion, diced

1 small bunch radishes, halved

2 cloves garlic, smashed

2 cups dry red wine (preferably Burgundy, see Notes)

½ tablespoon tomato paste

1 fresh bay leaf

4 sprigs fresh rosemary

6 sprigs fresh thyme

2 cups chicken bone broth or stock

1 pound cremini or button mushrooms, cut into bite-sized pieces

2 tablespoons minced fresh parsley

1. Warm a large, deep skillet or pot with a lid over medium-high heat. When the skillet is hot, add the bacon and cook, stirring frequently, until the fat has rendered out and the bacon becomes crisp, about 5 to 6 minutes. Use a slotted spoon to remove the bacon from the skillet, leaving the rendered fat behind. Set aside.

2. Pat the chicken dry and season on all sides with salt and pepper. Place the chicken skin side down in a single layer in the skillet with the bacon fat, working in batches so as not to overcrowd the pan. Cook until the skin becomes well browned, about 6 minutes per side. Remove the chicken to a dish and set aside.

3. Pour off all but 2 tablespoons of fat, reserving the poured-off fat to use in step 5. Add the carrot, celery, onions, radishes, and garlic to the skillet. Reduce the heat to medium and cook, stirring frequently, for 5 minutes until the vegetables are just softened. Reduce the heat further if necessary in order to prevent the garlic from browning and becoming bitter.

4. Once the vegetables have cooked, pour in the wine and deglaze the skillet by scraping up any browned bits on the bottom of the pan. Stir in the tomato paste until dissolved. Increase the heat to medium-high and cook until the wine has reduced by half, about >>

5 minutes. Meanwhile, use a length of butcher's twine to create a bouquet garni by tying together the bay leaf, rosemary, and thyme (see Notes). When the wine has reduced, add the bouquet garni and broth to the skillet and bring to a simmer. Place the chicken pieces in the broth skin side up so that they are only partially submerged. Reduce the heat to medium-low and simmer for 45 minutes until cooked through (but see next step).

5. When the chicken has been cooking for about 30 minutes, heat 2 tablespoons of the reserved rendered fat in a large skillet or pot over medium-high heat. (If you do not have enough reserved fat to total 2 tablespoons, add avocado oil as needed.) Sauté the mushrooms in the oil, stirring frequently, until softened and browned, about 6 to 8 minutes.

6. Add the cooked mushrooms to the pan with the chicken and stir gently to combine. Simmer for 5 minutes to allow the flavors to meld. Check that the internal temperature of the chicken has reached 165°F and remove from heat.

7. Remove and discard the bouquet garni. Transfer the chicken to a serving dish and spoon the pan sauce over top. Garnish with fresh parsley. Serve hot.

NOTES: *If you choose not to cook with red wine, you can substitute 2 cups beef stock or additional chicken stock, plus 2 tablespoons red wine vinegar or apple cider vinegar.*

Using a bouquet garni makes the herbs easy to remove prior to serving. However, if you do not have butcher's twine on hand, you may also simply add the herbs to the pot loose and remove individually in step 6.

Coq au Vin can be made in advance and kept refrigerated for up to 3 days. In fact, letting the dish rest for at least 24 hours develops and improves the flavor and is the preferred method. This makes it a great option for dinner parties or holidays, when preparing food in advance is desirable. When ready to serve, reheat the coq au vin in a 350°F oven for 30 minutes.

MACRONUTRIENTS PER SERVING
CALORIES: 803 KCAL FAT: 50 G, 447 KCAL CARBOHYDRATE: 11 G (9 G NET), 43 KCAL PROTEIN: 61 G, 242 KCAL

210   KETO PASSPORT

SAUERKRAUT

MAKES ABOUT 1 PINT

If you've never tried your hand at fermenting vegetables before, sauerkraut is a great place to start! This simple recipe requires no special equipment, just a quart-sized glass jar or similar vessel to hold the sauerkraut while it ferments.

INGREDIENTS
1 large head cabbage (about
   2 ½ pounds)
1½ tablespoon canning or fine sea salt

Equipment

1 wide-mouth quart-size jar

Non-metal tamper (optional)

1 glass fermentation weight (see page xv)

1. Before beginning, clean and sanitize any equipment that will come into contact with your sauerkraut, such as the cutting board, slicer or knife, mixing bowl, fermentation jar, and utensils. Once your work area is cleaned, remove any damaged outer leaves from the cabbage head and discard. Rinse the cabbage well under fresh water, then peel off one or two large outer leaves, keeping them in one piece if possible. Set aside.

2. Cut the cabbage into quarters, then remove and discard the core. Shred the cabbage leaves using a sharp knife, mandolin slicer, the slicing edge of a box grater, or similar. Smaller pieces will result in a more soft-textured sauerkraut.

3. Place the shredded cabbage into a large nonreactive mixing bowl and sprinkle with 1 tablespoon of salt. Using your hands, knead, squeeze, and wring the shredded cabbage for 3 minutes or longer. During this process, the cabbage will release water from its leaves. This will cause salted brine to collect at the bottom of the bowl.

4. Taste both the cabbage and the brine. Both should have the same level of saltiness. If not, continue kneading. The cabbage should be pleasantly but not overpoweringly salty. If your cabbage is not salty enough, sprinkle in additional salt and knead until the desired taste is achieved. If your cabbage is over-salted, add a couple tablespoons of purified water and mix well to dilute.

5. Firmly pack the cabbage into the jar, tamping down the contents with your hands or a non-metal tamper so that there are no air bubbles. Continue to pack the jar until it is nearly filled, leaving an inch or so of headspace at the top. Reserve the brine at the bottom of the mixing bowl.

6. Once the jar is packed, tear several pieces of the reserved cabbage leaves so that they are larger than the mouth of the jar. Use these torn leaves to completely cover the shredded sauerkraut, tucking the edges under as best as possible. If using, place a fermentation >>

weight atop the leaves. Press down firmly to submerge the leaves beneath the level of the brine. Pour additional brine from the mixing bowl into the jar until it is nearly filled.

7. Place the lid over the mouth of the jar, securing it only halfway so that air may escape. Alternatively, you may cover the mouth of the jar with an overturned tea saucer or small plate. Place the jar in a shallow dish to catch any brine that bubbles out during fermentation. Leave the sauerkraut in a cool, temperature-stable place away from direct sunlight, fresh fruits, vegetables, plants, or trash receptacles.

8. Allow the sauerkraut to ferment for several days up to several weeks, until the desired level of sourness has been reached. If you live in a relatively warm climate, you may begin tasting your sauerkraut after about the third day. As the sauerkraut ferments, periodically check the top of the jar to ensure that the cabbage is still submerged beneath the brine (and not floating on top) and also that no mold has begun to grow. If your brine has begun to evaporate, you may add a tablespoon or more of purified water to keep the cabbage from drying out, which is to be avoided. If your cabbage begins to grow mold or takes on an offensive odor, you must discard it and start over with a new batch.

9. Once your sauerkraut is fermented to your liking, seal the with an airtight lid and store in the refrigerator. Refrigerated sauerkraut will keep for several months.

NOTE: *It is impossible to get accurate nutritional information for home-fermented vegetables. These values are provided as an estimate. Read the "Fermenting" section on page xiv before fermenting for the first time.*

MACRONUTRIENTS PER SERVING (½ CUP)
CALORIES: 10 KCAL FAT: 0 G, 0 KCAL CARBOHYDRATE: 2 G (0 G NET), 10 KCAL PROTEIN: 0 G, 0 KCAL

GRIBENES

Gribenes are fried-out poultry skins that are typically made as part of rendering Schmaltz (page 227). They are crispy, airy, and delicious served fresh from the stove as a snack or used as a crunchy topping for salads, soups, and other dishes. Think chicharrones but chicken.

INGREDIENTS

Fried-out chicken skin (from making Schmaltz, page 227)

½ medium yellow onion, sliced ¼-inch thick

¼ teaspoon fine sea salt

Pinch freshly ground black pepper

Pinch smoked paprika

1. Heat a large skillet over medium heat. If you have the skillet used for making schmaltz, use that; there is no need to clean or wipe it. Add the chicken skin and onions to the skillet and season with sea salt and pepper. Sauté for 20 minutes, using a splatter screen over the skillet if possible and stirring frequently, until the chicken pieces and onions become crisp and turn a rich golden brown. Be sure to watch the pan closely as it cooks; the chicken skin (gribenes) will darken rapidly.

2. Once the gribenes are crisp to your liking, remove them from the pan with a slotted spoon and drain on a paper towel. Sprinkle with smoked paprika and serve immediately, or place in an airtight container and store in the refrigerator. If desired, reheat by quickly frying in a pan with a small amount of oil to return to original crispiness.

NOTE: *The macronutrient values for this recipe are our best guesstimates. It is impossible to predict exactly how much fried-out skin each batch of schmaltz will yield, and nutritional information for fried-out skin is imprecise at best. The exact values for your batch might differ in terms of fat and protein (the carbohydrate will remain the same).*

MACRONUTRIENTS PER SERVING
CALORIES: 217 KCAL FAT: 16 G, 144 KCAL CARBOHYDRATE: 1 G (1 G NET), 3 KCAL PROTEIN: 19 G, 75 KCAL

MOULES MARINIÈRE

MAKES 4 SERVINGS

Mussels are incredibly nutrient dense—an excellent source of vitamin B12, as well as selenium and manganese. Plus, they cook in just 3 minutes! Moules marinière is a classic French preparation. Most recipes call for heavy cream, but we got the decadent idea to use crème fraîche from J. Kenji López-alt of Serious Eats. Either way is fantastic.

INGREDIENTS

4 pounds mussels (see Notes)

2 tablespoons unsalted butter or ghee

1 tablespoon avocado oil

1 shallot, diced

1 leek, white and green parts thinly sliced, or 1 additional shallot, diced

2 cloves garlic, chopped

3 sprigs fresh thyme

1 dried bay leaf

1 cup chicken bone broth or stock (see Notes)

1½ tablespoons lemon juice, plus more to taste

¼ cup crème fraîche, or use heavy whipping cream or full-fat coconut milk (optional)

3 tablespoons parsley leaves, chopped

¼ teaspoon fine sea salt

¼ teaspoon ground black pepper

1. Prepare the mussels: Wash the mussels under cold running water and use a stiff brush to clean any sand or barnacles off the shell. Pull off any beards (the "tuft" that sticks out of the shell, which the mussel uses to tether itself to hard surfaces). Discard any mussels with broken shells or that do not close when you tap them gently on the counter. Rinse them once more under cold water, then set aside.

2. Heat the butter and avocado oil in a large, deep wok or pot over medium heat. When the butter stops foaming, add the shallot, leek, garlic, thyme, and bay leaf. Turn down the heat a bit and sauté stirring frequently for 5 to 7 minutes, until the leeks are soft.

3. Pour in the broth and lemon juice and increase the heat to high. Let the broth come to a boil. Add the mussels. Place a lid on the pan and cook for 3 minutes, shaking the pan a couple times to "stir" the mussels. Begin checking the mussels at 3 minutes—you want to stop cooking them as soon as all the mussels have opened. If they are still closed, replace the lid and continue cooking, checking every minute to see if they are ready.

4. When the mussels have opened, use tongs or a slotted spoon to transfer them to a serving bowl. Discard any mussels that did not open.

5. Remove and discard the thyme sprigs and the bay leaf. Whisk the crème fraîche, parsley, salt, and pepper into the broth. When the crème fraîche are completely incorporated, taste and adjust the lemon juice and salt as needed. Pour the sauce over the mussels. Serve immediately.

NOTES: *Four pounds looks like a lot of mussels, but the usual recommendation is 1 pound per diner because the actual meat yield is so small per mussel. Live mussels need to breathe, so transport them home from the store in an open plastic bag, then place them in colander with ice in the fridge. Set the colander inside a larger bowl and pour off the melting water so the mussels are not submerged.*

This recipe generally calls for dry white wine. If you wish, you can use wine in place of the chicken stock and omit the lemon juice.

MACRONUTRIENTS PER SERVING
CALORIES: 416 KCAL FAT: 22 G, 197 KCAL CARBOHYDRATE: 16 G (15 G NET), 63 KCAL PROTEIN: 38 G, 151 KCAL

PORK WITH CAMEMBERT

MAKES 4 TO 6 SERVINGS

Camembert is a quintessential example of French cheesemaking. It was first produced in the 1800s in the village of Camembert, France. If you are outside the United States look for AOC-protected "Camembert de Normandy," which is handmade made of raw milk from heritage cattle in the Normandy region of France (the American FDA prohibits the importation of young raw milk cheeses, see Notes). This is Camembert in its "true" form, with its full depth of buttery, mushroomy flavor.

INGREDIENTS

1 pork tenderloin, about 2 pounds in weight

¼ tablespoon coarse sea salt, plus more to taste

¼ teaspoon freshly ground black pepper

2 tablespoons avocado oil

¼ cup dry white wine or chicken bone broth

1 teaspoon Dijon mustard

Leaves from 4 sprigs of thyme

3 tablespoons crème fraîche

4 ounces Camembert cheese, rind removed, cubed (see Notes)

1. Preheat the oven to 425°F.

2. Pat the pork tenderloin dry and season all over with salt and pepper. Heat the oil in a skillet over medium-high heat. When the oil begins to shimmer, add the pork tenderloin and cook for 1 to 1½ minutes per side until browned all over. Remove from heat.

3. Place the pork tenderloin in a baking dish and set aside the skillet to use to make the Camembert sauce in step 4. Bake the pork in the oven for 20 to 25 minutes until an instant-read thermometer inserted into the center of the thickest portion of the roast reads 145°F. (After about 15 minutes, move on to the next step.)

4. About 5 minutes before the tenderloin finishes cooking, prepare the Camembert sauce: Briefly heat the skillet over medium heat and pour the wine into the pan to deglaze, scraping up any browned bits off the bottom. Allow the wine to come a boil, then whisk in the Dijon and thyme leaves until well mixed. Lower the heat to medium-low and gently stir in the crème fraîche until it is well mixed. Add the Camembert cubes into the mixture, 1 or 2 at a time, until they have melted into the sauce, stirring gently as they melt. Remove from heat.

5. Remove the tenderloin from the oven and let it rest for at least 5 minutes. Slice the pork into thick medallions and pour any pan juices from the tenderloin into the Camembert sauce. Stir the pan juices into the sauce until blended and smooth. Arrange the pork on a serving platter and pour the Camembert sauce over top. Serve immediately.

NOTES: *In the USA, look for a pasteurized-milk Camembert from France, or seek out any of the local, organic, single-source Camembert-style producers that have been popping up domestically.*

The rind of Camembert is edible; in fact, it is meant to be eaten. If you wish, you may consume the rind that is not used in this recipe.

MACRONUTRIENTS PER SERVING (¼ RECIPE)
CALORIES: 315 KCAL FAT: 16 G, 145 KCAL CARBOHYDRATE: 1 G (1 G NET), 5 KCAL PROTEIN: 37 G, 147 KCAL

RABBIT STEW

At the risk of dredging up a tired cliché, rabbit really does taste a lot like (dark meat) chicken. If you can, get your butcher to section the rabbit for you. Take care not to overcook the meat, as it can get tough.

INGREDIENTS

1 pound thick-cut bacon or bacon ends

Pinch kosher salt

Generous pinch pepper

1 young rabbit (about 2½ pounds), sectioned into 8 pieces, or use 8 legs of rabbit

1 leek, white and light green parts sliced

2 shallots, chopped

4 cloves garlic, chopped

1½ cups chicken bone broth or stock

2 tablespoons apple cider vinegar

6 sprigs fresh thyme

3 sprigs fresh rosemary

2 dried bay leaves

1. Preheat the oven to 350°F.

2. Heat a large oven-proof skillet (cast-iron works well) over medium heat. Cook the bacon until just crisp. Use tongs to remove it to a plate, reserving the fat in the pan.

3. Season the rabbit with a pinch of salt (not too much, the bacon is salty) and pepper. Brown the rabbit about 3 minutes per side until lightly browned, working in batches if necessary. Remove the rabbit to the plate.

4. Pour off all but about 2 tablespoons of fat (reserve for a future use). Add the leek and shallots. Sauté 4 to 5 minutes until soft. Add the bacon and sauté another 30 seconds until fragrant.

5. Pour in the chicken stock and use a wooden spoon to scrape any browned bits off the bottom of the pot. Stir in the vinegar and the cooked bacon. Place the rabbit in the pot in a single layer if possible. Nestle the thyme, rosemary, and bay leaves around the rabbit.

6. Transfer the pan to the oven and cook 30 minutes. Check the rabbit in the thickest part of the meat to ensure the internal temperature is 160°F.

7. To serve, transfer the rabbit to a serving platter. Remove and discard the thyme and rosemary stems and the bay leaf. Optionally, place the skillet back on the stove and simmer the cooking liquid for a few minutes to thicken it. Spoon the liquid, along with the bacon and vegetables, over the rabbit. Serve hot.

MACRONUTRIENTS PER SERVING
CALORIES: 615 KCAL FAT: 42 G, 378 KCAL CARBOHYDRATE: 6 G (5 G NET), 25 KCAL PROTEIN: 50 G, 200 KCAL

ROTKOHLSALAT MIT SPEK (RED CABBAGE WITH BACON)

Rotkohlsalat (red cabbage salad) exists in a dizzying number of varieties in German cookery. This version uses savory bacon ("spek") for smokiness and is served with a red wine vinaigrette for a hint of sweetness. It's delicious as a side for virtually any meal—especially those that include pork—but we recommend you try it as a topping on hamburgers or meatballs.

INGREDIENTS

2 tablespoons fine sea salt

4 cups boiling water

1 pound red cabbage (about ½ of a medium-sized head), shredded

¼ cup olive oil

2 tablespoons red wine vinegar

½ tablespoon apple cider vinegar

½ teaspoon Dijon mustard

2 to 5 drops liquid stevia, or equivalent keto-friendly sweetener of choice

Pinch ground black pepper

Pinch caraway seeds (optional)

2 small shallots, diced small, or use ¼ cup diced yellow onion

4 thick slices smoky bacon

1. Dissolve the sea salt in the boiling water. Place the cabbage in a large colander over the sink and pour the salted water over the cabbage. Allow it to cool until safe to handle.

2. While the cabbage cools, make the vinaigrette. In a medium bowl, whisk together the avocado oil, vinegar, Dijon mustard, stevia, black pepper, and caraway seeds (if using) until a smooth emulsion forms.

3. Once the cabbage is cool enough to handle, knead and squeeze any excess water from the leaves. In a large bowl toss together the cabbage, vinaigrette, and shallots. Allow to marinate for 30 minutes to an hour. While it rests, cook and dice the bacon.

4. Before serving, stir the cabbage mixture and top with diced bacon. Serve warm or chilled.

MACRONUTRIENTS PER SERVING
CALORIES: 146 KCAL FAT: 12 G, 108 KCAL CARBOHYDRATE: 7 G (5 G NET), 27 KCAL PROTEIN: 4 G; 16 KCAL

SAUCE GRIBICHE

MAKES ABOUT 1 CUP

Sauce gribiche is a classic French recipe that always includes eggs, cornichons (tiny pickled gherkins), capers, and herbs. However, there are lots of variations on this theme that are all considered gribiche; refer to the recipe note for ideas on mixing it up. Serve gribiche on beef tongue (page 168), steak, or grilled or roasted vegetables. For a unique twist, check out Smoked Salmon and Gribiche Benedict (page 273).

INGREDIENTS

¼ cup plus 2 tablespoons olive oil

1 tablespoon Dijon mustard

2 teaspoons white wine vinegar

6 cornichons, chopped

2 tablespoons chopped fresh tarragon, plus more to taste

1 tablespoon capers, drained

⅛ teaspoon ground black pepper

⅛ teaspoon ground cayenne pepper (optional)

3 hard-boiled large eggs, peeled and finely chopped

Sea salt to taste

1. In a medium bowl, whisk together the olive oil, mustard, and vinegar until well combined. Stir in the cornichons, tarragon, capers, pepper, and cayenne.

2. Fold in the hard-boiled eggs, optionally smashing them with a fork depending on desired consistency. Taste and add salt and additional black pepper as needed. Store in an airtight container in the refrigerator.

NOTE: *There are many ways to vary this recipe. Try using red wine vinegar or sherry vinegar instead of white. Increase or decrease the Dijon. Add chopped fresh parsley or chervil. Substitute avocado oil mayonnaise in place of some of the olive oil. Chop the eggs into bigger pieces, or go the other way and blend the sauce with an immersion blender.*

MACRONUTRIENTS PER ¼ OF RECIPE
CALORIES: 244 KCAL FAT: 25 G, 221 KCAL CARBOHYDRATE: 1 G (1 G NET), 3 KCAL PROTEIN: 5 G, 20 KCAL

SCHMALTZ

MAKES ABOUT 1 CUP RENDERED FAT

Schmaltz is a staple cooking fat in European Jewish cooking. Made from rendered poultry skin, it is pleasantly mild and has an irresistibly savory fried chicken flavor. Making schmaltz is an excellent way to use chicken skin that otherwise might go to waste. Simply collect pieces of raw chicken skin in the freezer until you are ready to render a batch.

INGREDIENTS
1 pound chicken skin (see Note)

1. Optionally, rinse the chicken skin under fresh water and pat dry.

2. Cut the skin in into small pieces 1-inch square or so. If you intend to make Poutine (page 245) with the chicken skins from this recipe and prefer "french fry"-shaped strips, cut the skins into ½-inch by 2-inch pieces. Kitchen shears work well for this. It is easiest to cut the chicken skin when it is partially frozen.

3. Heat a large skillet over medium-low heat. Lay the chicken skin in a single layer at the bottom of the skillet and cover with a lid. Cook for 15 minutes until rendered fat begins to collect.

4. Uncover and increase the heat to medium. If you have a large enough splatter screen, set it over top of the skillet at this time. Continue to cook for another 15 minutes until the chicken skins begin to turn golden at the edges. Stir frequently and use a spatula to break apart any pieces that have begun to stick together.

5. Carefully remove the skillet from heat. Use a wire frying skimmer or similar to remove the skins from the fat. If desired, reserve the skins to use in another recipe such as Gribenes (page 215) or Poutine (page 245). Allow the fat left in the skillet to cool for a few minutes. Set a fine mesh strainer lined with a piece of cheesecloth over a heatproof bowl, then strain the rendered fat through to separate any solids. Allow the fat to cool thoroughly before transferring the schmaltz to an airtight container. Schmaltz can be kept refrigerated for about a week or in the freezer for several months.

NOTE: *We recommend using pastured chicken (or organic) to make this recipe. Whenever you are rendering fat or eating fatty cuts of meat (for example, well-marbled beef), it is advisable to select the best quality meat possible for your budget to avoid chemicals and contaminants that can be stored in the animal's fat.*

MACRONUTRIENTS PER SERVING (1 TABLESPOON)
CALORIES: 115 KCAL   FAT: 13 G, 115 KCAL   CARBOHYDRATE: 0 G, 0 KCAL   PROTEIN: 0 G, 0 KCAL

SCHWEINEHAXE

MAKES 2 GENEROUS SERVINGS OR 4 SMALLER SERVINGS

Schweinshaxe ("pork shank") is a traditional dish from Bavaria. Although this recipe takes a while to prepare, it requires relatively little hands-on time and produces hearty, fall-apart-tender roasted meat encased in crispy, melty pork crackling. It's perfect for late autumn celebrations and is an Oktoberfest favorite. We recommend serving this with a side of Sauerkraut (page 211) or Rotkohlsalat (page 223).

INGREDIENTS

2 pounds fresh pork hocks (2 to 4 hocks depending on size, see Note)

Filtered water

1 medium yellow onion, roughly chopped (leave the roots and skin if organic)

4 bay leaves

4 cloves garlic, halved

2 teaspoons caraway seeds

½ tablespoon black peppercorns

½ tablespoon fine sea salt

1 to 2 tablespoons coarse sea salt

1. Place the pork hocks in a large pot. Fill with enough water to completely cover the hocks, then add the onion, bay leaves, garlic, caraway seeds, peppercorns, and fine sea salt. Turn the heat to high and bring to a boil. Once boiling, reduce the heat to a very gentle simmer and cook uncovered for 90 minutes. Drain and discard the water. Set the hocks aside to cool.

2. Preheat the oven to 375°F. Once the hocks are cool enough to safely handle, use a very sharp knife to score through the skin, creating a diamond pattern. Sprinkle the coarse sea salt over the hocks and rub the granules into the cuts. Place the hocks on a rack inside of a roasting pan and bake for 90 minutes, rotating the pan once after 45 minutes. Larger hocks may need additional cooking time to become fully tender.

3. When the meat on the hocks is fork-tender, turn the broiler to high heat and broil for 5 to 10 minutes in order to crisp the skin. Keep a close watch on the meat to prevent scorching.

4. To plate, set the hocks so that the thicker portion is at the bottom. Serve immediately.

NOTE: *For this recipe, you will need fresh (not smoked) pork hocks, which are also known as pork knuckles and sometimes pork shanks. These may be a special-order item in some regions, so be sure to ask your butcher. Pork hocks will have about half or slightly more of their weight in bone. Macronutrients were calculated using a yield of 16 ounces of edible meat and skin.*

MACRONUTRIENTS PER SERVING (½ OF RECIPE)
CALORIES: 609 KCAL FAT: 35 G, 313 KCAL CARBOHYDRATE: 8 G (6 G NET), 32 KCAL PROTEIN: 63 G, 251 KCAL

SHRIMP PROVENÇAL

MAKES 4 SERVINGS

Pair this simple yet flavorful shrimp dish with a serving of Ratatouille (page 235) for a lovely French meal.

INGREDIENTS

¼ cup avocado oil

1½ pounds peeled and deveined extra large shrimp, fresh or defrosted

Fine sea salt

Freshly ground black pepper

1 tablespoon capers, drained, left whole if small or diced if large

2 cloves garlic, smashed and minced

8 to 10 pitted olives, either kalamata, green, or a mixture of both, diced small

¼ cup fresh lemon juice

2 tablespoons minced flat-leaf parsley

1. Heat 2 tablespoons of the oil in a large skillet with a lid over high heat. Pat any excess moisture off of the shrimp and season well with salt and pepper. Once the oil begins to shimmer, lay the shrimp into the skillet and sauté very briefly for 1 minute per side.

2. Pour the remaining 2 tablespoons of avocado oil over the shrimp and stir in the capers, garlic, and olives. Sauté for no longer than 30 seconds to 1 minute, stirring frequently and turning the shrimp over once.

3. Add the lemon juice and 1 tablespoon of the parsley. Reduce the heat to low and cover the skillet with the lid. Cook for 4 or 5 minutes, until the shrimp is cooked through. The shrimp will turn opaque and curl into a c-shape when they are done. (If they curl into tight o-shapes, they are overcooked.)

4. Transfer the shrimp and olive mixture to a serving platter and serve immediately topped with a generous drizzle of the pan sauce and garnished with the remaining parsley.

MACRONUTRIENTS PER SERVING
CALORIES: 261 KCAL FAT: 17 G, 150 KCAL CARBOHYDRATE: 4 G (3 G NET), 15 KCAL PROTEIN: 24 G, 94 KCAL

STEAK AND KIDNEY PIE

MAKES 6 SERVINGS

Lindsay's dad was born in Scotland, and her Scottish grandmother always had steak and kidney pies in the freezer, so this is nostalgia food for Lindsay. If you've never had kidney, it does have a distinct flavor that is perhaps an acquired taste; but kidneys are also mineral-rich and nutrient-dense, definitely worth adding to your diet.

INGREDIENTS

For the filling

- 6 ounces ox kidney, or substitute beef kidney
- 1 pound beef stew meat or rump roast, cut into 1- to 2-inch cubes
- 1½ teaspoon + ¾ teaspoon coarse sea salt
- ½ + ½ teaspoon ground black pepper
- 3 sprigs fresh thyme
- 1 bay leaf
- 2 cups beef stock
- 3 tablespoons beef tallow or fat of choice
- 1 small onion, chopped
- 8 ounces cremini mushrooms, thinly sliced

For the crust

- 1½ cups shredded mozzarella cheese
- ½ cup blanched almond flour
- 2 tablespoons coconut flour
- 1 teaspoon ground psyllium husks (optional but recommended)
- ½ teaspoon aluminum-free baking powder
- ½ teaspoon fine sea salt
- 3 tablespoons full-fat cream cheese
- 2 large eggs

Equipment: 2 approximately 12-inch pieces of parchment paper

1. *In the morning, prepare the kidney:* Going along the natural "lobes" of the kidney, cut away the meat from the fatty white center. You will end up with pieces about 1 inch in diameter. Discard the fat.

2. Place the kidney and the beef in a slow cooker. Season with 1½ teaspoons salt and ½ teaspoon pepper and stir well to coat. Place the thyme and bay leaf in the slow cooker. Pour the beef broth over everything. Cook on low 8 hours.

3. In the evening, preheat the oven to 375°F.

4. When the beef is tender, use a slotted spoon to remove the meat to a large bowl and set it aside to cool. (It is a good idea to stir it periodically so it cools evenly.) Strain the broth through a fine mesh strainer and reserve for later. Set aside. >>

5. *Make the crust:* Place the mozzarella cheese in a medium microwave-safe glass bowl. Stir in the almond and coconut flours, along with the psyllium husks, baking powder, and salt. Place the cream cheese on top. Microwave on high for 1 minute. Remove from the microwave and stir well. Microwave on high another 30 seconds. Stir well again. If the cheese is melted and the dough comes together in a uniform ball, add the eggs. Otherwise, continue to microwave in 15 second increments until fully melted, then add the eggs. Mix the eggs into the dough until fully incorporated. Place the dough in the freezer to chill while you finish the filling.

6. Heat the tallow in a large skillet over medium-high heat. When melted, add the onions and cook until starting to soften, 3 to 4 minutes. Turn the heat to medium and stir in the mushrooms. Season with the remaining ¾ teaspoon salt and ½ teaspoon pepper. Cook, stirring frequently, until the onions and mushrooms are soft, about 6 minutes.

7. Measure 1 cup of the reserved broth from the slow cooker and pour it over the onions and mushrooms. Allow it to come to a boil, then reduce the heat to maintain a low boil until the liquid reduces by half, about 8 to 10 minutes.

8. Carefully transfer about half the contents of the skillet into a high-powered blender (you can also use an immersion blender). Blend on low for 20 seconds, then increase the speed and continue blending until the mixture is smooth (it will be thick). Pour the purée back into the skillet.

9. Cut the beef and kidney into small bite-sized pieces. (The kidney is more pleasant when the pieces are smaller!) Add the meat to the skillet and stir thoroughly. Taste and adjust the salt and pepper as needed. Transfer the mixture to a pie pan.

10. Remove the crust from the freezer and quickly knead the dough with your hands. Form the crust into a ball and place it in the center of one of the sheets of parchment paper. Flatten it to about 1-inch thick with your hands and neaten the edges of the circle so it forms a large puck. (This will help it roll out nicely.) Place the other sheet of parchment paper on top and roll the dough to the size of your pie pan. Carefully peel off the top sheet of parchment, then replace it, carefully flip the crust between both pieces of parchment, and peel off the other sheet.

11. Gently place the crust atop the meat filling, discarding the parchment paper. Trim off any areas that hang off the sides. Cut a few slits in the top. Place the pie on a baking sheet and bake in the oven for 20 to 25 minutes until the crust is deeply golden and the filling is bubbling. Remove from the oven and allow the pie to rest for 15 minutes before serving.

NOTE: *You can also make the crust in the morning and place it in the refrigerator during the day. Take it out of the fridge when you start to cook the filling so it warms a bit before rolling it out.*

MACRONUTRIENTS PER SERVING
CALORIES: 574 KCAL FAT: 42 G, 379 KCAL CARBOHYDRATE: 9 G (6 G NET), 37 KCAL PROTEIN: 39 G, 158 KCAL

RATATOUILLE

MAKES 12 SERVINGS AS A SIDE

Ratatouille is a rustic braised vegetable dish from the Provence region of France. Although it is traditionally served with the vegetables cut into rounds and carefully arranged in a casserole, this less labor-intensive preparation is just as delicious. Ratatouille can be enjoyed warm or chilled, as a main course, a side, or even as a starter. Leftovers keep well in the fridge, making them an excellent option for packing into weekday lunches.

INGREDIENTS

½ cup avocado oil

1 pound eggplant, cut into 1-inch cubes

1 pound zucchini, cut into 1-inch cubes

2 bell peppers, red or yellow, cut into 1-inch dice

1 medium onion, cut into 1-inch cubes

2 medium ripe, flavorful tomatoes, peeled if desired, seeded and roughly cubed

6 cloves of garlic, smashed and minced

2 teaspoons fine sea salt

¼ teaspoon ground black pepper to taste

1 tablespoon tomato paste

½ cup water or bone broth

2 bay leaves

4 to 6 small sprigs of fresh thyme

6 to 10 small sprigs of fresh parsley

6 to 8 fresh basil leaves, chopped, to garnish

1. Warm 6 tablespoons of avocado oil in a large heavy-bottomed pot over medium heat. Add the eggplant to the pot and sauté stirring occasionally until just golden on all sides, about 8 minutes. The eggplant will absorb most (if not all) of the cooking oil initially, but will release much of it back into the pan as it softens. Remove the eggplant with a slotted spoon and set aside in a large bowl. In the same pot, sauté the zucchini until just browned on all sides, about 8 minutes. Remove the zucchini with a slotted spoon and place it in the bowl with the eggplant.

2. Add the remaining 2 tablespoons of avocado oil to the pot, then the add bell peppers and onions. Sauté, stirring frequently, until the onions become soft and lightly brown, about 5 or 6 minutes.

3. Add the tomatoes, garlic, pepper, sea salt, tomato paste and water to the pot. Stir well. Return the cooked eggplant mixture to the pot and stir to coat.

4. Use a square of cheesecloth tied with butcher's twine to create a bouquet garni (or herb sachet) with the bay leaves, thyme, and parsley inside. Add the bouquet garni to the pot and submerge into the vegetables (see Note). Bring the liquid to a boil, then reduce the heat to a simmer. Cover and cook over low heat for 1 hour. Remove the lid and increase >>

the heat to medium. Cook for about 20 minutes to thicken the ratatouille, stirring the bottom of the pot occasionally to prevent scorching. When the desired consistency is reached, remove and discard the bouquet garni.

5. Optionally allow the ratatouille to rest for 15 minutes before serving (but it may be eaten immediately if desired). Alternately, chill before serving. Serve garnished with fresh basil.

NOTE: *Using a bouquet garni makes the herbs easy to remove prior to serving. However, if you do not have cheesecloth and butcher's twine on hand, simply add the herbs to the pot loose and remove individually in the fourth step.*

MACRONUTRIENTS PER SERVING
CALORIES: 169 KCAL FAT: 14 G, 127 KCAL CARBOHYDRATE: 10 G (7 G NET), 41 KCAL PROTEIN: 2 G, 9 KCAL

WESTERN EUROPE   237

UNITED STATES

CANADA

UNITED STATES

MEXICO

THE
BAHAMAS

CUBA

HAITI

JAMAICA

PUERTO RICO
(U.S.)

BELIZE

GUATEMALA
HONDURAS

EL SALVADOR

NICARAGUA

COSTA RICA

No

VENEZUELA

COLOMBIA

ECUADOR

PERU

HAWAIIAN ISLANDS (U.S.)

Pacific Ocean

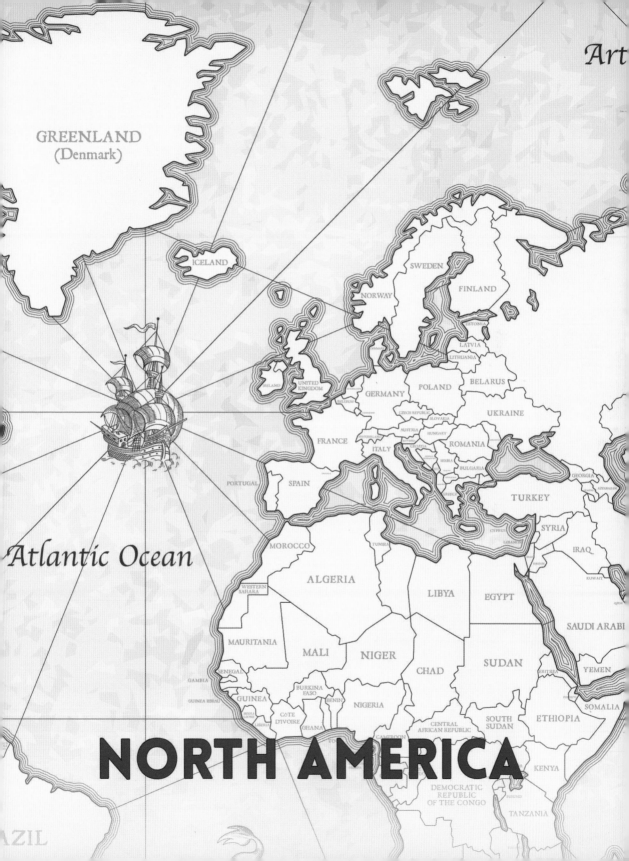

GREENLAND
(Denmark)

ICELAND

Art

SWEDEN

NORWAY

FINLAND

ESTONIA

LATVIA

LITHUANIA

IRELAND

UNITED
KINGDOM

BELARUS

POLAND

GERMANY

BELGIUM

CZECH REPUBLIC

SLOVAKIA

UKRAINE

FRANCE

SWITZERLAND

AUSTRIA

HUNGARY

ITALY

CROATIA

ROMANIA

SERBIA

BULGARIA

GEORGIA

PORTUGAL

SPAIN

GREECE

AZERBAIJAN

TURKEY

CYPRUS

SYRIA

LEBANON

IRAQ

MOROCCO

TUNISIA

IRAQ

KUWAIT

Atlantic Ocean

ALGERIA

LIBYA

EGYPT

SAUDI ARABIA

WESTERN
SAHARA

MAURITANIA

MALI

NIGER

CHAD

SUDAN

YEMEN

SENEGAL

ERITREA

GAMBIA

BURKINA
FASO

NIGERIA

GUINEA BISSAU

GUINEA

BENIN

SIERRA LEONE

CÔTE
D'IVOIRE

GHANA

LIBERIA

CAMEROON

SOUTH
SUDAN

ETHIOPIA

SOMALIA

CENTRAL
AFRICAN REPUBLIC

NORTH AMERICA

KENYA

DEMOCRATIC
REPUBLIC
OF THE CONGO

BURUNDI

TANZANIA

AZIL

AVOCADO CREMA

MAKES A SCANT ⅔ CUP

This creamy avocado sauce can elevate Mexican dishes, but don't stop there! Avocado crema is delicious on eggs and salads, and it can even be used as a dip. Because the avocado oxidizes, this crema does not keep well in the fridge, so make it shortly before you intend to use it.

INGREDIENTS

1 medium avocado

¼ cup Mexican crema (see Note)

2 tablespoons lime juice

¼ teaspoon fine sea salt or more, to taste

¼ teaspoon ground cumin (optional)

1. Place the flesh of the avocado in a food processor or blender. Add the crema, lime juice, and salt. Process until smooth. Taste and adjust seasoning to your preference, adding cumin if desired.

2. Transfer the mixture to a serving dish. Optionally cover and chill in the refrigerator for 1 to 2 hours or serve immediately.

NOTE: *You can substitute sour cream, plain full-fat Greek yogurt, crème fraîche, or strained coconut yogurt for the crema.*

MACRONUTRIENTS PER SERVING (¼ RECIPE, ABOUT 2 HEAPING TABLESPOONS)
CALORIES: 105 KCAL FAT: 10 G, 86 KCAL CARBOHYDRATE: 4 G (2 G NET), 16 KCAL PROTEIN: 1 G, 3 KCAL

BEEF CHEEK BARBACOA

MAKES 6 SERVINGS

Fun fact: barbacoa is the origin of the word barbecue. Barbacoa refers generally to a variety of slow-cooked shredded meat dishes of Mexican origin. Beef cheek is a traditional Mexican ingredient, as is goat. In fact, if you can find goat meat, try it in this recipe! Sheep and pork are also used in some regional variations. Try serving the barbacoa piled atop cauliflower rice or zucchini noodles.

INGREDIENTS

3 dried guajillo chiles, stems and seeds removed

2 cups chicken bone broth or stock, plus more as needed

2 tablespoons avocado oil

1 medium onion, thinly sliced

4 cloves garlic, smashed

2 teaspoons ground cumin

2 teaspoons dried oregano

¼ teaspoon ground cloves

2 tablespoons apple cider vinegar

2 chipotles canned in adobo, plus 2 tablespoons of the adobo sauce

3 pounds beef cheeks or another well-marbled cut of beef such as chuck roast or brisket

2 bay leaves

1 teaspoon fine sea salt

1 tablespoon lime juice

Optional toppings

Double batch of Avocado Crema (page 241)

1½ cups crumbled cotija cheese

¾ cup diced red onion

1. Preheat the oven to 350°F. Cut the stem ends of the guajillo chiles off and shake out the seeds if desired. Lay the chiles on a cookie sheet and bake for 4 minutes, turning once. Do not allow the chiles to burn.

2. Place the chiles in a small saucepan with 1 cup of the chicken broth. Bring to a boil and allow to simmer for 10 minutes or longer, until soft. Meanwhile, move on to the next step.

3. Heat the avocado oil in a deep, oven-safe casserole over medium-high heat. (See Note for slow cooker instructions.) When the oil begins to shimmer, add the onions and cook for 5 to 7 minutes, until they become soft and translucent. Add the garlic and cook for an additional minute. Add the cumin, oregano, and cloves, and stir well to coat the onions. Cook for 30 seconds, stirring frequently.

4. Deglaze the bottom of the casserole with the remaining 1 cup of chicken broth, scraping up any browned bits. Carefully pour the contents into a blender along with the softened guajillo chiles and the broth in which they were simmered. Add the vinegar, chipotles, and adobo sauce. Purée until smooth, about 2 minutes. >>

5. Place the beef cheeks into the casserole and add the bay leaves, salt, lime juice, and the sauce from the blender. Stir well to coat and cover the casserole with a lid.

6. Simmer over low heat for 2 hours or longer, stirring occasionally. The meat is done when it is fork-tender and can easily be pulled apart. If the sauce becomes too thick during cooking, you may add additional chicken broth as needed.

7. To serve, cut the beef into small chunks and shred with two forks or tongs, mixing the shredded beef with the sauce.

8. Spoon the shredded meat and sauce into individual serving bowls and optionally top each with a generous dollop of avocado crema, 3 tablespoons of cotija, and 2 tablespoons of diced red onion.

NOTE: *To prepare the barbacoa in a slow cooker, follow steps the first four steps as written. Place the beef cheeks, bay leaves, salt, lime juice, and the sauce from the blender in the slow cooker. Stir well and cook covered on low for 6 to 7 hours, until tender. Finish and serve as described in the final two steps.*

MACRONUTRIENTS PER SERVING (NO OPTIONAL TOPPINGS)
CALORIES: 451 KCAL FAT: 23G, 205 KCAL CARBOHYDRATE: 8 G (6 G NET), 30 KCAL PROTEIN: 50 G, 201 KCAL

MACRONUTRIENTS PER SERVING (WITH OPTIONAL TOPPINGS)
CALORIES: 730 KCAL FAT: 47 G, 419 KCAL CARBOHYDRATE: 16 G (11 G NET), 64 KCAL PROTEIN: 59 G, 236 KCAL

CHICKEN CRACKLING POUTINE

MAKES 4 SERVINGS

Layla spent her college winter breaks traipsing around the Laurentian mountains in Quebec. Although her fluency in French never improved beyond the very basic, she did develop a deep love for the unique, hearty food of the province. The chicken cracklings in this recipe provide the "crunch" of the twice-fried potatoes traditionally used in poutine.

INGREDIENTS

¼ cup heavy whipping cream, or substitute full-fat coconut milk

2 tablespoons unsalted butter or ghee

2 teaspoons minced shallot or onion

1 cup sliced cremini or button mushroom

¼ cup dry white wine (see Note)

¾ cup chicken bone broth

Pinch fine sea salt or more, to taste

Pinch freshly ground black pepper or more, to taste

1 batch fried chicken skin leftover from making Schmaltz (page 227)

1 cup white cheddar cheese curds or bite-sized chunks of mozzarella cheese

1. In a small saucepan over medium-low heat, gently simmer the cream until it is reduced by half. (Coconut milk may separate if heated too quickly, so heat gently if using.) Remove from heat and set aside.

2. In a medium-sized saucepan, melt 1 tablespoon of the butter over medium heat. When the butter is melted, add the shallots or onions and cook for 30 seconds to 1 minute, until fragrant and translucent. Increase the heat to high and add the mushrooms. Cook, stirring frequently, until the water released from the mushrooms has evaporated and the mushrooms turn golden brown, about 3 to 5 minutes.

3. Pour the wine into the pan and deglaze, scraping up any browned bits on the bottom of the pan. Allow the wine to cook until reduced by half, about 2 minutes. Stir in the broth and reduce the heat to medium. Cook until the flavor is melded and the sauce has reduced slightly, about 5 minutes.

4. Gently stir in the remaining 1 tablespoon of butter and the reduced cream from step 1. Remove from heat and add salt and pepper to taste. Cover and set aside.

5. Heat a large skillet over medium heat. (If you still have the skillet used for making schmaltz, use it here; there is no need to clean or wipe it.) Add the fried chicken skin to the skillet and sauté for 10 to 15 minutes, using a splatter screen over the skillet if possible and stirring frequently, until the chicken pieces become crisp and turn a rich golden brown. Be sure to watch the pan closely as it cooks; the chicken skin will darken rapidly. >>

6. Remove the chicken from the pan and drain. Return the pan with the gravy to the burner and gently reheat until it is just steaming.

7. To assemble the poutine, place a layer of chicken cracklings at the bottom of a serving dish, top with cheese curds, and pour the warm gravy over top. Season with additional salt and fresh pepper if desired. Serve immediately.

NOTES: *If you choose not to cook with wine, you can substitute an additional ¼ cup chicken broth plus ¾ teaspoon apple cider vinegar.*

The macronutrient values for this recipe are our best guesstimates. It is impossible to predict exactly how much fried-out skin each batch of schmaltz will yield, and nutritional information for fried-out skin is imprecise at best. The exact values for your batch might differ in terms of fat and protein (the carbohydrate will remain the same).

MACRONUTRIENTS PER SERVING
CALORIES: 640 KCAL FAT: 49 G, 437 KCAL CARBOHYDRATE: 6 G (5 G NET), 23 KCAL PROTEIN: 46 G, 182 KCAL

NORTH AMERICA   247

BLUE CHEESE DIP

Blue cheese dip is the obligatory accompaniment for Buffalo Wings (page 256). Both blue cheese and buttermilk (or kefir) are delicious ways to get some extra probiotic goodness into your food. Try a dollop of this dip atop a grilled steak or follow the dressing instructions for a pourable version to top your favorite salad.

INGREDIENTS

½ cup full-fat sour cream

½ cup blue cheese crumbles

2 tablespoons buttermilk or plain kefir (increase to 4 tablespoons for dressing)

½ cup avocado oil mayonnaise

½ tablespoon fresh lemon juice

Pinch fine sea salt

Pinch freshly ground black pepper

1. In a medium bowl, mix together the sour cream, ¼ cup of the blue cheese crumbles, the buttermilk, mayonnaise, lemon juice, sea salt, and pepper. Stir until well combined.

2. Add in the remaining ¼ cup of the blue cheese and stir until it reaches the desired consistency (chunky or creamy). Store in an airtight container in the refrigerator until ready to use.

MACRONUTRIENTS PER SERVING (2 TABLESPOONS)
CALORIES: 92 KCAL FAT: 9 G, 84 KCAL CARBOHYDRATE: 1 G (1 G NET), 2 KCAL PROTEIN: 1 G, 5 KCAL

BOLICHE

MAKES 8 TO 10 SERVINGS DEPENDING ON SIZE OF ROAST

Boliche is a Cuban dish in which a roast is stuffed with sausage (or ham) and olives, marinated in a citrusy marinade, and slow roasted. Intriguing, no? In this recipe we offer a quicker method using your countertop pressure cooker, but if you prefer to prepare your roast in the oven, refer to the recipe notes for directions.

INGREDIENTS

2 approximately 2-pound boneless eye of round beef roasts (see Notes)

8 ounces Spanish dried chorizo sausage, diced (see Notes)

8 large pitted green olives, chopped small

Juice of 1 small orange

Juice of 1 lime

3 tablespoons avocado oil

6 cloves garlic, pressed or very finely minced

2 teaspoons sea salt

½ teaspoon ground black pepper

½ teaspoon dried oregano

⅛ teaspoon paprika

2 bay leaves

1 cup beef broth or stock

1. Using a sharp knife with a long, narrow blade, insert the knife into one end of a roast. Carefully stick the knife through the center of the roast almost to the other end. Twist the knife back and forth. Remove the knife and insert it again perpendicular to your first cut, making a cross shape. As before, insert it almost all the way through the center, rotate it back and forth, and remove it. Repeat with the other roast.

2. Mix the chorizo and olives in a small bowl. Stuff each roast with half the chorizo, pushing the stuffing all the way to the bottom of the pocket you created. You should use all the stuffing, but if you have any leftover, place it in an airtight container in the refrigerator.

3. Use the tip of the knife to poke holes in the surface of the roasts and place them in a deep roasting pan or bowl to marinate. Pour the orange juice and lime juice over the surface and turn the roasts to coat.

4. In a small bowl, make a paste by mixing the oil, garlic, salt, pepper, oregano, and paprika. Spread the paste as evenly as possible over the surface of the roasts. Cover and place in the refrigerator to marinate at least 3 hours or overnight.

5. Place both roasts in your countertop pressure cooker and pour any remaining marinade over top. Place the bay leaves on top of the roasts and pour the beef broth around the roasts. If you have any extra stuffing, you may place it atop the roasts. Secure the lid and cook using high pressure for 50 minutes. Allow the pressure to release naturally for 15 minutes, then manually release the pressure valve and open the lid. >>

6. Carefully remove the roasts to a cutting board to rest for about 10 minutes. If desired, you may reduce the cooking liquid using the Sauté function on the pressure cooker or by pouring the liquid into a saucepan and simmering on the stove.

7. To serve, thinly slice the roasts and arrange the slices on a serving platter. Strain the cooking liquid and spoon it over the sliced roast. Serve any remaining cooking liquid in a gravy pitcher on the side.

NOTES: *If you cannot find smaller roasts, use one roast weighing about 3 pounds. If you use a larger roast, you might need to adjust the cooking time up.*

Spanish chorizo is sold cured and dried, so it can be easily cubed (like salami). If you cannot find this variety, Portuguese linguiça makes a better substitute than Mexican chorizo. The latter is usually uncured ground meat in a casing—i.e., raw sausage. Alternately use any spicy or mild cured sausage you wish.

To prepare your boliche in the oven, place the roasts in a heavy roasting pan with a lid. Increase the beef broth to 2 cups and add it to the roasting pan along with the bay leaves. Cook covered in a 350 °F oven for 2½ to 3 hours. Allow to rest before slicing as described above.

MACRONUTRIENTS PER SERVING (1/10 OF RECIPE)
CALORIES: 407 KCAL FAT: 22 G, 202 KCAL CARBOHYDRATE: 3 G (2 G NET), 10 KCAL PROTEIN: 46 G, 184 KCAL

252   KETO PASSPORT

CURTIDO ROJO

MAKES ABOUT 2 QUARTS DEPENDING ON THE SIZE OF YOUR CABBAGE

This delightful pickled or fermented slaw is most often associated with Guatemala—we think of it as Guatemalan sauerkraut. It makes an excellent side to a big plate of carnitas or carne asada, and it's fantastic on fish tacos. If you choose not to eat beets on a keto diet, simply substitute an extra cup or two of red or green cabbage; but remember that the fermentation reduces the sugar content of the beets.

INGREDIENTS

1 small head or ½ large head red cabbage

1 small beet, peeled and shredded

1 small red onion, thinly sliced

½ jalapeño, ribs and seeds removed, minced (or more or less to taste)

2 cloves garlic, minced

Grated zest of 1 lime, preferably organic

2 teaspoons dried oregano

1 teaspoon ground cumin

2 to 4 teaspoons coarse sea salt

Equipment

Wide-mouth jars: 1 half-gallon jar, 2 quart-size jars, or 4 pint-size

Non-metal tamper (optional)

1 to 4 glass fermentation weights (see page xv)

1. Before beginning, clean and sanitize any equipment that will come into contact with your curtido, such as the cutting board, slicer or knife, mixing bowl, fermentation jar(s), and utensils. Once your work area is cleaned, remove any damaged outer cabbage leaves, and set aside one healthy whole leaf.

2. Cut the cabbage into quarters, then remove and discard the core. Shred the cabbage leaves using a sharp knife, mandolin slicer, the slicing edge of a box grater, or similar. Smaller pieces will result in a more soft-textured curtido.

3. Place the sliced cabbage in a large mixing bowl. Add the beet, red onion, jalapeño, garlic, lime zest, oregano, and cumin to the cabbage. Stir well to combine. Sprinkle 2 teaspoons of salt over the vegetables. Use your hands to massage, squeeze, and knead the mixture. Do not be gentle here. This will cause salted brine to collect at the bottom of the bowl.

4. Taste the cabbage and beets. Ideally you will be able to taste the salt, but the mixture won't be overpoweringly salty. If you can't taste any salt, sprinkle in another teaspoon and massage it in for a minute. Taste again and repeat if necessary.

5. Once the vegetables have started to soften and the bottom of the bowl is covered with brine, tightly pack the prepared vegetables into the jar(s), tamping down the contents with your hands or a non-metal tamper so that there are no air bubbles. There should >>

be a couple inches of headspace at the top of your jar. Reserve the brine at the bottom of the mixing bowl.

6. Once packed, cover the surface of the vegetables with pieces of the large cabbage leaf you saved in the first step (cut or tear it to fit). If using, place a fermentation weight atop the leaves. Press down firmly to submerge the leaves beneath the level of the brine. Pour additional brine from the mixing bowl into the jar until it is nearly filled.

7. Set the jar(s) on a rimmed plate (pie plates or small baking pans work well), cover the jar lightly with a kitchen towel or coffee filter, or set an overturned plate over the mouth, and place the jar aside to ferment in a dark, temperature-stable area away from any trash cans, houseplants, or fresh fruits and vegetables.

8. Every day, check your curtido to make sure the vegetables are still submerged. Press down on the fermentation weight to release more brine as needed. Do not be surprised if your curtido bubbles over! Also check for the presence of mold. Any mold on the surface means you must discard the curtido and start again.

9. On day 3 or 4, start taste-testing your curtido (do not use a metal utensil). Your ferment is ready whenever the taste and texture are pleasing to you; depending on your ambient temperature and the time of year, this might be 4 or 5 days, or it might be a couple weeks! When you are ready to stop the fermentation process, remove the fermentation weight and place an airtight lid on the jar(s). You can safely store your ferment in the refrigerator for several months.

NOTES: *If your vegetables are not completely covered with liquid, juice the lime and add that to the jar. The vegetables must be completely covered with liquid to safely ferment them. You can always remove a bit of the cabbage/beet mixture as well, or add a bit of brine from a previous batch of curtido or store-bought kraut (although that will impact the flavor of the final product).*

It is impossible to get accurate nutritional information for home-fermented vegetables. These values are provided as an estimate. Read the "Fermenting" section on page xiv before fermenting for the first time.

MACRONUTRIENTS PER SERVING (½ CUP)
CALORIES: 40 KCAL FAT: 0 G, 0 KCAL CARBOHYDRATE: 8 G (4 G NET), 32 KCAL PROTEIN: 0 G, 0 KCAL

BUFFALO WINGS

MAKES 6 SERVINGS

Layla's husband was born and raised in Buffalo, New York, as were several generations of family before him. Unsurprisingly, he has strong opinions on how "chicken wings" (they're not called Buffalo wings there, it's redundant) should taste. After much tinkering, we've managed to create a traditional wing recipe that satisfies even the most dyed-in-the-wool Buffalonian. For the authentic experience, be sure to serve this with plenty of Blue Cheese Dip (page 249).

INGREDIENTS

3 pounds chicken wings cut into drums and flats (See Note)

1 tablespoon aluminum-free baking powder

1 tablespoon fine sea salt

⅓ cup cayenne-pepper-based hot sauce (Frank's RedHot Sauce Original is traditional)

⅓ cup melted unsalted butter or ghee

2 tablespoons apple cider vinegar

¼ teaspoon ground cayenne pepper, or to taste (optional)

1 teaspoon paprika

For serving

6 stalks celery, cut into sticks

1 batch Blue Cheese Dip (page 249)

1. Pat the chicken dry and place it in a large bowl. Mix the baking powder and salt in a small bowl and, working a little bit at a time, sprinkle the chicken with this mixture, tossing to coat evenly.

2. Place a wire rack inside of a large rimmed baking sheet and arrange the chicken in a single layer with a small space between pieces (use two baking sheets if necessary). For the crispiest wings, place the baking sheet in the refrigerator and allow the wings to air dry overnight. Otherwise, place an oven rack in the upper-middle position and preheat the oven to 250°F.

3. Bake the chicken for 30 minutes, then increase the heat to 425°F.

4. Once the heat has reached 425°F, bake the chicken for 20 minutes. Rotate the pan and bake for an additional 20 to 25 minutes, until the chicken skin becomes crisp with bubbles and turns golden brown.

5. Meanwhile, in a medium bowl whisk together the hot sauce and melted butter until smooth. Whisk in the apple cider vinegar, cayenne pepper, and paprika, using more or less cayenne to adjust the heat of the wing sauce.

6. When the wings are cooked, transfer to a large bowl and pour the wing sauce over top. Toss until well coated. Serve immediately with celery sticks and Blue Cheese Dip for dipping.

NOTE: *Pre-separated chicken wings are often sold as "party wings." If you are cutting the chicken wings yourself, simply cut each wing through each of its two joints. This will create a drum, flat, and tip. The tips are not used in this recipe, but save them as they are ideal for making bone broth.*

MACRONUTRIENTS PER SERVING (WINGS ONLY)
CALORIES: 602 KCAL FAT: 46 G, 414 KCAL CARBOHYDRATE: 1 G (1 G NET), 3 KCAL PROTEIN: 42 G, 167 KCAL

MACRONUTRIENTS PER SERVING (WITH CELERY AND BLUE CHEESE SAUCE)
CALORIES: 823 KCAL FAT: 68 G, 611 KCAL CARBOHYDRATE: 3 G (3 G NET), 14 KCAL PROTEIN: 45 G, 180 KCAL

CRETONS

MAKES 8 SERVINGS

The best way to describe cretons is Canadian pork pâté. Sounds a little odd, eh? It's quite tasty actually, and great to have on hand as a fat- and protein-rich snack or small meal, or to serve as a party spread. Usually cretons is eaten on toast, but for keto-friendly options try it on celery sticks or sliced bell pepper, or atop a toasted Basic Mug Muffin (page 271).

INGREDIENTS

1½ pounds ground pork

¾ cup finely chopped yellow onion

2 cloves garlic, finely minced

¾ teaspoon ground black pepper

½ teaspoon ground cloves

¼ teaspoon ground cinnamon

¼ teaspoon allspice

¼ teaspoon fine sea salt

½ cup heavy whipping cream

¼ cup filtered water

¼ cup pork rind crumbs (see Note)

1. Heat a large skillet over medium heat. Add the pork and cook until only a little pink remains, about 5 minutes. While it cooks, break up the meat with a spoon or meat chopper.

2. Stir in the onions and garlic. Cook a few minutes more until the meat is cooked through. Add the pepper, cloves, cinnamon, allspice, and salt. Stir well, then cook for 1 minute more.

3. Add the cream, water, and pork rind crumbs. Allow the liquid to come to a boil, then cover and reduce heat to a simmer. Cook, stirring occasionally, for 1½ hours. Remove the lid and cook uncovered, stirring occasionally, until the mixture is thick and all the liquid is evaporated, about 15 minutes.

4. Remove from heat and adjust the salt and pepper to taste. Transfer to a decorative bowl or several smaller ramekins, smoothing the top with a rubber spatula.

5. Cover tightly with plastic wrap and refrigerate until well chilled and firm, at least 4 hours or overnight.

NOTE: *If you can't find pork rind crumbs in the store, simply get plain chicharrones (pork rinds) and grind them yourself in a food processor or crush them with a rolling pin.*

MACRONUTRIENTS PER SERVING
CALORIES: 285 KCAL FAT: 19 G, 170 KCAL CARBOHYDRATE: 3 G (2 G NET), 11 KCAL PROTEIN: 25 G, 100 KCAL

CALDO DE RES

SERVES 6

Layla became obsessed with this soup after tasting it in a taqueria in Philadelphia's Italian Market neighborhood. (Despite the name, some of Philly's best Mexican cuisine is found in the small mom-and-pop shops there!) The textures of the fall-apart-tender beef and the crisp, bright vegetables combine delectably with the taste of the smoky chile-tomato sauce. It's also packed with micronutrients.

INGREDIENTS

2 bay leaves

1½ pounds beef soup bones

6 cloves garlic, smashed

1 pound beef oxtails or bone-in beef shank

1 medium onion

8 cups filtered water

4 dried guajillo chiles, stems removed and seeds shaken out

1 Roma tomato

1 tablespoon apple cider vinegar

½ small head of green cabbage, quartered

2 small carrots, roll cut or chopped into 2-inch pieces

2 medium stalks celery, chopped into 2-inch pieces

1 small chayote squash, sliced into 2-inch strips

1 cup green beans, chopped into 2-inch pieces

1 teaspoon dried oregano

2 tablespoons fine sea salt

1. Place the bay leaves, soup bones, 2 cloves of garlic, and oxtails, into a large stockpot. Roughly chop half the onion and add it to the pot. Pour in the water and bring it to a boil over high heat. Reduce the heat and simmer for 2 to 2½ hours, until the meat is fork-tender. Meanwhile, move on to the next step.

2. While the soup simmers, preheat the oven to 350°F. Lay the guajillo chiles flat on a baking sheet and roast for 2 minutes per side. Once roasted, transfer the chiles to a small saucepan and cover with 2 cups of water. Bring to a low boil, then simmer for 30 minutes. Transfer the chiles and cooking liquid to a blender. Add the tomato, remaining half onion, and garlic cloves. Purée until smooth, about 1 minute or longer. Set aside.

3. When the meat is cooked, remove the oxtails to a bowl and set aside. Skim excess fat from the top of the broth if desired, then strain the stock into a separate bowl and set aside. You may save the soup bones for another use. Discard the cooked vegetables.

4. Return the beef stock to the stockpot. Add the puréed chile mixture and stir well, then stir in the apple cider vinegar, cabbage, carrots, celery, chayote, green beans, oregano, and salt. Add the oxtails back to the pot. Simmer the mixture until the vegetables are tender, about 15 minutes.

5. Taste and adjust the salt if needed. Serve immediately.

MACRONUTRIENTS PER SERVING
CALORIES: 257 KCAL FAT: 12 G, 106 KCAL CARBOHYDRATE: 12 G (8 G NET), 46 KCAL PROTEIN: 27 G, 108 KCAL

DEVILED EGGS (3 WAYS)

Your Mama's Deviled Eggs
MAKES 6 EGGS

Ok, maybe not your mama's deviled eggs, but this is a pretty classic deviled egg recipe that would be welcome at any American picnic or barbeque!

INGREDIENTS
6 hard-boiled large eggs, peeled

¼ cup avocado oil mayonnaise

1 teaspoon yellow mustard

¼ teaspoon fine sea salt, plus more to taste

Pinch black pepper, plus more to taste

Dash keto-friendly hot sauce (optional)

Paprika to garnish (optional)

1. Cut the eggs in half lengthwise. Gently scoop the yolks into a small bowl without tearing the whites. Mash the yolks with a fork. Add the mayonnaise, mustard, salt, pepper, and hot sauce (if using). Continue to mash the yolks and stir the ingredients together until smooth.

2. Arrange the egg whites on a serving tray with the cut sides facing up. Fill the divots in the eggs with the egg yolk mixture, dividing equally between the eggs. If not serving immediately, store in the refrigerator. Before serving, sprinkle paprika over the eggs.

MACRONUTRIENTS PER SERVING (2 PIECES = 1 WHOLE EGG)
CALORIES: 145 KCAL FAT: 13 G, 114 KCAL CARBOHYDRATE: 1 G (1 G NET), 3 KCAL PROTEIN: 6 G, 25 KCAL

Not Your Mama's Deviled Eggs: Bacon and Butter Eggs
MAKES 6 EGGS

The keto diet is derisively called the "bacon and butter diet," so why not occasionally live up to the name? These eggs are best eaten fresh, so prepare them just before serving.

INGREDIENTS

2 slices bacon

¼ cup salted butter

6 hard-boiled large eggs, peeled

1 tablespoon minced fresh chives

Sea salt to taste

1. In a small skillet, cook the bacon over medium heat until crispy, flipping frequently. Remove the bacon to a plate to cool. Measure 1½ teaspoons of bacon grease into a small bowl.

2. Place the butter in the bowl with the bacon grease. Stir to melt the butter in the hot grease. If needed, microwave the butter and bacon grease in 10-second increments.

3. Cut the eggs in half lengthwise. Carefully remove the yolks without tearing the whites and place the egg yolks in the bowl with the butter mixture. Mash the yolks with a fork and stir the ingredients together until smooth. Stir in the chives. Taste and adjust salt as needed.

4. Arrange the egg whites on a serving tray with the cut sides facing up. Fill the divots in the eggs with the egg yolk mixture, dividing equally between the eggs. Serve immediately.

MACRONUTRIENTS PER SERVING (2 PIECES = 1 WHOLE EGG)
CALORIES: 158 KCAL FAT: 14 G, 125 KCAL CARBOHYDRATE: 1 G (1 G NET), 2 KCAL PROTEIN: 6 G, 29 KCAL

Not Your Mama's Deviled Eggs: Wasabi Eggs
MAKES 4 EGGS

Wasabi packs a punch, but it is balanced by the saltiness of the marinated Shoyu Tamago in this recipe. Maybe your taste buds just get distracted? If burning nostrils aren't your thing, you can reduce the wasabi powder to suit your tastes.

INGREDIENTS

1 tablespoon wasabi powder or 2 tablespoons wasabi paste

2 teaspoons filtered water

3 tablespoons avocado oil mayonnaise

1 batch Shoyu Tamago (page 57)

1 teaspoon marinade from Shoyu Tamago (optional)

2 teaspoons pickled ginger, chopped (to garnish, optional)

1. If using wasabi powder, in a small bowl, mix together the wasabi powder and filtered water. Add the mayo and stir to combine. Set aside to rest for 5 minutes. Meanwhile, cut the Shoyu Tamago in half lengthwise. Carefully remove the yolks without tearing the whites.

2. When the wasabi mayo is ready, add the egg yolks. Mash the yolks with a fork. Optionally add 1 teaspoon of marinade. Continue to mash the yolks and stir the ingredients together until smooth.

3. Arrange the egg whites on a serving tray with the cut sides facing up. Fill the divots in the eggs with the egg yolk mixture, dividing equally between the eggs. Optionally garnish with pickled ginger. If not serving immediately, store in the refrigerator.

MACRONUTRIENTS PER SERVING (2 PIECES = 1 WHOLE EGG)
CALORIES: 176 KCAL FAT: 14 G, 128 KCAL CARBOHYDRATE: 3 G (2 G NET), 10 KCAL PROTEIN: 7 G, 30 KCAL

DILLY BEANS

MAKES ABOUT 2 QUARTS

The southern United States is home to an impressive collection of recipes for pickled and fermented vegetables, meats, roots, and eggs. One of the most crowd-pleasing and easy to make are fermented string beans done in the style of dill pickles, commonly known as "Dilly Beans." Dilly Beans taste great with keto burgers, chopped up into chicken or tuna salads, or eaten alone as a snack.

INGREDIENTS

1 quart non-chlorinated filtered water

2 tablespoons canning or fine sea salt

4 to 6 sprigs fresh dill weed

1 or 2 jalapeño peppers, halved (optional, to taste)

4 cloves garlic, halved

1 teaspoon black peppercorns

2 bay leaves

1 pound string beans, ends trimmed

Equipment

2 wide-mouth jars

2 glass fermentation weights (see page xv)

1. Clean and sanitize all of the equipment that will come into contact with your vegetables, such as the mixing bowl, utensils, weights, and jars. Pour the water into a nonreactive mixing bowl and add the sea salt to make the brine. Stir until fully dissolved, then set aside.

2. Divide the dill, jalapeño peppers, garlic, peppercorns and bay leaves between the two jars. Pack the green beans vertically into the jars, on top of the spices. Try to pack the beans as tightly as possible to keep the spices from floating out.

3. Pour the brine into the packed jars, leaving 1 inch of headspace at the top. Place the fermentation weight atop the beans and cover with the lid, leaving it partially unscrewed so that gas can escape. Set the jars inside of a shallow dish or on a plate.

4. Leave the jars to ferment for a week or longer in a temperature-stable area away from direct sunlight, fruits, vegetables, plants, or trash receptacles (placing them in a cabinet works well). As they ferment, check under the lid of the jar every day or every other day to ensure that no mold has grown. If the beans have grown mold or have begun to smell offensive, throw them away and start over with a new batch.

5. After 7 days, begin tasting the beans. Once they are fermented to your liking, seal the jars with an airtight lid and store in the refrigerator, where they should keep for several months. Once you have eaten all of the beans, you can enjoy the leftover fermentation brine as a refreshing probiotic/electrolyte tonic similar to pickle juice.

NOTE: *It is impossible to get accurate nutritional information for home-fermented vegetables. These values are provided as an estimate. Read the "Fermenting" section on page xiv before fermenting for the first time.*

MACRONUTRIENTS PER SERVING (2 OUNCES)
CALORIES: 14 KCAL FAT: 0 G, 0 KCAL CARBOHYDRATE: 3 G (2 G NET), 14 KCAL PROTEIN: 0 G, 0 KCAL

EGGS BENEDICT

MAKES 2 SERVINGS

This classic breakfast involves a lot of steps, but it's a lovely dish that is worth the work when serving a nice breakfast or brunch. Poaching eggs takes a bit of skill, but we provide a handy trick in this recipe. (If poaching is too troublesome, you can always fry the eggs.) To save time in the morning, prepare the Hollandaise the night before.

INGREDIENTS

Hollandaise

½ cup unsalted butter, melted

3 egg yolks, room temperature

2½ teaspoons fresh lemon juice

Pinch sea salt

Pinch ground black pepper

Pinch cayenne pepper (optional)

Recommended equipment: 4 small canning rings (see Note)

Other ingredients

4 slices Canadian bacon or bacon

Filtered water

1 teaspoon white vinegar

4 medium eggs

1 batch Basic Mug Muffins (recipe follows on page 271)

1½ tablespoons unsalted butter, melted

2 tablespoons fresh parsley, finely chopped

1. *Make the Hollandaise:* In a wide-mouthed jar, combine the egg yolk, lemon juice, salt, pepper, and cayenne (if using). Use an immersion blender to blend about 10 seconds just to combine. With the immersion blender running in the egg yolk mixture, pour in the melted butter in a steady stream. Move the immersion blender up and down to let the butter fully emulisify. Taste the hollandaise and adjust the seasoning. If not using immediately, place a lid on the jar and store in the refrigerator. Stir before using. (See Notes)

2. Heat a skillet over medium heat. Cook the bacon on both sides until done to desired crispness. Remove to a plate and set aside.

3. Place an oven rack about 6 inches below the broiler and preheat the broiler on low heat. While it heats, in a wide, deep skillet, heat about 1 inch of water and the vinegar over high heat. When the water boils, drop the canning rings upside-down in the water so they lie flat on the bottom of the pan. (If they do not all fit, only use as many as can sit flat on the bottom and poach your eggs in batches). Remove the pan from the heat.

4. One at a time, crack an egg into a small bowl, then gently pour it into the water over one of the canning rings. It will settle into the ring; use a spoon if necessary to gently coax it into place. Repeat for all the eggs. Place the lid on the pan and set a timer for 3½ minutes for runny yolks, 4 minutes for jammy yolks, or 4½ minutes for more well-done yolks. While they cook, move on to the next step.

5. Place the muffin slices on a heavy baking sheet and brush them with the melted butter. Place them under the broiler. Toast them about 1 minute, keeping a close eye on them so they do not burn. Remove from the oven and place on 2 serving plates (2 muffin halves per plate). Place 1 piece of Canadian bacon or bacon (cut in half) on each muffin half.

6. When the egg timer goes off, use a slotted spatula to lift the eggs out of the water, keeping them inside their canning rings, removing them in the order in which you placed them in the water, and gently shaking off excess water.

7. Gently pop the eggs out of the canning rings and place one on each muffin. Top each with a generous dollop (about 2 tablespoons) of Hollandaise. Garnish with parsley. Serve immediately.

NOTES: *This makes more Hollandaise than you need for this recipe. Store leftovers in the refrigerator and use within a few days. Hollandaise is excellent on asparagus!*

Canning rings are not necessary for poaching eggs, but they help keep the eggs together. If you do not have rings, simply pour each egg slowly and gently from the small bowl directly into the water. The first time you poach eggs, you should start with one to check the timing necessary to get the egg cooked to your liking.

MACRONUTRIENTS PER SERVING
CALORIES: 748 KCAL FAT: 68 G, 608 KCAL CARBOHYDRATE: 6 G (4 G NET), 22 KCAL PROTEIN: 32 G, 126 KCAL

BASIC MUG MUFFINS

MAKES 2 SERVINGS

INGREDIENTS

1 tablespoon unsalted butter

3 tablespoons blanched almond flour

½ teaspoon aluminum-free baking powder

Pinch salt

1 large egg, room temperature

1. Put in the butter in a straight-sided coffee mug and microwave on high for 20 seconds; continue cooking in 10-second increments as needed until just melted.

2. With a fork, mix the almond flour, baking powder, and salt into the butter, removing as many lumps as possible. Add the egg and stir until well combined.

3. Microwave on high for 90 seconds. Remove from the microwave. Let sit for 1 minute, then invert the mug over a plate and tip out the muffin.

4. To use, cut the muffin crossways into 4 rounds. Optionally toast under a low-heat broiler before serving (as directed in the Keto Eggs Benedict recipe).

Suggested toppings:

Raw almond butter with a few very ripe raspberries, smashed

Kajmak (page 185) or softened cream cheese with minced fresh chives

Melted butter with cinnamon sprinkled on top

MACRONUTRIENTS PER SERVING (½ RECIPE)
CALORIES: 150 KCAL FAT: 14 G, 123 KCAL CARBOHYDRATE: 3 G (2 G NET), 11 KCAL PROTEIN: 5 G, 22 KCAL

SMOKED SALMON AND GRIBICHE BENEDICT

MAKES 2 SERVINGS

And now for something a little different…

INGREDIENTS

1 batch Basic Mug Muffins (page 271)

1½ tablespoons unsalted butter, melted

4 ounces smoked salmon

1 batch Sauce Gribiche (page 225)

2 tablespoons fresh parsley, finely chopped

1. Place an oven rack about 6 inches below the broiler and preheat the broiler on low heat. Place the muffin slices on a heavy baking sheet and brush them with the melted butter. Place them under the broiler. Toast them about 1 minute, keeping a close eye on them so they do not burn. Remove from the oven and place 2 slices on each of 2 serving plates.

2. Place 1 ounce of smoked salmon on each of the muffin slices. Top each with an even helping of Sauce Gribiche. Garnish with parsley and serve immediately.

MACRONUTRIENTS PER SERVING
CALORIES: 783 KCAL FAT: 74 G, 663 KCAL CARBOHYDRATE: 4 G (3 G NET), 18 KCAL PROTEIN: 26 G, 104 KCAL

JERK CHICKEN

MAKES 4 SERVINGS

Jerk chicken is not the national dish of Jamaica (that honor belongs to ackee and saltfish if you're wondering), but it might as well be. No trip to the Caribbean island would be complete without the spicy, smoky dish. Scotch bonnet chiles, thyme, and allspice are the quintessential flavor undertones of jerk-style cooking (but see recipe note). Serve jerk chicken with cauliflower rice and a basic cabbage slaw or salad.

INGREDIENTS

6 scallions, white and green parts roughly chopped

6 cloves garlic, crushed

1-inch piece fresh ginger, peeled and grated or minced

1 Scotch bonnet pepper, ribs and seeds removed (see Note)

2 tablespoons fresh thyme leaves

1 tablespoon granulated monkfruit sweetener (optional)

2 teaspoons ground allspice

1 teaspoon ground cinnamon

½ teaspoon ground nutmeg

½ teaspoon white pepper, or substitute ground black pepper

2 tablespoons tamari or coconut aminos

1 tablespoon filtered water

¼ cup avocado oil

4 bone-in skin-on chicken thighs

4 bone-in skin-on chicken drumsticks

1. *Make the marinade:* Place the scallions, garlic, ginger, Scotch bonnet pepper thyme, monkfruit (if using), allspice, cinnamon, nutmeg, white pepper, tamari, and water in a high-powered blender. Pulse about 10 times to combine. Scrape down the sides of the blender then, with the blender running, stream in the avocado oil. Blend on high until smooth.

2. Place the chicken pieces in a deep glass dish or bowl. Use your fingers to gently separate the skin from the meat. Spoon some of the marinade under the skin and massage it around, then pour the rest over top of the meat, flipping to coat. Place in the refrigerator to marinate at least 2 hours, but 24 is better.

3. Heat a grill over medium heat (see Notes for oven instructions). Shake off the excess marinade and place the chicken on the grill with the thighs skin side up. Grill for about 25 minutes, flipping the drumsticks every 5 minutes or so and the thighs after 10 minutes. (Stay by the grill—the marinade tends to cause flare-ups, so you want to watch the meat. If necessary, move the chicken to indirect heat and add a bit more cooking time.)

4. Use a meat thermometer to check the internal temperature of the drumsticks and thighs. If they are cooked to 165°F, remove to a dish and cover; otherwise continue to cook. When they reach the proper temperature, remove from heat and let rest for a few minutes before serving warm.

NOTES: *Scotch bonnet peppers are traditionally used in Jamaican jerk chicken, but if you can't find them in the store, you can substitute a habanero pepper or, for less heat, a jalapeno pepper. If you want your jerk extra spicy, leave the ribs and seeds of the pepper in the marinade.*

To prepare in the oven, place the oven rack in the center position and preheat the oven to 400°F. Set a wire rack inside a rimmed baking sheet and place the chicken pieces on the rack. Bake for 15 to 20 minutes per side, until the chicken skin becomes browned and the meat is cooked through to an internal temperature of 165°F.

MACRONUTRIENTS PER SERVING (NO SWEETENER)
CALORIES: 473 KCAL FAT: 34 G, 306 KCAL CARBOHYDRATE: 7 G (5 G NET), 28 KCAL PROTEIN: 32 G, 128 KCAL

SNAPPER VERACRUZ

MAKES 6 SERVINGS

While many people probably think rice, beans, tortillas, beef, and meat are typical "Mexican food," we would argue that this is one of the more emblematic dishes in Mexican cuisine. Coastal cities such as Veracruz (also the name of a Mexican state) have access to fabulous fresh seafood; and the simple yet flavorful preparation of this huachinango veracruzano is a delicious representation of what Mexican cuisine has to offer.

INGREDIENTS

2 pounds red snapper fillets, cut into 6 portions

Juice of 2 small limes

3 tablespoons avocado oil

1 medium onion, finely chopped

3 cloves garlic, chopped

1 fresh jalapeño or serrano pepper, ribs and seeds removed, minced

2 bay leaves

½ cup chopped pitted green olives

2 tablespoons brine from the olives

2 tablespoons capers, drained

1½ teaspoons dried oregano

2 large very ripe tomato, chopped, juices reserved

3 tablespoons fresh cilantro, finely chopped

1 lime, cut into 6 wedges

1. Preheat the oven to 425°F.

2. Place the snapper in a shallow bowl and pour 2 tablespoons of lime juice over top. Toss gently to coat and set aside.

3. Heat the avocado oil in a skillet over medium heat. Add the onion, garlic, jalapeño, and bay leaves and sauté about 3 minutes, until just starting to brown. Stir in the olives and their brine and the capers. Crush the oregano between your palms and add that to the pan with the tomato and its juices. Cook for an additional 3 to 4 minutes, crushing the tomatoes with a wooden spoon as they cook. When the onions are soft and the tomatoes are mostly broken down, remove the pan from the heat and stir in the rest of the lime juice.

4. Spoon about ⅓ of the tomato mixture into the bottom of a baking dish large enough to hold the fish in a single layer (slight overlap is ok if necessary). Place the fish in the dish, then spoon the remaining tomato mixture evenly over the top (it will not coat the fish). Pour any juices from the fish bowl over top.

5. Bake the fish for 15 to 18 minutes, until the meat is opaque and flakes when tested with a fork. Remove from the oven and let sit for a few minutes, then carefully transfer the fillets to serving plates. Spoon the tomato mixture from the baking dish over the fish. Garnish each serving with fresh cilantro and a slice of lime.

MACRONUTRIENTS PER SERVING
CALORIES: 254 KCAL FAT: 11 G, 96 KCAL CARBOHYDRATE: 7 G (6 G NET), 29 KCAL PROTEIN: 32 G, 128 KCAL

AJI DE GALLINA

The uniquely-flavored aji amarillo paste gives this Peruvian chicken dish its rich golden color. It is readily available in Latin markets or can be ordered online. Aji paste can also be used to make Causa Limeña (page 285, see the recipe note).

INGREDIENTS

2 pounds bone-in skinless chicken thighs

4 cups chicken bone broth or stock

¼ cup avocado oil

1 medium onion, chopped

2 cloves garlic, minced

½ cup heavy whipping cream, or substitute full-fat coconut milk

2 to 4 tablespoon aji amarillo paste, use less for a milder dish

½ cup walnuts, chopped

3 tablespoons grated Parmesan cheese or nutritional yeast

¼ teaspoon fine sea salt, plus more to taste

For serving

2 hard-boiled large eggs, sliced

½ cup pitted kalamata olives, halved lengthwise

1 lime, cut into wedges

1. Place the chicken and bone broth in a large pot and bring to a boil over high heat. Reduce the heat to a simmer and cook for 35 to 40 minutes until cooked through. Remove the chicken and set aside. Strain the broth and reserve 2 cups. Save the remaining broth may be saved for another use.

2. While the chicken cooks, heat 2 tablespoons of oil in a skillet over medium-high heat. Add the onions and sauté, stirring frequently, until the onions become golden, about 5 minutes. Add the garlic and sauté for an additional 1 to 2 minutes until fragrant. Remove from heat.

3. In a blender or a food processor, process the cream, aji amarillo paste, walnuts, Parmesan cheese, and the remaining 2 tablespoons of oil until smooth. Add the cooked onion mixture and process until smooth, watching for hot splatter.

4. Pour the blended sauce back into the skillet and bring to a gentle simmer. Separate the chicken meat from the bones, shred, and add to the sauce, stirring well to coat (save the bones to make bone broth). Stir in the reserved broth a half cup at a time until the sauce reaches the desired consistency. Stir in salt to taste. Simmer the chicken in the sauce until heated through. Serve warm, garnished with slices of egg, olives, and lime wedges.

NOTE: *If you buy bone-in skin-on chicken and remove the skin yourself, freeze the skin to use later for Gribenes (page 215).*

MACRONUTRIENTS PER SERVING (CHICKEN AND SAUCE ONLY)
CALORIES: 530 KCAL FAT: 35 G, 311 KCAL CARBOHYDRATE: 6 G (5 G NET), 25 KCAL PROTEIN: 49 G, 194 KCAL

MACRONUTRIENTS PER SERVING (WITH SERVING ACCOMPANIMENTS)
CALORIES: 589 KCAL FAT: 40 G, 356 KCAL CARBOHYDRATE: 8 G (6 G NET), 32 KCAL PROTEIN: 51 G, 204 KCAL

BRAZILIAN CHOPPED SALAD

This recipe is loosely based on a Brazilian salad, which typically comprises hearts of palm, avocado, and tomatoes. We don't call for tomatoes in this recipe so as to allocate the carbs to other veggies, but feel free to add some if you want! Top with chopped chicken and/or hard-boiled eggs for a complete meal.

INGREDIENTS

Dressing

- ½ cup extra-virgin olive oil
- ¼ cup packed fresh cilantro leaves, finely chopped
- ¼ cup packed fresh mint leaves, finely chopped
- 1 clove garlic, chopped
- 2 tablespoons fresh lime juice
- 1 tablespoon balsamic vinegar
- ½ teaspoon ground cumin
- ½ teaspoon fine sea salt
- ½ teaspoon white pepper or ground black pepper

Salad

- 10 ounces shredded red cabbage, green cabbage or broccoli slaw
- 1 14-ounce can hearts of palm, drained, rinsed, and chopped
- 4 cups baby spinach, baby kale, or a mix, roughly chopped
- 1 small bell pepper, any color, diced
- 1 medium cucumber, diced
- 1 medium zucchini, diced
- 2 scallions, white and green parts thinly sliced
- 2 medium avocados, cubed

1. Make the dressing by putting all the dressing ingredients in a jar with a tight-fitting lid. Shake well.

2. Place the cabbage, hearts of palm, spinach, bell pepper, cucumber, zucchini, and scallions in a large bowl. Pour in half the dressing. Toss very well to combine.

3. Transfer the salad to a serving bowl, top with the avocado, and drizzle with additional dressing to taste.

MACRONUTRIENTS PER SERVING
CALORIES: 291 KCAL FAT: 26 G, 230 KCAL CARBOHYDRATE: 15 G (8 G NET), 61 KCAL PROTEIN: 5 G, 18 KCAL

SOUTH AMERICA   283

CAUSA LIMEÑA

MAKES 8 SERVINGS

Causa limeña is a Peruvian dish in which potatoes are mashed with lime juice and aji chile paste, then the mixture is layered with seafood or chicken salad and other ingredients to make a delicious and beautiful all-in-one dish. Because it is traditionally made specifically with waxy potatoes, our version differs in texture, but it has all the flavors one expects from the original!

INGREDIENTS

1 tablespoon kosher salt

1 pound cauliflower florets

1 celeriac (aka celery root), peeled and cut into 1-inch chunks

8 ounces lump crab meat, or substitute cooked shredded chicken

$\frac{1}{4}$ cup avocado oil mayonnaise

$\frac{1}{4}$ cup finely diced red bell pepper, plus more for garnish (optional)

$\frac{1}{4}$ cup finely diced onion

$\frac{1}{4}$ teaspoon ground black pepper

2 tablespoons freshly squeezed lime juice

$\frac{1}{2}$ teaspoon fine sea salt, plus more to taste

$\frac{1}{4}$ teaspoon black pepper, plus more to taste

1 to 2 tablespoons aji amarillo paste (to taste, see Notes)

1 tablespoon avocado oil for greasing the ring (see Notes)

1 avocado, very thinly sliced

Equipment: Metal ring mold $3\frac{1}{2}$- to 4-inches in diameter (see Note)

1. Bring a large pot of water to a boil with the kosher salt. Add the cauliflower and celeriac and boil for 10 to 12 minutes until the vegetables are easily pierced with a fork. Drain in a colander and run under cold water to quickly cool. Shake of any excess water and set aside.

2. In a small bowl, stir together the crab meat, mayonnaise, bell pepper, onion, and black pepper until thoroughly combined. Place in the refrigerator if not assembling the causa limeña right away.

3. When the cauliflower and celeriac are room temperature, place them in a food processor or high-powered blender with the lime juice, $\frac{1}{2}$ teaspoon salt, and the black pepper, plus $\frac{1}{2}$ tablespoon of the aji amarillo paste. Blend until smooth, then taste the mixture. Continue adding aji amarillo paste to your liking, blending to combine. When the mixture is as spicy as you want, adjust the salt and pepper as needed and set aside.

4. Grease the inside of the ring mold and place it on a flat plate you will use for serving. Spoon 2 tablespoons of the cauliflower mash into the ring and smooth to create an even >>

layer. Arrange ⅛ of the sliced avocado on top of the cauliflower to make a second layer, covering the cauliflower as completely as possible. Cover the avocado evenly with 2 tablespoons of cauliflower mash. Spoon 3 tablespoons of the crab mixture over top and carefully smooth. Finish with 2 tablespoons of cauliflower mash. Smooth the top of the cauliflower mash, then carefully slide the ring mold off.

5. Repeat to assemble the remaining servings (8 total). Optionally garnish with finely diced red bell pepper. Serve immediately or place in the refrigerator and serve chilled.

NOTES: *Aji amarillo paste is also an ingredient in Ají de Gallina (page 281). In the recipe, you may substitute a fresh aji chili (or a cayenne pepper or jalapeño) plus ¼ cup avocado oil. Remove the ribs and seeds if desired, then blend the pepper and the oil together until smooth (an immersion blender in a jar works well for this). Use this mixture to season the cauliflower in place of the aji amarillo paste.*

If you do not have a ring mold, options for assembling the causa limeña are:
Line a 4-inch straight-sided ramekin with plastic wrap. Assemble the layers as instructed above. Place a small plate upside-down on top of the ramekin and invert them both together. Holding the edges of the plastic wrap against the plate, lift the ramekin straight up. Remove the plastic wrap and, optionally, use an icing spatula to smooth the top and sides. Repeat for the remaining servings.

Line a mini loaf pan with plastic wrap. Layer thusly: ½ cup cauliflower mash, ½ of the avocado slices, ½ cup cauliflower mash, ½ of the crab mixture, and ½ cup cauliflower mash. Unmold as above, then repeat for the remaining ingredients (will make 2 mini-loaves). To serve, carefully cut portions and transfer to serving plates (this is easier if you chill the causa limeña before serving).

If you'd rather not use plastic wrap, use eight 4-inch ramekins and do not unmold, simply serve the causa limeña in the ramekins. Layer the ingredients as instructed in the recipe.

MACRONUTRIENTS PER SERVING
CALORIES: 141 KCAL FAT: 10 G, 91 KCAL CARBOHYDRATE: 8 G (5 G NET), 32 KCAL PROTEIN: 7 G, 27 KCAL

EMPANADAS

MAKES 8 SERVINGS

Empanadas are stuffed meat pies that are common across Central and South America. Our version uses a ground beef filling based on Argentinian recipes with keto-friendly fathead dough in place of the usual pastry. Serve these with Chimichurri (page 291) or Fermented Chimichurri (page 294) for dipping.

INGREDIENTS

For the dough

1½ tablespoons avocado oil

2 cups shredded mozzarella

1 cup almond flour

⅛ teaspoon fine sea salt

½ teaspoon aluminum-free baking powder (optional, see Note)

2 ounces cream cheese

2 eggs, lightly beaten

For the filling

1 tablespoon bacon fat or fat of choice

¼ small onion, diced

½ small red bell pepper, diced

1 clove garlic, minced

6 ounces ground beef

1 teaspoon ground cumin

½ teaspoon dried oregano

½ teaspoon sweet paprika

⅛ teaspoon fine sea salt

⅛ teaspoon ground black pepper

Pinch cayenne pepper, or more to taste

4 large pitted green olives, chopped

½ cup shredded mozzarella cheese or 1 large egg, lightly beaten

1. Preheat the oven to 425°F. Use the avocado oil to grease a rimmed baking sheet very well. (Alternately, line a baking sheet with parchment paper, but greasing the sheet helps the empanadas crisp up on the bottom.)

2. Make the dough: Mix together the mozzarella, almond flour, ⅛ teaspoon salt, and baking powder (if using) in a microwavable glass bowl. Place the cream cheese in the bowl. Microwave on high for 1 minute. Remove from the microwave and stir well. Microwave on high another 30 seconds. Stir well again. If the cheese is melted and the dough has come together in a uniform ball, add the eggs. Otherwise, continue to microwave in 15 second increments until fully melted, then add the eggs.

3. Mix the eggs into the dough until fully incorporated. Place the dough in the freezer to chill while you move on to the filling. >>

4. Make the filling: Heat the bacon fat in a medium skillet over medium heat. Add the onion, bell pepper, and garlic. Sauté 3 to 4 minutes until the vegetables are just soft. Crumble in the ground beef. Cook about 5 minutes until the meat is almost cooked through. While it cooks, combine the cumin, oregano, paprika, salt, black pepper, and cayenne pepper in a small bowl.

5. Season the beef with the spice mixture and stir very well to combine. When the meat is just cooked through, remove the skillet from the heat and stir in the olives. Taste and adjust the salt and cayenne as needed. Set aside.

6. Remove the dough from the freezer. Divide it into 8 equal portions. Roll each portion into a ball. One at a time, place a dough ball between two sheets of parchment paper. Press down with a cutting board or flat-bottomed metal bowl to flatten (or roll out with a rolling pin) to form a circle a little less than ¼-inch thick. Place a heaping tablespoon of the meat mixture on one half of the circle, avoiding the edges. Carefully fold the other half of the dough over the meat mixture. Fold the edges of the empanada together and crimp the edges sealed with a fork. Transfer the empanada to the greased baking sheet. Repeat with the rest of the ingredients.

7. Sprinkle each empanada with 1 tablespoon of mozzarella or brush the empanadas with the beaten egg. Bake in the oven for 10 to 12 minutes until golden brown on top.

8. Remove from the oven and allow to cool for a few minutes on the baking sheet, then transfer to a wire rack to cool for at least 5 minutes before serving. Serve warm.

NOTE: *Adding the baking powder makes the dough a bit drier, while omitting it results in a slightly chewier final product. If your dough tears while forming the empanada, just pinch and smooth the dough back together.*

MACRONUTRIENTS PER SERVING (1 empanada, with baking powder)
CALORIES: 295 KCAL FAT: 22 G, 199 KCAL CARBOHYDRATE: 6 G (4 G NET), 24 KCAL PROTEIN: 19 G, 76 KCAL

CHIMICHURRI

Chimichurri is one of our favorite ways to add healthy fats and tons of flavor to keto meals. This Brazilian and Argentinian sauce is perhaps best associated with the grilled beef of churrasco, but it's also great on raw and cooked veggies and even as a salad dressing. You can also use it to marinate beef, chicken, lamb, or even seafood.

INGREDIENTS

1 cup packed fresh flat-leaf parsley leaves

1 cup packed fresh cilantro leaves, or substitute additional parsley

4 cloves garlic, smashed

2 tablespoons dried oregano

¼ cup red wine vinegar

½ teaspoon fine sea salt

¼ teaspoon ground black pepper

¼ teaspoon red pepper flakes (or more or less to taste)

1 cup extra-virgin olive oil

1. In a high-powered blender or food processor, combine the parsley, cilantro, garlic, oregano, vinegar, salt, black pepper, and pepper flakes (if using). Pulse 5 to 10 times to combine. Scrape down the sides of the bowl and pour in a few tablespoons of oil. Blend on high about 30 seconds until combined. Scrape down the sides again.

2. With the blender running, add the remaining oil in a slow, steady stream. (You can use more or less to make a thicker or more diluted sauce.)

3. Transfer the chimichurri to a jar and store in the refrigerator.

MACRONUTRIENTS PER SERVING (2 TABLESPOONS)
CALORIES: 329 KCAL FAT: 36 G, 325 KCAL CARBOHYDRATE: 2 G (1 G NET), 7 KCAL PROTEIN: 1 G, 2 KCAL

CHARQUICAN (JERKY STEW)

MAKES 6 SERVINGS

While most keto eaters might eschew butternut and acorn squash, they are nutrient dense and can be consumed in modest quantities by people who do not have medical reasons to eat ultra-low-carb. Do select the lowest-sugar jerky you can find. The directions below are for preparing this dish in a countertop pressure cooker, but refer to the recipe note for alternatives.

INGREDIENTS

1½ pounds beef stew meat

2 teaspoons arrowroot powder (optional)

Generous pinch sea salt and ground black pepper

2 tablespoons beef tallow or fat of choice

1 medium onion, diced

8 ounces butternut or acorn squash, cubed

2 medium turnips, peeled and diced

3 cloves garlic, chopped

1 tablespoon dried oregano

1 tablespoon smoked paprika

1 teaspoon ground cumin

¼ to ½ teaspoon dried chili flakes, or to taste (optional)

6 ounces beef jerky, chopped into bite-sized pieces

6 cups beef stock

Salt, to taste

3 tablespoons parsley leaves, chopped, for garnish

1. Optionally toss the stew meat in the arrowroot powder to coat. Season generously with salt and pepper.

2. Press the Sauté button on your countertop pressure cooker. Add the tallow. When hot, brown the stew meat for about 2 minutes per side, working in batches so as not to crowd the pressure cooker. Transfer the meat to a bowl.

3. Place the onion, squash, and turnips in the pressure cooker. Sauté for about 5 minutes until starting to brown. Stir in the garlic, oregano, paprika, cumin, and chili flakes. Sauté one minute more, then stir in the beef jerky.

4. Pour in about 1 cup of the broth and use a wooden spoon to scrape any browned bits off the bottom of the pan. Stir in the rest of the broth. Return the stew meat and any juices collected in the bowl to the pressure cooker and stir well.

5. Press the Cancel button on the pressure cooker. Secure the lid. Cook using the Manual or Pressure Cook feature for 35 minutes. Allow the pressure to release naturally for 10 minutes, then carefully release the pressure steam valve. Remove the lid and stir the stew. Taste and adjust the salt as needed.

6. Ladle the stew into serving bowls, garnish with fresh parsley, and serve immediately.

NOTE: *This stew can also be cooked on the stovetop. Follow steps 1 through 4 in a large pot on the stove over medium heat, then simmer for about 1½ hours until the stew meat is very tender. Alternately, brown the meat in a skillet, transfer to a slow cooker, add the rest of the ingredients except the parsley, and cook on low for 6 to 8 hours. Serve as directed.*

MACRONUTRIENTS PER SERVING
CALORIES: 591 KCAL FAT: 41 G, 369 KCAL CARBOHYDRATE: 14 G (10 G NET), 54 KCAL PROTEIN: 42 G, 166 KCAL

FERMENTED CHIMICHURRI

MAKES ABOUT 1⅓ CUPS

Fermenting chimichurri adds a whole new flavor dimension, not to mention the beneficial bacteria associated with ferments!

INGREDIENTS

1 cup packed fresh flat-leaf parsley leaves

1 cup packed fresh cilantro leaves, or substitute additional parsley

4 cloves garlic, smashed

2 small shallots, roughly chopped

½ serrano pepper, ribs and seeds removed, chopped (or more or less to taste)

2 tablespoons fresh lime juice

2 tablespoons dried oregano

½ teaspoon fine sea salt

¼ teaspoon ground black pepper

After fermenting

1 cup extra-virgin olive oil

Red pepper flakes to taste (optional)

Equipment

1 wide-mouth pint-sized jar, sterilized

Non-metal tamper (optional)

1 glass fermentation weight, sterilized

1. In a high-powered blender or food processor, combine the parsley, cilantro, garlic, shallots, serrano pepper, lime juice, oregano, salt, and black pepper. Pulse 5 to 10 times to combine. Continue pulsing and scraping down the sides as needed until the herbs are finely chopped and the mixture is well combined.

2. Transfer the mixture to the jar and use a non-metal tamper or your first to pack it down to remove any air pockets. Brine should appear on the surface. Place the fermentation weight on the surface. Cover the jar with a clean kitchen towel or double layer of paper towel.

3. Place the jar on a plate and set it in a cool, dark place (such as a cabinet). Allow it to ferment for 1 week, pressing down gently on the weight every day to release brine to the surface. After a week, taste the mixture. It should be pleasantly tangy. If you wish, you can leave it to ferment for longer until it reaches the desired tanginess.

4. When the herbs are fermented to your liking, mix the herbs and brine with the olive oil. When combined, taste and add red pepper flakes if you want spicier chimichurri. Store in the refrigerator.

NOTE: *It is impossible to get accurate nutritional information for home-fermented recipes. The macronutrients provided for the unfermented chimichurri are a conservative estimate for this fermented chimichurri. The carbohydrates will be reduced during the fermentation process, but we are unable to know by exactly how much. Read the "Fermenting" section on page xiv before fermenting for the first time.*

MACRONUTRIENTS PER SERVING (2 TABLESPOONS)
CALORIES: 329 KCAL FAT: 36 G, 325 KCAL CARBOHYDRATE: 2 G (1 G NET), 7 KCAL PROTEIN: 1 G, 2 KCAL

CREMA DE AGUACATE (AVOCADO SOUP)

Avocado soup is served throughout Latin America in several different forms. This crowd-pleasing recipe includes cream to add richness and a hint of sweet to balance out the savory notes. You may serve this soup either hot or cold, although we typically serve it warm because it's simply too irresistible to wait for!

INGREDIENTS

2 tablespoons avocado oil

1 tablespoon unsalted butter, ghee, or additional avocado oil

2 tablespoons finely minced onion

1 clove garlic, minced

½ serrano pepper, ribs and seeds removed, minced

2 large avocados

2 cups chicken bone broth or vegetable stock

1 small tomatillo, fresh or canned, quartered

¼ teaspoon fine sea salt

Pinch ground white pepper

½ cup heavy whipping cream, or substitute full-fat coconut milk

¼ cup queso fresco or other unripened cheese such as farmer's cheese or ricotta (optional)

To garnish

4 fresh cilantro sprigs

Additional serrano pepper, thinly sliced, to taste

1. In a skillet, warm the avocado oil and butter over medium-high heat. When the butter has stopped foaming (or once the oil is heated, if using ghee or additional avocado oil), add the onion and garlic. Sauté stirring frequently until just softened but not browned, about 2 to 3 minutes. Add the minced serrano pepper and sauté 2 minutes more. Remove from heat and set aside.

2. Scoop the avocado flesh into a blender or food processor. Add the broth, tomatillo, salt, white pepper, and sautéed onion mixture. Puree until smooth.

3. Pour the avocado purée into a large pot and stir in the cream or coconut milk. Warm the soup gently over medium heat stirring frequently until hot but not boiling, about 5 to 7 minutes. If the soup is allowed to boil, it may splatter.

4. Serve immediately, topped with crumbled queso fresco and cilantro sprigs. Alternatively, you may chill the soup in the refrigerator for several hours to serve cold.

MACRONUTRIENTS PER SERVING
CALORIES: 355 KCAL FAT: 34 G, 308 KCAL CARBOHYDRATE: 9 G (4 G NET), 36 KCAL PROTEIN: 6 G, 26 KCAL

CHURRASCO CHICKEN HEARTS

MAKES 4 SERVINGS

If you've ever been to a Brazilian barbeque restaurant, you are familiar with churrasco: basically, grilled meat served off long skewers ("churrasco" can refer to the meat itself or the barbequing technique). While the term is used across Central and South America, churrasco chicken hearts are usually considered a Brazilian dish. In keeping with the churrasco tradition, serve these with Chimichurri (page 291) or Fermented Chimichurri (page 294), or go outside the box and dip these in Spicy Mayo (page 63).

INGREDIENTS

1½ pounds chicken hearts

¼ cup avocado oil

2 cloves garlic, finely minced

Zest and juice of 1 lemon

½ habanero or jalapeño pepper, ribs and seeds removed, minced

¼ to ½ teaspoons coarse salt, to taste

Equipment: 4 to 6 metal or bamboo skewers

1. If there are membranes on the hearts, remove and discard them. Optionally trim off the fatty sections. Squeeze the hearts to remove any blood (there might not be any), then rinse the hearts under cold water and pat dry.

2. In a glass container with a lid, whisk together the avocado oil, garlic, lemon zest and juice, and habanero. Toss the chicken hearts in the marinade. Cover and marinate at least 1 hour up to 12 hours in the refrigerator. Stir after 30 minutes if marinating on the shorter side, or every few hours if marinating longer.

3. Slide the hearts onto skewers. They may touch, but do not pack them together. Discard any leftover marinade.

4. TO BROIL: Heat the broiler to high and place a rack about 6 inches from the heating element. (If using an under-oven broiler, heat to low.) Broil the skewers for about 8 minutes, turning once about halfway through, until cooked through.

   TO GRILL: Heat a grill over medium-high heat. Grill for 10 to 15 minutes, turning every 4 to 5 minutes, until cooked through.

5. Transfer the skewers to a serving tray and sprinkle with coarse salt. Serve hot.

NOTES: *If you are using bamboo skewers, soak them in warm water for a minimum of 30 minutes prior to cooking in order to prevent them from burning.*

The macronutrient values provided include all of the marinade to be conservative. If you want more precise values, you will need to weigh your marinade before and after marinating the meat to determine how much is being discarded.

MACRONUTRIENTS PER SERVING
CALORIES: 386 KCAL FAT: 30 G, 266 KCAL CARBOHYDRATE: 3 G (2 G NET), 10 KCAL PROTEIN: 27 G, 106 KCAL

MOQUECA (BRAZILIAN SEAFOOD STEW)

MAKES 6 SERVINGS

This hearty (and incredibly easy) Brazilian stew can be made with any type of seafood. Try adding scallops or squid for delicious variations.

INGREDIENTS

1 pound mild-tasting fish such as snapper or cod

2 tablespoons avocado oil

Juice of 1 large lime

1¼ teaspoon fine sea salt

¾ teaspoon ground black pepper

2 tablespoons coconut oil (see Note)

1 medium yellow onion, diced

1 medium bell pepper (any color), diced

2 cloves garlic, minced

3 scallions, white and green parts chopped

1 cup diced tomatoes, fresh or canned

½ cup fresh cilantro leaves, chopped

1½ teaspoons paprika

1 teaspoon ground cumin

¼ teaspoon red pepper flakes, or to taste (optional)

1 14-ounce can full-fat coconut milk

1 pound medium shrimp, peeled or unpeeled

1. Slice the fish into large chunks about 2 inches wide. In a medium bowl, whisk the avocado oil, lime juice, and ¼ teaspoon each of the salt and pepper. Place the fish in the bowl and toss gently to coat. Set aside to marinate at room temperature while you move on to the next step, stirring the fish occasionally as it marinates.

2. Heat the coconut oil in a deep skillet or wok over medium-high heat. Add the onion and bell pepper, and sauté until soft, about 5 minutes. Add the garlic and scallions and sauté 2 minutes. Stir in the tomatoes and sauté 3 minutes until the tomatoes start to break down.

3. If desired, set aside a couple tablespoons of the cilantro to use as a garnish for the finished dish. Stir the remaining cilantro into the vegetables, along with the paprika, cumin, red pepper flakes, and the remaining 1 teaspoon salt and ½ teaspoon pepper. Pour in the coconut milk and stir well to combine. Allow the liquid to come to a boil.

4. If the fish is thick (an inch or more), nestle the pieces of fish into the vegetables and pour the marinade over top. Cook for 5 minutes, then nestle the shrimp into the stew as well. Cook for about 5 minutes more until the shrimp are just cooked through.

5. If the fish is less than an inch or so thick, nestle both the fish and shrimp into the vegetables. Pour the marinade from the fish over top. Cook for about 5 minutes until both are cooked through.

6. Taste the broth and adjust the salt and pepper. Ladle into individual serving bowls and garnish with cilantro if reserved. Serve hot.

NOTE: *Moqueca is traditionally made with palm oil. Although unrefined palm oil and palm kernel oil are both "good fats" according to our go-to expert Dr. Cate Shanahan, we are concerned about the environmental impact of sourcing palm oil. If you can find a sustainable product, use it in place of the coconut oil.*

MACRONUTRIENTS PER SERVING
CALORIES: 359 KCAL FAT: 24 G, 213 KCAL CARBOHYDRATE: 10 G (8 G NET), 38 KCAL PROTEIN: 28 G, 111 KCAL

POLLO ASADO COLUMBIANO

MAKES 8 SERVINGS

This Colombian-style chicken is marinated in a irresistible blend of fresh herbs and savory spices. If you prepare the marinade the night before, this recipe makes for an excellent no-fuss weekday dinner when paired with sliced avocado and a simple salad.

INGREDIENTS

½ medium onion, roughly chopped

¼ cup chopped cilantro leaves

4 green onions, white and green parts roughly chopped

3 cloves garlic, smashed

1½ tablespoons avocado oil

1 tablespoon apple cider vinegar

1 tablespoon fresh lime juice

1 tablespoon ground cumin

1 tablespoon paprika

2 teaspoons dried oregano

1 teaspoon dried thyme

¼ teaspoon fine sea salt

Pinch freshly ground black pepper

4 pounds bone-in skin-on chicken drumsticks, thighs, or a mixture of both

1. In a food processor or blender, combine the onion, cilantro, green onions, garlic, avocado oil, vinegar, lime juice, cumin, paprika, oregano, thyme, salt, and pepper. Process until a thick paste forms, stopping to scrape down the sides of the bowl as necessary.

2. Place the chicken pieces into a dish or bowl and pour the marinade over top. Mix to coat the chicken pieces, then cover the dish. Marinate in the refrigerator for a minimum of 1 hour and preferably overnight, turning the chicken pieces once or twice.

3. TO BAKE: Place the oven rack in the center position and preheat the oven to 400°F. Set a wire rack inside a rimmed baking sheet. Remove the chicken from the marinade, shake off any excess, and place the chicken pieces on the rack. Bake for 15 to 20 minutes per side, until the chicken skin becomes browned and the meat is cooked through to an internal temperature of 165°F. If you wish to further crisp the skin, you may broil the chicken for 3 to 5 minutes once they are cooked through.

   TO GRILL: Heat the grill to medium. Shake off any excess marinade. Grease the grates and lay the chicken directly on the grates, skin side up. Grill for about 25 minutes total until the chicken reaches an internal temperature of 165°F, flipping the drumsticks every 5 minutes or so and the thighs after 10 minutes.

4. Allow the chicken to rest for 5 minutes prior to serving.

MACRONUTRIENTS PER SERVING
CALORIES: 464 KCAL FAT: 29 G, 262 KCAL CARBOHYDRATE: 3 G (2 G NET), 11 KCAL PROTEIN: 42 G, 166 KCAL

SHRIMP CEVICHE

MAKES 8 SERVINGS

Traditional recipes called for the shrimp to be "cooked" in lime juice, but it is faster (and maybe safer, depending on who you ask) to precook the shrimp before marinating. Our favorite way to serve this is over an artfully arranged bed of raw baby spinach and thinly sliced avocado (yes, in addition to the avocado in the ceviche—you can never have too much!) with garden-fresh cherry tomatoes on the side.

INGREDIENTS

- 8 cups filtered water
- 1 tablespoon plus ¼ teaspoon coarse sea salt
- 2 pounds small to medium raw shrimp, peeled, tails removed, and deveined
- ¼ cup fresh lemon juice
- ¼ cup fresh lime juice
- ⅛ teaspoon ground black pepper
- 1 cucumber, lightly peeled, seeded, diced small
- ½ cup finely chopped red onions
- 1 jalapeño pepper, ribs and seeds removed, finely chopped (or more or less to taste)
- ¼ cup plus 2 tablespoons chopped fresh cilantro leaves
- 2 avocados, cubed

1. Heat the water and 1 tablespoon salt over high heat. When it just starts to boil, add the shrimp. Watch the shrimp carefully. As soon as they turn opaque, which happens quickly, drain them in a colander and run cold water over them to stop the cooking.

2. In a glass bowl with a lid, combine the lemon juice, lime juice, ¼ teaspoon salt, pepper, cucumber, onions, and jalapeños. Shake the excess water off the shrimp, then roughly chop them and add them to the bowl. Stir well to coat the shrimp. Cover and marinate in the refrigerator at least 1 hour, stirring once or twice.

3. Just before serving, stir in ¼ cup cilantro leaves, then gently fold in the avocado. Transfer to a serving bowl and garnish with the remaining 2 tablespoons cilantro. Serve cold.

VARIATION: Creamy ceviche? We got the idea from the packaging on Bellwether Farms brand crème fraîche to mix crème fraîche—a favorite ingredient of ours—into ceviche, something we never would have thought of ourselves. For keto folks looking to bump up the fat, that's a great option. Stir ½ to ⅔ cup crème fraîche into the ceviche to taste before adding the avocado in the third step, or simply serve the ceviche with a hearty dollop of crème fraîche on top.

MACRONUTRIENTS PER SERVING
CALORIES: 182 KCAL FAT: 6 G, 50 KCAL CARBOHYDRATE: 7 G (4 G NET), 26 KCAL PROTEIN: 28 G, 113 KCAL

MACRONUTRIENTS PER SERVING (WITH ⅔ CUP CRÈME FRAÎCHE)
CALORIES: 246 KCAL FAT: 13 G, 113 KCAL CARBOHYDRATE: 7 G (4 G NET), 28 KCAL PROTEIN: 29 G, 115 KCAL

SOPA DE ACEITUNAS (BLACK OLIVE SOUP)

Black olive soup is a very simple South American soup that really highlights the flavor of olives. If you don't like olives, this isn't the recipe for you! The egg yolks serve to thicken the soup a bit and add some healthy fat and protein, but feel free to omit them. The soup will still be delicious.

INGREDIENTS

2 tablespoons avocado oil

½ small yellow onion, finely chopped

3 cloves garlic, minced

3 cups chicken stock or vegetable broth

1½ cups pitted black olives, or use a mix of green and black olives, sliced or chopped

2 large egg yolks, lightly beaten (optional)

⅔ cup heavy whipping cream or full-fat coconut milk

Salt and pepper to taste

1. In a large soup pot, heat the avocado oil over medium heat. Add the onion and garlic, and sauté about 3 minutes until starting to soften. Add in the chicken stock and olives and stir well. Allow the broth to come to a boil, then reduce the heat and simmer for 20 minutes.

2. In a medium bowl, lightly beat together the egg yolks and cream. Spoon a few tablespoons of broth from the soup into a small cup. Allow it to cool for a minute, then slowly pour it into the cream mixture, whisking constantly. Next, slowly pour the cream mixture into the soup, whisking constantly. Allow the soup to come to a boil and boil gently for 1 minute.

3. Optionally, use an immersion blender to partially (or fully) blend the soup. Season to taste with salt and pepper. Serve hot.

MACRONUTRIENTS PER SERVING
CALORIES: 336 KCAL FAT: 32 G, 286 KCAL CARBOHYDRATE: 7 G (5 G NET), 29 KCAL PROTEIN: 7 G, 29 KCAL

INDEX

A

Africa, 1
  Bamya Alich'a (Ethiopian-style Okra), 3
  Berbere Spice Blend. *See* Berbere Spice
    Blend
  Bobotie, 6–7
  Doro Wat, 11
  Jollof Rice with Chicken, 12–13
  Malata, 15–16
  Nigerian Meat Stew, 17–19
  Niter Kibbeh. *See* Niter Kibbeh
  Ras el Hanout Spice Blend, 23
  Shrimp Piri Piri, 24
  Suya, 27
  Tibs Wat, 29
Aioli, 162
aji amarillo paste
  Aji Dd Gallina, 281
  Causa Limeña, 285–286
aji chilis, substitute for aji amarillo paste, 286
Aji Dd Gallina, 281
alcohol, cooking with, xiv
  mirin. *See* mirin
  substituting for, 155
arrowroot powder, as thickening agent, xiii
asparagus
  Asparagus and Celery Root Vichyssoise, 207
  Asparagus and Serrano Ham, 163
avocado
  Avocado Crema, 241
  Brazilian Chopped Salad, 283
  Causa Limeña, 285–286
  Crema de Aguacate (Avocado Soup), 297
  Saffron Avocado Lassi, 94
  Salted Margarita Lassi, 95
  Shrimp Ceviche, 305

B

bacon
  Bacon and Butter Eggs, 264
  Bacon Borscht, 173
  Coq au Vin, 209–210
  Eggs Benedict, 268–269
  Kapusta (Cabbage and Mushrooms), 187
  Rotkohlsalat mit Spek (Red Cabbage with
    Bacon), 223
  Zrazy, 202–203
Baked Cod with Tahini Sauce, 107
baking powder, xiv
Bamya Alich'a (Ethiopian-style Okra), 3
barbacoa, Beef Cheek Barbacoa, 243–244
Basic Mug Muffins, 271
  Eggs Benedict, 268–269
  Smoked Salmon and Gribiche Benedict,
    273
béchamel sauce, Moussaka, 154–155
beef
  Beef Cheek Barbacoa, 243–244
  Beef Khoresh, 109
  Beef Tongue with Tonnato Sauce (Vitello
    Tonnato), 168–169
  Bobotie, 6–7
  Boliche, 251–252
  Bulgogi, 39
  Charquican (Jerky Stew), 292–293
  Empanadas, 287–289
  Nigerian Meat Stew, 17–19
  Porcini Mushroom Beef Stew, 156–157
  Sokkori Gomtang (Oxtail Soup), 59–61
  Steak and Kidney Pie, 233–234
  Suya, 27
  Tibs Wat, 29
  Zrazy, 202–203

beets
 Bacon Borscht, 173
 Beet Kvass, 175
 Chlodnik, 183
 Curtido Rojo, 253–255
Berbere Spice Blend, 5
 Bamya Alich'a, 3
 Doro Wat, 11
 Tibs Wat, 29
Bhindi Pyaz (Okra with Onions), 77
bird's eye chilis. *See* piri piri chilis; Thai chilis
Black Olive Soup (Sopa de Aceitunas), 307
Blini, 179
Blini with Smoked Salmon and Herbed
 Crème Fraîche, 181
Blue Cheese Dip, 249
Bobotie, 6–7
Bok Choy with Mushroom, 33–34
Boliche, 251–252
bouquet garni, 210, 237
Brazilian Chopped Salad, 283
Brussels sprouts, Indian-spiced Roasted Brus-
 sels Sprouts, 89
Buffalo Wings, 256–257
Bulgogi, 39
butter
 Bacon and Butter Eggs, 264
 Ghee, 87
 Niter Kibbeh. *See* Niter Kibbeh

C

cabbage
 Brazilian Chopped Salad, 283
 Cabbage and Mushrooms (Kapusta), 187
 Curtido Rojo, 253–255
 Rotkohlsalat mit Spek (Red Cabbage with
 Bacon), 223
 Sauerkraut, 211–213
Caldo de Res, 260–261
Caldo Verde, 139
Camembert, Pork with Camembert, 218–219
Caprese Salad (Insalata Caprese), 141
cauliflower rice
 Cauliflower Tabbouleh, 111
 Chicken Biryani, 78–79

 Indian-style Cauliflower Rice, 91
 Jeweled Cauliflower Rice, 124–125
 Jollof Rice with Chicken, 12–13
 Omurice, 47–49
Causa Limeña, 285–286
cayenne peppers
 aji amarillo paste substitution, Causa
 Limeña, 286
 jalapeño substitution, Keto-Friendly
 Sriracha, 37
celery root (celeriac)
 Asparagus and Celery Root Vichyssoise, 207
 Causa Limeña, 285–286
Champinones al Ajillo (Garlic Mushrooms),
 161
Charquican (Jerky Stew), 292–293
Chasu Pork Belly, 41
 Zoodle Ramen, 72–73
cheese
 Blue Cheese Dip, 249
 Camembert, Pork with Camembert,
 218–219
 Crema de Aguacate (Avocado Soup), 297
 Fried Halloumi with Za'atar, 121
 Kajmak, 185
 Palačinke, 191
 Palak Paneer, 97
 Paneer, 99
 Parmesan, 177
 spinach and cheese Palačinke filling, 192
 Spinach Ricotta Dumplings, 159
chicken
 Aji Dd Gallina, 281
 Buffalo Wings, 256–257
 Chicken "Groundnut" Stew, 8–9
 Chicken Biryani, 78–79
 Chicken Cacciatore, Umbrian Style, 143
 Chicken Crackling Poutine, 245–247
 Chicken Kebabs, 113–114
 Chicken Korma, 81
 Churrasco Chicken Hearts, 298–299
 Coq au Vin, 209–210
 Doro Wat, 11
 Gribenes, 215
 Jerk Chicken, 274–275
 Jollof Rice with Chicken, 12–13

Omurice, 47–49
Pollo Asado Columbiano, 303
Schmaltz, 227
Tak Bokkeum Tang, 64–65
Tandoori Chicken, 103
chili peppers, xii–xiii
 aji, 286. *See also* aji amarillo paste
 gochugaru chili flakes, 45–46, 64
 guajillo chiles, 243–244, 260
 habanero peppers. *See* habanero peppers
 hatch chilis (New Mexico chilis), 5
 jalapeños. *See* jalapeño peppers
 Korean gochu chili flakes, 64
 Korean gochujang, 64–65
 piri piri. *See* piri piri chilis; Thai chilis
 sambol (sambal), 101
 Scotch bonnet. *See* Scotch bonnet peppers
 Scoville scale, xiii
 serrano peppers. *See* serrano peppers
 Thai chilis. *See* Thai chilis; piri piri chilis
Chimichurri, 291
 Fermented Chimichurri, 294–295
Chlodnik, 183
clams, Malata, 15–16
Coconut Sambal (Pol Sambol), 101
condiments. *See also* sauces
 Japanese-style Mayonnaise, 53
 Pol Sambol (Coconut Sambal), 101
 Spicy Mayo, 63
 Tahini, 129
 Toum, 133
Coq au Vin, 209–210
Coquilles St. Jacques (Scallops in Mushroom
 Cream Sauce), 144–145
Crema de Aguacate (Avocado Soup), 297
crème fraîche (sour cream)
 Bacon Borscht, 173
 Blini with Smoked Salmon and Herbed
 Crème Fraîche, 181
 Blue Cheese Dip, 249
 Kajmak, 185
 Moules Marinière, 216–217
 Mushroom Julienne, 189
 Pork with Camembert, 218–219
 Shrimp Ceviche, 305
Cretons, 259

Cucumber Yogurt Sauce
 Chicken Kebabs, 113–114
 Kebab-e Barg, 127
curry
 Bobotie, 6–7
 Curried Fish, 84–85
 Madras Curry Spice Blend. *See* Madras
 Curry Spice Blend
 Nigerian Meat Stew, 17–19
 Palak Paneer, 97
 Tom Yum Goong, 69
Curtido Rojo, 253–255

D

Deviled Eggs
 Not Your Mama's Deviled Eggs: Bacon and
 Butter Eggs, 264
 Not Your Mama's Deviled Eggs: Wasabi
 Eggs, 265
 Your Mama's Deviled Eggs, 263
Dilly Beans, 266–267
dips. *See also* sauces
 Blue Cheese Dip, 249
 Cucumber Yogurt Sauce, 119
Do Chua (Vietnamese Pickled Vegetables), 43
Dolmas, 146–147
Doro Wat, 11
dressings. *See also* sauces; condiments
 Blue Cheese Dip, 249
 Greek Salad, 149
 Tahini, 129
 Tahini Turmeric Dressing, 131
dumplings, Spinach Ricotta Dumplings, 159

E

East Asia
 Bok Choy with Mushroom, 33–34
 Bulgogi, 39
 Chasu Pork Belly, 41
 Do Chua (Vietnamese Pickled Vegetables),
 43
 Japanese-style Mayonnaise, 53
 Keto-Friendly Sriracha, 35–37
 Kimchi, 45–46

Larb Lettuce Cups, 51
Okonomiyaki Sauce, 53
Omurice, 47–49
Pork Satay, 54–55
Quail Shoyu Tamago, 57–58
Shoyu Tamago, 57
Sokkori Gomtang (Oxtail Soup), 59–61
Spicy Mayo, 63
Tak Bokkeum Tang, 64–65
Thit Heo Nuong Xa (Vietnamese-style
    Pork Chops), 67
Tom Yum Goong, 69
Yogurt Probiotic Shots, 71
Zoodle Ramen, 72–73
Eastern Europe, 171
Bacon Borscht, 173
Beet Kvass, 175
Bigos, 176–177
Blini, 179, 181
Chlodnik, 183
Kajmak, 185
Kapusta (Cabbage and Mushrooms), 187
Mushroom Julienne, 189
Palačinke, 191–192
Polish Dill Pickles, 193–195
Russian Mushroom Soup, 197
Salata od Hobotnice (Octopus Salad), 199
Tarator, 201
Zrazy, 202–203
eggplant
Moussaka, 154–155
Ratatouille, 235–237
eggs
Basic Mug Muffins, 271
Deviled Eggs (3 Ways), 263–265
Eggs Benedict, 268–269
Omurice, 47–49
Quail Shoyu Tamago, 57–58
Sauce Gribiche, 225
Shoyu Tamago, 57
as thickening agent, xiii
Empanadas, 287–289

F
fat-adapted, viii–x
Faux Patatas Bravas, 164
fenugreek seeds, 5
Berbere Spice Blend, 5
Niter Kibbeh, 20
fermented foods
Beet Kvass, 175
Bigos, 176–177
Curtido Rojo, 253–255
Dilly Beans, 266–267
Fermented Chimichurri, 294
fermenting, xiv–xv
Keto-Friendly Sriracha, 35–37
Kimchi, 45–46
Polish Dill Pickles, 193–195
Sauerkraut, 211–213
Yogurt Probiotic Shots, 71
yogurt, 115–117
fermenting, xiv–xv
flours, xiv
Fried Halloumi with Za'atar, 121

G
Garlic Mushrooms (Champinones al Ajillo),
    161
gelatin, as thickening agent, xiii
Ghee, 87
Niter Kibbeh, 20–21
glycogen, vi–vii
gnocchi. *See* Spinach Ricotta Dumplings
gochugaru/gochu chili flakes
Kimchi, 45–46
sourcing, 46
Tak Bokkeum Tang, 64
gochujang
sourcing, 65
Tak Bokkeum Tang, 64
grain-free flours, xiv
grape leaves, Dolmas, 146–147
Greek Salad, 149

Gribenes, 215
guajillo chiles
  Beef Cheek Barbacoa, 243–244
  Caldo de Res, 260
guindilla peppers, Gildasm, 165

H

habanero peppers
  Churrasco Chicken Hearts, 298–299
  Nigerian Meat Stew, 17–19
  piri piri chili substitute, 3
halloumi, Fried Halloumi with Za'atar, 121
hatch chilis (New Mexico chilis), Berbere
  Spice Blend, 5
Hollandaise sauce (Eggs Benedict), 268–269
hot peppers. *See* chili peppers

I

Indian-spiced Roasted Brussels Sprouts, 89
Indian-style Cauliflower Rice, 91
  Chicken Biryani, 78–79
Insalata Caprese (Caprese Salad), 141
Instant Pot, xiv
Israeli Salad, 123

J

jalapeño peppers
  aji amarillo paste, 286
  Causa Limeña, 285–286
  Churrasco Chicken Hearts, 298–299
  Keto-Friendly Sriracha, 35–37
  Larb Lettuce Cups, 51
  Shrimp Ceviche, 305
  Snapper Vercruz, 277
  Tibs Wat, 29
Japanese-style Mayonnaise, 53
  Spicy Mayo, 63
Jerk Chicken, 274–275
Jerky Stew (Charquican), 292–293
Jeweled Cauliflower Rice, 124–125
Jollof Rice with Chicken, 12–13

K

Kajmak, 185
  Palačinke filling, 192
Kapusta (Cabbage and Mushrooms), 187
Kearns, Brad, ix
kebabs. *See also* skewers
  Chicken Kebabs, 113–114
  Kebab-e Barg, 127
keto, vi–viii
  becoming fat- and keto-adapted, viii–x
  macros, ix
Keto-Friendly Sriracha, 35–37
  Spicy Mayo, 63
The Keto Reset Diet, ix, x
Kimchi, 45–46
Korean gochujang
  sourcing, 65
  Tak Bokkeum Tang, 64
Korean red pepper powder (gochugaru/
  gochu chili flakes), 64
  Kimchi, 45–46
  sourcing, 46
  Tak Bokkeum Tang, 64

L

lamb
  Bobotie, 6–7
  Kebab-e Barg, 127
  Lamb Souvlaki, 151
  Moussaka, 154–155
Larb Lettuce Cups, 51
lassi, 93–95
Lemon Garlic Sardines, 153

M

macros, ix
Madras Curry Spice Blend, 83
  Bobotie, 6–7
  Nigerian Meat Stew, 17–19
Malata, 15–16
mayonnaise
  Aioli, 162
  Japanese-style Mayonnaise, 53
  Spicy Mayo, 63

Mediterranean, 137
 Aioli, 162
 Asparagus and Serrano Ham, 163
 Caldo Verde, 139
 Caprese Salad (Insalata Caprese), 141
 Champinones al Ajillo (Garlic Mushrooms),
  161
 Chicken Cacciatore, Umbrian Style, 143
 Coquilles St. Jacques (Scallops in Mushroom
  Cream Sauce), 144–145
 Dolmas, 146–147
 Faux Patatas Bravas, 164
 Gildas, 165
 Greek Salad, 149
 Lamb Souvlaki, 151
 Lemon Garlic Sardines, 153
 Moussaka, 154–155
 Porcini Mushroom Beef Stew, 156–157
 Spinach Ricotta Dumplings, 159
 Tonnato Sauce, 167
 Vitello Tonnato (Beef Tongue with Tonnato
  Sauce), 168–169
Middle East, 105
 Baked Cod with Tahini Sauce, 107
 Beef Khoresh, 109
 Cauliflower Tabbouleh, 111
 Chicken Kebabs, 113–114
 Cucumber Yogurt Sauce, 119
 Fried Halloumi with Za'atar, 121
 Israeli Salad, 123
 Jeweled Cauliflower Rice, 124–125
 Kebab-e Barg, 127
 Tahini, 129
 Tahini Turmeric Dressing, 131
 Toum, 133
 Yogurt, 115–117
 Za'atar Spice Blend. *See* Za'atar Spice Blend
milk
 pasteurization, 99, 117
 Yogurt, 115–117
Mint Lassi, 93
mirin
 Chasu Pork Belly, 41
 Do Chua, 43
 Okonomiyaki Sauce, 53

sourcing, 41
 Zoodle Ramen, 72–73
Moqueca (Brazilian Seafood Stew), 300–301
Moules Marinière, 216–217
Moussaka, 154–155
mushrooms
 Bigos, 176–177
 Bok Choy with Mushroom, 33–34
 Champinones al Ajillo (Garlic Mushrooms),
  161
 Chicken Cacciatore, Umbrian Style, 143
 Coquilles St. Jacques (Scallops in Mushroom
  Cream Sauce), 144–145
 Kapusta (Cabbage and Mushrooms), 187
 Mushroom Julienne, 189
 Porcini Mushroom Beef Stew, 156–157
 Russian Mushroom Soup, 197
 as thickening agent, xiii
mussels, Moules Marinière, 216–217
mustard seeds, sourcing, 77

N

New Mexico chilis (hatch chilis), Berbere
 Spice Blend, 5
Nigerian Meat Stew, 17–19
Niter Kibbeh, 20–21
 Bamya Alich'a, 3
 Doro Wat, 11
 Tibs Wat, 29
North America, 239
 Avocado Crema, 241
 Basic Mug Muffins, 271
 Beef Cheek Barbacoa, 243–244
 Blue Cheese Dip, 249
 Boliche, 251–252
 Buffalo Wings, 256–257
 Caldo de Res, 260–261
 Chicken Crackling Poutine, 245–247
 Cretons, 259
 Curtido Rojo, 253–255
 Deviled Eggs (3 Ways), 263–265
 Dilly Beans, 266–267
 Eggs Benedict, 268–269
 Jerk Chicken, 274–275

Smoked Salmon and Gribiche Benedict, 273
Snapper Veracruz, 277
Not Your Mama's Deviled Eggs
    Bacon and Butter Eggs, 264
    Wasabi Eggs, 265
nutritional ketosis, vii

O

Octopus Salad (Salata od Hobotnice), 199
offal
    Beef Tongue with Tonnato Sauce (Vitello
        Tonnato), 168–169
    Churrasco Chicken Hearts, 298–299
    Steak and Kidney Pie, 233–234
Okonomiyaki Sauce, 53
    Omurice, 47–49
okra
    Bamya Alich'a (Ethiopian-style Okra), 3
    Bhindi Pyaz (Okra with Onions), 77
olives
    Chicken Cacciatore, Umbrian Style, 143
    Gildas, 165
    Greek Salad, 149
Omurice, 47–49
onions, Bhindi Pyaz (Okra with Onions), 77
oxtails
    Caldo de Res, 260–261
    Nigerian Meat Stew, 17–19
    Sokkori Gomtang (Oxtail Soup), 59–61

P

Palačinke, 191
    filling ideas, 192
Palak Paneer, 97
Paneer, 99
peppers. *See* chili peppers
Pickled Vegetables (Do Chua), 43
piri piri chilis, 3, 13. *See also* Thai chilis
    Bamya Alich'a, 3
    Jollof Rice with Chicken, 12
    Shrimp Piri Piri, 24
Pol Sambol (Coconut Sambal), 101
Polish Dill Pickles, 193–195

Pollo Asado Columbiano, 303
Porcini Mushroom Beef Stew, 156–157
pork
    Asparagus and Serrano Ham, 163
    Bacon Borscht, 173
    Bigos, 176–177
    Boliche, 251–252
    Chasu Pork Belly, 41
    Cretons, 259
    Kapusta (Cabbage and Mushrooms), 187
    Larb Lettuce Cups, 51
    Omurice, 47–49
    Pork Satay, 54–55
    Pork with Camembert, 218–219
    Rotkohlsalat mit Spek (Red Cabbage with
        Bacon), 223
    Schweinshaxe, 229
    Thit Heo Nuong Xa (Vietnamese-style Pork
        Chops), 67
    Zoodle Ramen, 72–73
pork rind crumbs
    Coquilles St. Jacques, 144–145
    sourcing, 145
pressure cookers, xiv

Q

Quail Shoyu Tamago, 57–58

R

Rabbit Stew, 221
ramen, Zoodle Ramen, 72–73
Ras el Hanout Spice Blend, 23
Ratatouille, 235–237
Russian Mushroom Soup, 197

S

Saffron Avocado Lassi, 94
salads
    Brazilian Chopped Salad, 283
    Caprese Salad (Insalata Caprese), 141
    Greek Salad, 149

Israeli Salad, 123
Salata od Hobotnice (Octopus Salad), 199
salmon
  Blini with Smoked Salmon and Herbed
    Crème Fraîche, 181
  Smoked Salmon and Gribiche Benedict, 273
Salted Margarita Lassi, 95
sambol (sambal), 101
sardines, Lemon Garlic Sardines, 153
sauces. See also condiments
  Aioli, 162
  Avocado Crema, 241
  béchamel (Moussaka), 154–155
  Blue Cheese Dip, 249
  Chimichurri, 291
  Cucumber Yogurt Sauce, 119
  Fermented Chimichurri, 294–295
  Hollandaise (Eggs Benedict), 268–269
  Okonomiyaki Sauce, 53
  Sauce Gribiche, 225
  Tahini, 129
  Tahini Turmeric Dressing, 131
  Tonnato Sauce, 167
Sauerkraut, 211–213
  Bigos, 176–177
Scallops in Mushroom Cream Sauce
  (Coquilles St. Jacques), 144–145
Schmaltz, 227
  Chicken Crackling Poutine, 245–247
  Gribenes, 215
Schweinshaxe, 229
Scotch bonnet peppers
  Chicken "Groundnut" Stew, 8–9
  Jerk Chicken, 274–275
  piri piri chili substitute, 3
Scoville scale, xiii
seafood
  Baked Cod with Tahini Sauce, 107
  Blini with Smoked Salmon and Herbed
    Crème Fraîche, 181
  Causa Limeña, 285–286
  Coquilles St. Jacques, 144–145
  Curried Fish, 84–85
  Gildas, 165
  Lemon Garlic Sardines, 153
  Malata, 15–16

Moqueca (Brazilian Seafood Stew), 300–301
Moules Marinière, 216–217
Salata od Hobotnice (Octopus Salad), 199
Shrimp Ceviche, 305
Shrimp Piri Piri, 24
Shrimp Provençal, 231
Smoked Salmon and Gribiche Benedict, 273
Snapper Veracruz, 277
Tom Yum Goong, 69
Tonnato Sauce, 167
serrano peppers
  Asparagus and Serrano Ham, 163
  Chicken Biryani, 78
  Chicken Korma, 81
  Crema de Aguacate, 297
  Curried Fish, 84
  Fermented Chimichurri, 294
  jalapeño substitution, Keto-Friendly
    Sriracha, 37
  Palak Paneer, 97
  piri piri chili substitute, 3
  Snapper Vercruz, 277
  Tom Yum Goong, 69
Shoyu Tamago, 57
  Wasabi Eggs, 265
shrimp
  Moqueca (Brazilian Seafood Stew), 300–301
  Shrimp Ceviche, 305
  Shrimp Piri Piri, 24
  Shrimp Provençal, 231
  Tom Yum Goong, 69
Sisson, Mark, ix
skewers
  Chicken Kebabs, 113–114
  Churrasco Chicken Hearts, 298–299
  Kebab-e Barg, 127
  Lamb Souvlaki, 151
  Pork Satay, 54–55
  Suya, 27
Smoked Salmon and Gribiche Benedict, 273
Snapper Veracruz, 277
Sopa de Aceitunas (Black Olive Soup), 307
soup
  Asparagus and Celery Root Vichyssoise, 207
  Bacon Borscht, 173
  Caldo de Res, 260–261

Caldo Verde, 139
Chlodnik, 183
Crema de Aguacate (Avocado Soup), 297
Russian Mushroom Soup, 197
Sokkori Gomtang (Oxtail Soup), 59–61
Sopa de Aceitunas (Black Olive Soup), 307
Tarator, 201
thickening agents, xiii
Tom Yum Goong, 69
sour cream. *See* crème fraîche
sourcing ingredients, xii
  gochugaru chili flakes, 46
  gochujang, 65
  mirin, 41
  mustard seeds, 77
  pork rind crumbs, 145
  tuna, 167
South America, 279
  Aji Dd Gallina, 281
  Brazilian Chopped Salad, 283
  Causa Limeña, 285–286
  Charquican (Jerky Stew), 292–293
  Chimichurri, 291
  Churrasco Chicken Hearts, 298–299
  Crema de Aguacate (Avocado Soup), 297
  Empanadas, 287–289
  Fermented Chimichurri, 294–295
  Moqueca (Brazilian Seafood Stew), 300–301
  Pollo Asado Columbiano, 303
  Shrimp Ceviche, 305
  Sopa de Aceitunas (Black Olive Soup), 307
South Asia, 75
  Bhindi Pyaz (Okra with Onions), 77
  Chicken Biryani, 78–79
  Chicken Korma, 81
  Curried Fish, 84–85
  Ghee, 87
  Indian-spiced Roasted Brussels Sprouts, 89
  Indian-style Cauliflower Rice, 91
  lassi, 93–95
  Madras Curry Spice Blend. *See* Madras
    Curry Spice Blend
  Mint Lassi, 93
  Palak Paneer, 97
  Paneer, 99

Pol Sambol (Coconut Sambal), 101
Saffron Avocado Lassi, 94
Tandoori Chicken, 103
spice blends
  Berbere Spice Blend. *See* Berbere Spice Blend
  Madras Curry Spice Blend. *See* Madras
    Curry Spice Blend
  Ras el Hanout, 23
  Za'atar. *See* Za'atar Spice Blend
spinach
  Brazilian Chopped Salad, 283
  Greek Salad, 149
  Malata, 15–16
  Palačinke filling, 192
  Palak Paneer, 97
  Spinach Ricotta Dumplings, 159
sriracha, Keto-Friendly Sriracha, 35–37
  Spicy Mayo, 63
Steak and Kidney Pie, 233–234
stews
  Bigos, 176–177
  Charquican (Jerky Stew), 292–293
  Chicken "Groundnut" Stew, 8–9
  Doro Wat, 11
  Moqueca (Brazilian Seafood Stew), 300–301
  Nigerian Meat Stew, 17–19
  Porcini Mushroom Beef Stew, 156–157
  Rabbit Stew, 221
  thickening agents, xiii
  Tibs Wat, 29
Suya, 27

T

tabbouleh, Cauliflower Tabbouleh, 111
Tahini, 129
  Baked Cod with Tahini Sauce, 107
  Tahini Turmeric Dressing, 131
Tak Bokkeum Tang, 64–65
Tandoori Chicken, 103
tapas
  Aioli, 162
  Asparagus and Serrano Ham, 163
  Champinones al Ajillo (Garlic Mushrooms),
    161

Faux Patatas Bravas, 164
Gildas, 165
tapioca starch, as thickening agent, xiii
Tarator, 201
Thai chilis. *See also* piri piri chilis
  Pol Sambol, 101
  Tom Yum Goong, 69
thickening agents, xiii
Thit Heo Nuong Xa (Vietnamese-style Pork
  Chops), 67
Tibs Wat, 29
Tonnato Sauce, 167
  Vitello Tonnato (Beef Tongue with Tonnato
  Sauce), 168–169
Toum, 133
  Chicken Kebabs, 113–114
  Kebab-e Barg, 127
tuna
  sourcing, 167
  Tonnato Sauce, 167

V

vegetables
  Bhindi Pyaz (Okra with Onions), 77
  cauliflower rice. *See* cauliflower rice
  Cauliflower Tabbouleh, 111
  Curtido Rojo, 253–255
  Do Chua (Vietnamese Pickled Vegetables),
  43
  Dolmas, 146–147
  Indian-spiced Roasted Brussels Sprouts, 89
  Israeli Salad, 123
  Kimchi, 45–46
  Palak Paneer, 97
  Ratatouille, 235–237
  Spinach Ricotta Dumplings, 159
vichyssoise, Asparagus and Celery Root
  Vichyssoise, 207
Vietnamese Pickled Vegetables (Do Chua), 43
Vitello Tonnato (Beef Tongue with Tonnato
  Sauce), 168–169

W

Wasabi Eggs, 265
Western Europe, 205
  Asparagus and Celery Root Vichyssoise, 207
  Coq au Vin, 209–210
  Gribenes, 215
  Moules Marinière, 216–217
  Pork with Camembert, 218–219
  Rabbit Stew, 221
  Ratatouille, 235–237
  Rotkohlsalat mit Spek (Red Cabbage with
  Bacon), 223
  Sauce Gribiche, 225
  Sauerkraut, 211–213
  Schmaltz, 227
  Schweinshaxe, 229
  Shrimp Provençal, 231
  Steak and Kidney Pie, 233–234
wine, xiv
  mirin. *See* mirin
  substituting for, 155

Y

Yogurt, 115–117
  Chicken Korma, 81
  Chlodnik, 183
  Cucumber Yogurt Sauce, 119
  Mint Lassi, 93
  Saffron Avocado Lassi, 94
  Salted Margarita Lassi, 95
  Tandoori Chicken, 103
  Yogurt Probiotic Shots, 71
Your Mama's Deviled Eggs, 263

Z

Za'atar Spice Blend, 135
  Fried Halloumi with Za'atar, 121
Zoodle Ramen, 72–73
Zrazy, 202–203